C0-AOE-752

DE PROPRIETATIBUS LITTERARUM

edenda curat

C. H. VAN SCHOONEVELD

Indiana University

Series Maior, 7

THE WORD 'SUBLIME' AND ITS CONTEXT 1650-1760

by

THEODORE E. B. WOOD

1972
MOUTON
THE HAGUE · PARIS

LIBRARY OF CONGRESS CATALOG CARD NUMBER: 77-165151

Printed in The Netherlands by Mouton & Co., Printers, The Hague.

ACKNOWLEDGMENTS

I am grateful for the assistance that I received from the entire staff of the Folger Shakespeare Library, Washington, D.C., but would like to mention especially Dr. Louis B. Wright, Director of the Library, Miss Dorothy Mason, Miss Beverly Shell, and Miss Priscilla Randolph. They were invariably helpful and tolerant of my many questions and requests. Miss Mason also put me onto several leads I would not otherwise have discovered, as did Mr. Christopher Grose, a doctoral candidate and Milton specialist researching his dissertation at the Folger Library for Washington University, St. Louis, Mo.

I am mostly indebted to Dr. Arthur H. Scouten of the University of Pennsylvania for encouraging me to write on the elusive subject of the sublime.

I acknowledge here the permission given me to incorporate a considerable amount of scholarship from three sources in my study. The publishers and works are: The University of Chicago Press, *The Ballad Revival: Studies in the Influence of Popular on Sophisticated Poetry* by Albert B. Friedman; the Harvard University Press, *Philosophy in a New Key: A Study in the Symbolism of Reason, Rite, and Art* by Susanne K. Langer; and the University of Michigan Press, *The Sublime: A Study of Critical Theories in XVIII-Century England* by Samuel H. Monk.

T. E. B. W.
Atherton, California
May, 1971

PREFACE

During the Spring of 1963, while engaged in a program of independent study and research, I became interested in the problem of Longinus and the 'sublime' in the literature and criticism of the Restoration and eighteenth-century periods in England. Not surprisingly, the one work that played the greatest part in arousing my interest was *The Sublime: A Study of Critical Theories in XVIII-Century England* (*MLA*, 1935; Ann Arbor, 1960) by Samuel Holt Monk.

A subsequent re-reading of Monk's book inspired two realizations. The first was that, comprehensive as it is, *The Sublime* practically ignores in the period it covers a number of primary sources that might have complemented nicely the more formal contemporaneous references to the sublime. My second conclusion about Monk's study was in connection with what it does say; for although it has long been considered to be the most authoritative and complete treatment of the English eighteenth-century sublime, its approach struck me as being seriously biased and narrow. Thus it seemed that the present work could be made to the end of ameliorating these deficiencies in the text that is still a standard work for students of British eighteenth-century esthetics.

However, because of the complexity and subtlety of the problem of the sublime, I found it difficult during the early stages of investigation to settle on an approach that would be both effective in revealing the shortcomings of Monk's view and constructive in developing a more catholic and flexible interpretation. My impasse was presently rendered considerably less formidable, however, by a reading of a number of modern studies, headed by Susanne K. Langer's book *Philosophy in a New Key: A Study in the Symbolism of Reason, Rite, and Art* (Harvard University Press, 1942). A number of Mrs. Langer's observations support my two leading theses: (1) that classical oratory is not necessarily devoid of interest in the study of the eighteenth-century sublime, and (2) that the sublime of Longinus has several legitimate heirs in the eighteenth century. With regard to the first of these, Mrs. Langer suggests that the primary concern of much classical oratory is 'value', rather than bombastic exhortation to action on the basis of 'facts'. I have attempted to show that eighteenth-century discussions of oratory and rhetoric share common ground with the sublime in this general area of 'value'. My second thesis is strengthened by Mrs. Langer's point that ideas (like those in *On the Sublime*) formulated at a time early in the history of speculation on a subject like esthetics are, generally speaking, informal, flexible, and capable of spawning divergent offspring. Mrs. Langer also embarrasses critics who, like Monk, would argue for a single significant development for the eighteenth-century sublime in the direction of the 'natural sublime' when she points out that one attempt after another has failed to apply the post-Lockeian concept of causality to esthetics and psychology.

My interest in this study is to establish a context for the contemporaneous usage of a term by Restoration and early eighteenth-century writers. I do not champion any single narrow concept of what the sublime meant for that period, or for our own. (I will have something to say, however, regarding Longinus' intentions.) There are areas of agreement and disagreement in the commentary of the last three hundred years over the meaning of the sublime. Hence, it seemed that the most judicious method for attacking the amorphous problem of a context study was to examine a limited number of the most interesting critiques, books and learned articles on Longinus and the sublime that have appeared since 1900, and then in subsequent chapters to take up the matter of contemporaneous usage, the latter hopefully gaining added significance from the general discussion in the first chapter.

In organizing the original seventeenth- and eighteenth-century data by chapter, only two procedures seemed feasible. The first was to subject all of my material to the indiscriminate dictates of chronology and simply present the 120-odd documents in order of their first date of publication, making chapter divisions, perhaps, by decade. This method offered all the usual advantages accruing to the observance of chronology, chief of which is probably the most faithful possible rendition of development or progress of an idea. But since part of my quarrel with Monk and certain others concerned their injection of these very properties I deemed strict chronology as being of minimal importance, and selected the second way of handling my original sources: by genre or literary figure (under each heading of which, however, chronology is generally observed). Thus, if no overall trend in the usage of the sublime becomes apparent during the course of this context study, that is all right; it was never necessarily supposed that one would. Similarly, we should not be disturbed if Augustan references to the sublime, for example, lead obliquely to other matters of great interest not traditionally associated with the sublime as such.

Finally I come to the choice of writers included in this study. From the beginning there was no question of taking up the major Restoration and eighteenth-century critical figures, literary and philosophic; these had already been subjected to all the analysis they could profitably stand. For in addition to Monk, there is a doctoral dissertation by Alfred Rosenberg, *Longinus in England bis zur Ende des 18. Jahrhunderts* (Weimar and Berlin, 1917), and Walter J. Hipple, Jr., *The Beautiful, the Sublime, and the Picturesque in Eighteenth-Century British Aesthetic Theory* (Carbondale, 1957). Of Hipple's and several other studies I will have more to say in Chapter I, but it suffices to observe here that these studies, whatever their weaknesses, cover seventeenth- and eighteenth-century theories of the sublime quite thoroughly. That left me those contemporaneous writers who are either barely mentioned by Monk and others, or those whose writings are today only available in rare book collections and repositories, and which are therefore virtually unknown to the general student of the period.

I decided to omit Rosenberg from the general discussion in Chapter I because of the nature of his book, which, like mine, is basically an exposition of primary source material supported by a minimum of secondary theorizing on Rosenberg's part. Hence I saw fit to include certain items of interest from his book in Appendix 3,[1] and will merely summarize here the few leading theses thereof. Rosenberg says that until about 1612 England was uninterested in the sublime of Longinus, presumably because Longinus did not then have a popular tradition behind his name. One of Rosenberg's most telling points is that any number of passages by authors writing until 1800 that seem to have been inspired by Longinus actually stem from other sources. Rosenberg concludes from his investigation that English critical thought would have gone the same way without Longinus, but that his treatise helped it along its destined path. As with Monk's book, I do not include in the Context writers treated at any length by Rosenberg. However, in a case where he merely mentions an eighteenth-century author in passing, or discusses him in a milieu tangential to the literary sublime, I feel free

[1] I do this also for the reason that Rosenberg's book is available in this country only at Duke University and the University of Michigan.

to include his observations.

To return to the matter of the little-known writings of our period, I decided that they might supply an interesting, even enlightening, context of the sublime, and accordingly turned to the resources of the Folger Shakespeare Library, Washington, D.C., which were most graciously made available to me for the space of several months. I think a word is in order concerning the technique I used to determine what materials to scrutinize among the very many held in the Folger Library. My first objective was to approach the matter of source selection with as few pre-conceived ideas as possible. I therefore went through the Library's chronological card catalogue for the years between 1647 and 1767, merely jotting down a title that looked as if it might relate in some way to the sublime. The time span was designed to overlap the period between the appearance in 1652 of the first translation of Longinus in English by John Hall and the publication in 1757 (?) of Edmund Burke's *A Philosophical Enquiry into the Origin of our Ideas of the Sublime and the Beautiful.*

Next I read the documents selected to see if they mentioned the sublime. When I encountered such a reference I copied it as fully as seemed necessary, and with no concern at that time for its significance in a larger frame of reference. In every case I tried to preserve faithfully the original spelling, punctuation and format, changing the last two only in the very few cases where the original would have produced hopeless ambiguity. I sought throughout for authenticity. In the same spirit I present these materials, not so much to prove a thesis about the eighteenth century's conception of the sublime as to show the complexities of such a thesis.

In an effort to standardize the references to the treatise of Longinus throughout my study, I use whenever possible the chapter and section headings of the English translation by W. Rhys Roberts. Exceptions are noted. This does not mean that I prefer his version to the other three to be mentioned; his numbering is simply the best for the rapid locating of a given passage.

In connection with translations, I will refer to the treatise as *On the Sublime*, rather than *Peri Hupsous*, or *De Sublimitate*. Furthermore, I must assume on the part of the reader a certain familiarity with the treatise. I do not offer in this study my own analysis for two reasons: The sheer bulk of the primary material comprising the Context makes the confinement of the whole within reasonable limits a real problem. And various translations of Longinus are held by nearly every academic library, and, I am sure, by many public libraries. Limitations of space also preclude a discussion of the problem concerning the identity of the author of *On the Sublime*. The reader will find the intricacies of this 2,000-year-old enigma fully presented in Roberts' prefatory comments, as well as in those of most other modern translators of Longinus.

CONTENTS

I

MODERN CRITICS ON THE SUBLIME

The problem of the influence of Longinus and the sublime on the Restoration and eighteenth century in England is at once intriguing and difficult to assess. That there was such an influence has never been doubted, beginning with numerous writers in the Restoration itself. Indeed, the enormous volume of references to the sublime during the period 1650-1760 poses a problem of interpretation that remains to our own day. Not that there have not been studies undertaken by the last two generations of scholars that had as their purpose an explanation of exactly what the eighteenth-century sublime was. (For the sake of brevity I will hereafter so call the entire matter of the sublime for the years 1650-1760.) Each of these studies, however, has one or more shortcomings serious enough, I believe, to justify the appearance of yet another.

I should say at the outset that it is impossible in a book of this length to deal comprehensively with some sixty years of scholarship on a subject as important as the sublime,[1] just as it is unfeasible in the context study proper to do more than suggest what kind of context could

[1] Two well-known books which touch on the sublime, noticeable by their absence here, are Christopher Hussey, *The Picturesque: Studies in a Point of View* (London and New York, 1927) and Marjorie H. Nicolson, *Mountain Gloom and Mountain Glory* (Ithaca, 1959). I pass them by because the sublime is not their main concern, and neither author says anything about it that is not more fully set out by the critics I do discuss. Hussey treats the sublime as a countertrend to the picturesque school in the eighteenth century. Nicolson, on the other hand, is primarily concerned with the 'natural sublime' particularly as it relates to mountain scenery, and she covers a wider period of time than I do in this study.

Of the doctoral dissertations on the subject of Longinus and the sublime written within the last thirty years, the study most germane to my investigation in this chapter is probably Cora Lee Beers, *Longinus and the Disintegration of English Neo-Classicism* (Stanford University, 1939). Certainly it is worthy of summary in this footnote.

To begin with, Beers apparently believes that English letters in the last half of the seventeenth century were more restricted by the bondage of the rules than most critics now think. As examples of writers who helped to free English liter-

be established if a scholar had the time and patience to search all the rare book collections, and when he had finished that herculean task to persuade a publisher to publish the huge number of volumes that would be required. I can only hope that a faithful presentation of a part of the whole will have some value, and in that spirit I turn to the modern studies on Longinus and the sublime.

---

ature from this oppression, Beers presents lengthy chapters on the affinity for the sublime in Dryden, Addison, Akenside, Swift, Pope, Hurd, Young, Burke, Kames, and Gibbon. She finds that these and other critics formulated their own idea of 'ὕψους', with the result that eighteenth-century definitions of the term differed widely. Beers finds only three exceptions in English literature before Boileau's 1674 translation to the sublime style of ornateness and redundancy. (There are several others, however, in my Context alone.)

In her further discussion of the varying translations of 'ὕψους', Beers makes a remark that relates to a leading argument of my study, to wit, that they "seem to express the original meaning more accurately than does the English word 'sublime' with its suggestion of something beyond the reach of man's intellectual power". The key word is 'intellectual'. Evidently Beers' reasoning goes something like this: For the Augustans art and nature must go hand in hand if the former is to be estimable; nature embraces the faculty of rationality in its make-up and comprehensibility; rationality is logically verbalizable; and hence art can be verbalized. The trouble comes when man cannot use his supreme intellectual gift, this power of verbalizing concepts, to define the sublime. In terms of the foregoing argument, of course, the sublime becomes suspect as an ingredient in art. Yet the argument collapses if it can be shown that the strict association of art, nature, and rationality is specious. It would seem that a number of eighteenth-century critics intuited what we will discover explicit in Langer, that there is another criterion by which the sublime can be attributed to an art work without divesting the latter of its wellspring in the human mind. In other words, that the sublime need not belong entirely to the irrational domain, if indeed it belongs there at all.

I quote one passage that Beers takes from Edward Gibbon, *Gibbon's Journal to January 28th, 1763,* December 30, page 197 because it is instructive as to the kind of approach that leads critics of both the eighteenth century and our own astray on Longinus: "It [*On the Sublime*] is certainly a fine performance; the style is only faulty by being rather TOO POETICAL FOR A DIDACTIC WORK. [My emphasis, here and below.] In general, I should adopt most of his decisions; only I think that FOR WANT OF HAVING A CLEAR IDEA OF THE SUBLIME, he has sometimes blamed passages for being deficient in that respect, or praised them for excelling in it, whose nature and design neither had, nor required, that kind of beauty. I could likewise have wished Longinus had not always confined himself to SINGLE PASSAGES, but would have pointed that sublime which results from the choice and general disposition of a subject. The body of Chapter I will demonstrate why Gibbon's is an inadequate interpretation of Longinus.

And finally, I disagree with Beers' conclusion (p. 406) that Burke and Kames "read Longinus with understanding, and built a new aesthetic philosophy on the foundations laid in *De Sublimitate*". We hope to show that both writers failed to grasp the essence of Longinus, and ended up discussing a different kind of sublimity.

The fifteen scholars and critics with whom we will be concerned (in the Bibliography the reader can find them all at a glance) have probably provided most of the salient ideas on our subject. For the sake of convenience, and because they seem to be so oriented, these writers have been placed into three groups, representing the following viewpoints:

1. Sublimity of rhetoric and/or terror and vastness
2. Liberal view of Longinus' sublimity
3. Quasi-Langerian approach to Longinus' sublimity.

The third group refers, of course, to Susanne K. Langer, and specifically to her *Philosophy in a New Key*: *A Study in the Symbolism of Reason, Rite, and Art*.

In keeping with the intention expressed in the Preface, I will deal first with Mrs. Langer's book. An early caveat suggests the difficulty of attaining fruitful interpretations of centuries-old concepts through traditional epistemology:

> The end of a philosophical epoch comes with the exhaustion of its motive concepts. When all answerable questions that can be formulated in its terms have been exploited, we are left with only those problems that are sometimes called "metaphysical" in a slurring sense – insoluble problems whose very statement harbors a paradox. The peculiarity of such pseudoquestions is that they are capable of two or more equally good answers, which defeat each other. An answer once propounded wins a certain number of adherents who subscribe to it despite the fact that other people have shown conclusively how wrong or inadequate it is; since its rival solutions suffer from the same defect, a choice among them really rests on temperamental grounds. They are not intellectual discoveries, like good answers to appropriate questions, but *doctrines*. (p. 20)

Granted that Langer's remarks refer to philosophic tenets of more general applicability in cultural history than the idea of the sublime in the arts, it is striking how her words pertain to the debate over Longinus waged in both the eighteenth and twentieth centuries. It seems that each man sees in Longinus what he wants, often in apparent disregard of the treatise itself. One would expect many eighteenth-century writers to apply to the problem of the sublime the dichotomy, as recently formulated as the preceding century, of all reality as inner experience and outer world, and so they do, particularly the members of the school of the 'natural sublime'.[2] And, as Langer says (p. 31), this Cartesian

[2] When I say the 'school of the natural sublime', I refer to the theorists who filter their speculations on the sublime through the epistemological system that John Locke is generally given credit for initiating. Basically this system depends

epistemology is even now all too prevalent as we undertake the solutions of problems, esthetic and otherwise, that by their nature do not lend themselves to this 300-year-old approach. What then are we to do?

Mrs. Langer is not long in pointing the way. Notice how her concern with value parallels that of Longinus despite the obvious differences elsewhere.

> Now this is a mere declaration of faith, preliminary to a confession of heresy. The heresy is this: that I believe there is a primary need in man which other creatures probably do not have, and which actuates all his apparently unzoological aims, his wistful fancies, his consciousness of value, his utterly impractical enthusiasms, and his awareness of a "Beyond" filled with holiness. Despite the fact that this need gives rise to almost everything that we commonly assign to the "higher" life, it is not itself a "higher" form of some "lower" need; it is quite essential, imperious, and general, and may be called "high" only in the sense that it belongs exclusively (I think) to a very complex and perhaps recent genus. It may be satisfied in crude, primitive ways or in conscious and refined ways, so it has its own hierarchy of "higher" and "lower," elementary and derivative forms.
>
> This basic need, which certainly is obvious only in man, is the *need of symbolization.* (p. 45)

In positing that symbolization is the essential activity of the human brain, Langer gets to the heart of the problem that may well account for the critical fumbling over Longinus these past three hundred years. This is the ancient problem of artistic reconciliation of form and feeling.

---

on the dichotomy of an objective external reality of nature and an inner, subjective reality in the human mind that is not exactly the same in any two individuals. The mind starts its existence as a 'tabula rasa', and receives impressions upon which to build concepts only by the agency of the senses, which apprehend and transmit to the mind the phenomena of the natural world. Quite obviously this system caters no more to man's artistic functioning than it does to his other activities, the process of physical apprehension and association being essentially nonesthetic in that it really cannot be selective. We would say that selectivity is the next step after the mind's reception of and associative activities *vis-à-vis* sense impressions. But the eighteenth-century exponents of the natural sublime pretty much ignore the mind's powers of selectivity, and concentrate on its passive apprehension of the vast and awful in nature, which inspire various associations which in turn affect the psyche. Thus this school sees art primarily in psychological terms, which is striking in contrast to the classical view of art, which depends on such elements as form, genre, and decorum.

The eighteenth century is a complicated blend, if you will, of the traditional and psychological conceptions of what the artistic process and the art work are. This study will show clearly that the psychological school and the natural sublime by no means gain undisputed ascendency in literary criticism by mid-century. And in this chapter I try to illustrate the shortcomings of modern studies like Monk's that treat the sublime on the assumption that the true esthetic is prevailingly psychological.

One major reason that we find so many eighteenth- and twentieth-century critics of the sublime unsatisfactory (Samuel H. Monk chief among them) is that they make what seems more and more like a specious distinction between rhetoric (the arrangement of words) and esthetic (supposedly some psychological response different in mind and reference from 'mere' disposition of verbal entities). Langer, on the other hand, shows that each art form necessarily unites SYMBOLICALLY form (intellect) and feeling. I quote a short number of passages to this effect:

For there is an unexplored possibility of genuine semantic beyond the limits of discursive language. (p. 81)

Such reflection invites one to tackle anew, and with entirely different expectations, the whole problem of the limits of reason, the much-disputed life of feeling, and the great controversial topics of fact and truth, knowledge and wisdom, science and art. It brings within the compass of reason much that has been traditionally relegated to "emotion," or to that crepuscular depth of the mind where 'intuitions" are supposed to be born, without any midwifery of symbols, without due process of thought, to fill the gaps in the edifice of discursive, or "rational," judgment. (p. 90)

For, quite apart from all questions of the authenticity of intuitive, inherited, or inspired knowledge, about which I do not wish to cavil [neither, we note, did Longinus], the very idea of a *non-rational source* of any knowledge vitiates the concept of mind as an organ of understanding. ... Rationality is the essence of mind, and symbolic transformation its elementary process. It is a fundamental error, therefore, to recognize it only in the phenomenon of systematic, explicit reasoning. (p. 91)

Perhaps one of the best definitions we could form for the true intent of the Longinian sublime is suggested by a quotation by Langer from Donovan: "aural absorption trying to make ... [its] ... way among syllables which have been fixed by significance"[3] (p. 118). This incorporates the elements of sound, disposition of words, propriety, convention, and an overall pattern. Longinus, of course, touches on all of these elements.

I quote one final passage from *Philosophy in a New Key* to demonstrate how Langer apparently continually synthesizes form and feeling in her esthetic.

... the import of artistic expression is broadly the same in all arts as it is in music – the verbally ineffable, yet not inexpressible law of vital experience, the pattern of affective and sentient being. This is the "content" of what we perceive as "beautiful form"; and this formal element is the artist's "idea" which is conveyed by every great work. (p. 217)

[3] J. Donovan, "The Festal Origin of Human Speech", *Mind*, XVII (1892), 337.

I emphasize that Langer is not discussing here either Longinus or literature per se. Yet we see the Longinian ineffable, vital experience, sentient being, formal element, and so on.

There is something else that I want to emphasize also. My use of Mrs. Langer is in no way intended to prove that Longinus was one of the first symbolic logicians without knowing it. Neither do I have any intention of applying a Langerian test to the passages in the Context. Rather, I discuss her slant on esthetics because I believe that it helps to put the Context in clearer perspective, and affords a technique for organizing the approaches of the critics that comprise the balance of this chapter. Langer shows us that there are different epistemological assumptions made by Longinus, by the eighteenth century and some twentieth-century scholars, and by other twentieth-century scholars. She shows us the central importance of man's symbol-making urge and capacity. She shows us that the nature of literature very probably does not recognize the kind of fractionalizing process indulged in by eighteenth-century faculty psychologists, and modern scholars who classify a work as rhetoric or Romanticism. And, finally, Langer shows us the hazard of verbalizing symbolic perceptions that had more successfully been expressed by example than by precept.

The first group to be considered is the one I have termed "Sublimity of rhetoric and/or terror and vastness"; one could start with any of these writers, but I think it most constructive to begin with those of the first group. On the whole they reflect the most traditional and unimaginative scholarly estimation of Longinus and the sublime. And of this group, Samuel H. Monk is indisputably the towering figure, the one with whom any new study of the eighteenth-century sublime must reckon. As we will see, Monk's book *The Sublime*: *A Study of Critical Theories in XVIII-Century England* (*MLA*, 1935; Ann Arbor, 1960) is a pivotal document because it is the last word, so to speak, on the traditional view of the subject, and apparently the inspiration for a reopening of the investigation into the sublime that ultimately produced several critiques offering fresh ideas. It must be remembered, however, that *The Sublime* was originally written as a doctoral dissertation and hence does not represent quite what Monk would have written with a little more reflection on the subject. He says as much in his preface to the 1960 edition, and lists a half dozen studies between 1935 and 1960 that he says qualify or supplement his work. He does not, however, eschew the basic orientation of his original, and it is exactly that which will be my concern here.

It seems to me that *The Sublime* rests squarely on two fundamental postulates, both of which I intend to question. The first is that the 'pure' Longinian sublime is essentially rhetorical. The second is that the Kantian concept of imaginative literature is the universal desideratum, and that English poetry (which includes the sublime of course) since the Renaissance strives towards it, albeit unconsciously, until the beginnings of Romanticism in the last decades of the eighteenth century. The result of this double bias is a view of the eighteenth-century sublime as moving between the poles of the rhetorical conception of Longinus on the one hand, and the natural sublime of Edmund Burke on the other. A corollary to this bi-polarity is the dictum, so widely held even today, that the Longinian sublime emphasizes the artists, while the late eighteenth-century sublime, with its psychological involvement, is realized mainly in the responses of the audience. I cannot really agree with any of this unless qualified to the extent of removing its impact. In discussing these elements in Monk's appraisal of the sublime, I would hope to show their own insufficiency or accuracy, as well as to prepare the reader for those parts of the Context that simply will not conform to the history of the sublime as Monk sees it.[4]

In order to document Monk's attitude toward Longinus as being first of all a rhetorician, I submit the following five passages:

Only by stretching the meaning of the term [sublime] out of all conscience can Longinus's treatise be considered an essay on aesthetic . . . (p. 10)

It is evident that Longinus is well within the tradition of ancient rhetoric when he treats the sublime style as emotive in purpose and as capable of being expressed both in ornamental and in simple language. (p. 11)

The abiding interest of Longinus for the eighteenth century, and consequently for us, lay in his conception of the sublime that underlies sublimity of style and that is an expression of a quality of mind and experience. To write on the sublime style is to write on rhetoric; to write on sublimity is to write on aesthetic. The sublime style is a means to an end; sublimity is an end in itself.[5] (p. 12)

[4] See below p. 23 and p. 25.

[5] The second and third sentences of this passage will not stand up under close scrutiny when compared with what Longinus wrote. (This will come out more clearly when we turn to some other modern critics.) That Monk exaggerates the distinction between the sublime and the sublime style is apparent when we refer to a passage in *On the Sublime* as early as the first section: ". . . sublimity is a certain distinction and excellence in expression . . . we see skill in invention, and due order and arrangement of matter, emerging as the hard-won result not of one thing or two, but of the whole texture of the composition, whereas Sublimity flashing forth at the right moment scatters everything before it like a thunderbolt

In this sentence [Edward] Young goes far beyond Longinus, who had merely pleaded for the recognition of beauties which are attained by transcending the rules, and who was perfectly ready to state formulae for the creation of that rhetorical sublime with which he was chiefly concerned. (p. 102)

Throughout the eighteenth century Longinus was esteemed not only as a critic but as a rhetorician. We have followed his influence on critical and aesthetic thought to the neglect of the long survival of his dicta in the manuals of rhetoric that were taught to schoolboys until well into the nineteenth century. It was in rhetoric that the passions were of chief importance, and it was by the transfer of the rhetorical values of the pathetic and the sublime to the sphere of art that Boileau gave impetus, in the Augustan age, to the consideration of the aesthetic value of emotions. The acceptance of a rhetorician as a literary critic was made easy, not only by the fact that Longinus was, momentarily, a penetrating critic, but also by reason of the close alliance that existed between rhetoric and poetry. (p. 234)

Monk's estimation of Longinus as a critic probably rests to a great extent on two ideas, my appraisal of which will emerge during the course of this chapter and later, particularly in Chapter III on oratory and rhetoric. The first is that the eighteenth century made a sharp distinction between rhetorical and non-rhetorical expression. The second is Monk's concept of imaginative literature as cited above. Similarly, I find in the following quotation a certain rigidity, this time pertaining to what Longinus meant by the rules. While there is no doubt that he denied the universal validity of all man-made rules accruing to the arts, Longinus emphatically did not intend to say that art is therefore independent of rules. The point is that certain rules belong to art inherently.

Longinus' declaration that the sublime lay beyond the reach of the rules prepared the way for the alignment of the sublime on the side of original

. . ." (I.4.) There is no opposition here of sublime and sublime style, but rather of expression that is sublime and expression that is not.

Throughout his treatise Longinus stresses the mutual dependence of elements of style and spontaneous passion in his esthetic of the sublime. For instance: ". . . the expression of the sublime is more exposed to danger when it goes its own way without the guidance of knowledge . . . It is true that it often needs the spur, but it is also true that it often needs the curb. . . . Most important of all, we must remember that the very fact that there are some elements of expression which are in the hands of nature alone, can be learnt from no other source than art." (II.2,3.)

Of course Longinus discusses style; for him literary esthetics involves verbal expression and the mind of the artist, not the psyche alone. But he indicates that however important stylistic considerations are, they are subordinant to that *je ne sais quoi* which transports: "But our PARENTHETICAL [my emphasis] disquisition with regard to the use of figures as bearing upon the sublime has run to sufficient length, dear Terentianus." (XXIX.2.)

genius. It was a mere matter of deduction from this premise (sanctioned by every neo-classical critic) to the conviction that the rules were inimical to great art. (p. 235)

It is time to move toward the second of Monk's ruling biases. What follows serves nicely as a transition from matters rhetorical to the theories of Kant.

... Boileau endowed the word "sublime" with new significance. The idea that the sublime is not a matter of style opened the way for investigations into the inner quality of great art, into the experiences of artist and reader when the one perceives a sublime object and the other experiences a great work of art. It was a step away from Longinus. (p 36)

Hardly. In fact, it is just the opposite. This is precisely what Longinus was talking about. Elder Olson will help us to demonstrate this quite convincingly.[6] And while mentioning Boileau I might hazard the guess that one probable cause for the average reader's confusion over the opening chapters of *The Sublime* is the false distinction made by Monk between Longinus and Boileau, as illustrated by the above.[7]

I will restrict myself to two quotations from Monk that reveal his Kantian leanings. The reader can easily find many other passages.

... it is worth noticing that when the sublime was given to England it was already associated with the external world, as well as with literature and with rhetoric. Especially interesting, in the light of Kant's theory,[8] is the idea that the human understanding seeks to transcend the material world and to grasp infinity, and that the appreciation of sublimity is a token of the spiritual greatness of man. Is it not this idea which Kant expresses in his more technical language and which is, of course modified by his own philosophical system? (p. 17, footnote 21)

[6] See below pp. 44-47.
[7] Monk accounts for the disparity he finds between Longinus and Boileau on the grounds that Boileau did violence to the intent of the Greek critic while preparing his famous translation of 1674 (p. 30). But amusingly enough, the concensus of a group of more recent scholars, working straight from the Greek text, is that Longinus contains substantially the same ideas that Monk says are Boileau's unique contribution to his time's concept of the sublime! For such commentary on the part of four critics discussed in this chapter, see below T. R. Henn on Longinus' organic view of the sublime (p. 30), F. R. B. Godolphin's statement that *On the Sublime* is not a technical treatise on rhetoric, and that Longinus pointed out that works of genius do not lead the hearer to persuasion, the proper object of rhetoric (pp. 36, 39), C. B. Menuez on Longinus' formulation of the problem of a general esthetics, and her description of the psychological effect of art (pp. 45, 46), and E. Olson on Longinus' departure from the procedures of the Classical rhetoricians, and the impossibility for him of a theory of the rhetorical sublime (pp. 52-53).
[8] See my remarks on Iris Murdoch, pp. 42-44.

No doubt Longinus and Kant agree that the sublime involves 'the spiritual greatness of man', but Monk's qualifications toward the end of the passage remove any necessary connection between the earlier sublime and the sublime of Kant. A further blurring of the objective-subjective issue by Monk can be seen where he says

> Once it was seen that the sublime is a state of mind evoked by objects and ideas, the objective criteria of the rules were gradually invalidated and the perceptions of individuals, together with their personal emotions and their independent imaginative interpretation of experience could usurp the place of the older truth to nature. (p. 236)

In view of the modern predicament in the arts in which Romanticism had a leading role, it is instructive to compare this passage with those in Longinus that deal with the sublime as the echo of a great soul. The difference of the two positions is a bit subtle, but not difficult to see. The restraints that Longinus places on the writer's expressions of his noble thoughts are most of that difference, and may account for the fact that a judicious interpretation of *On the Sublime* makes most Romantic critical pronouncements sound pretty dated indeed.

Monk says (p. 25) that Silvain had complained that Longinus did not give a clear idea of the sublime, and Monk adds that a similar dissatisfaction was shared by all the more important theorizers. Perhaps Silvain puts his finger on the root of the trouble that Monk inherits from Kant. Longinus does not give an exact idea of the sublime because it is impossible, being essentially non-verbalizable in prose paraphrase or treatise. Longinus apparently knew this, consciously or subconsciously, but Kant, having the nature of most philosophers, cannot resist the temptation to verbalize his idea of the sublime. Thus, in this case, is the wisdom of the artist rendered superior to that of the philosopher, for there can be little doubt that Longinus, whoever he was historically, had the sensibilities of an artist. And, on the other side, the trouble with Kant's theory for the artist is its emphasis on non-sensuous factors, and its tendency to separate the art and esthetic response into discrete categories.

Faith in Monk's interpretation of Longinus is not encouraged by his statement that

> In the last section of his treatise, Longinus accounts for the decline of genius in his age on the grounds that liberty no longer existed, and that only in a state of freedom can great art be produced – an opinion that would naturally commend itself to the English in an age when they complacently contrasted their own constitutional monarchy with the despotism

that prevailed on the Continent, and when they prided themselves on the prevalence of individual liberty in the body politic. (p 26)[9]

Indeed, such an idea may have appealed to the English of the eighteenth century, but it is not Longinus' idea. A careful reading of the passage in his treatise[10] shows that he regards the external realities of politics and society as a partial explanation of his contemporary situation, but not the necessary cause. The sublime springs from within the artist, so that it is in the power of a great man to transcend completely the exigencies of his time. Longinus is borne out by the countless examples of just such artistic transcendence during the last two thousand years of Western life and art.

I will close this discussion of Monk by remarking that ironically he comes closest to realizing himself the meaning of *On the Sublime* in his section on John Dennis, whom he calls deprecatingly 'one of the minor critics of the age' (p. 45), and his interpretation of Longinus:

The striking thing to Dennis is that Longinus analysed the effects of the sublime on the soul. This statement would seem to support the idea that Longinus had some share in the founding of an aesthetic concept of the sublime; that he sought to turn criticism away from the rules, to turn men's minds away from the dogmas of the ancients, and to set them to analysing their own emotions in the presence of grandeur and beauty. By investigating the emotions consequent to sublimity, men began to learn that art is a matter, not of the rules, but of the individual's response to an object or an experience, and this knowledge led them gradually to that subjective view of art out of which an aesthetic was evolved. (p. 50)

But I cannot let Monk off before asking him whether, as it seems, he would restrict the use of the word 'aesthetic' to a subjectivist-psychological process of artistic production and response thereto. I deny that he has a valid right so to do, and cite the definition of 'aesthetic' in the *Oxford English Dictionary* and the contributions of Mrs. Langer and others to the science of beauty.

If I have been somewhat critical toward *The Sublime* it is only because I thought that such treatment might serve the useful purpose of

[9] Our confidence in Monk's powers of interpretation is further shaken when we compare statements he makes on pages 97 and 162. On the latter page he says that Edmund Burke is less sophisticated than Richard Payne Knight because he cannot distinguish between practical and esthetic aspects of the sublime in a case like that of a storm, with its terrifying elements of thunder and lightning; but on page 97 Monk presents a quotation from Burke's *Enquiry* that makes this very distinction. Neither of these references to Burke is in passing; Monk uses each in detailed discussion.

[10] XLIV, *passim*.

defining the problem of the sublime more clearly. Hopefully I can proceed with our other critics all the more constructively because of my examination of what I feel to be its inadequacies. Nevertheless, Monk's remains a very useful study. Certainly there is no other book on the subject that is so rich in contemporaneous references to the eighteenth-century sublime.[11]

I thought it interesting to see if, over the space of nearly twenty years, Monk did in fact change his view of the eighteenth-century sublime. Thus I turned to his introduction to John Baillie, *An Essay on the Sublime* (1747), number 43 in the series of Augustan Reprints (Berkeley and Los Angeles, 1953). Somewhat to my surprise I found hardly any change from the orientation of *The Sublime*, as the following quotations will show.

> Dr. John Baillie was one of many eighteenth-century theorists who found the origin of the sublime in man's imaginative response to the grandeur of nature. To these writers Longinus' emphasis upon matters of style was less important and fruitful than an analysis of the effects of sublimity in nature on the "soul" of man. The arts became sublime by representing sublime objects or by evoking effects analogous to those evoked by the objects themselves. (p. i)

> Baillie is in the Addisonian line. Turning away from the Longinian concern with "the Pathetic, or Figurative Manner," he begins with the sublime of natural objects. Locke provides him with the machinery of sensations, ideas, and association; Addison, with the category "great," or in Baillie's word "vast" objects. Like Addison, he finds that the effect of sublime objects is not related to the passions (as Longinus had hinted [!] and as John Dennis had asserted at length) since it is "a solemn *Sedateness*" or awe. (p. iii)

As in the case of *The Sublime* there seems no reason for disputing most of what Monk says about the eighteenth-century usage of the sublime, but equally no reason for accepting what he says about Longinus.

When *The Sublime* first appeared in 1935 it shortly received a review by Ronald S. Crane writing for *Philological Quarterly*. After criticizing Monk for failing "to show the effects of the critical theorizing he has studied on the contemporary production of works of art" (*P.Q.*, XV [1936], p. 165), Crane further condemns him for confusing and intermixing certain writers like Dennis, the Wartons, Lowth, Young, and

[11] And, of course, Monk offers generally comprehensive discussions of such leading eighteenth-century writers on the sublime as Boileau, Silvain, Dryden, Dennis, Addison, Hume, Akenside, Baillie, Lowth, Burke, Gerard, Kames, Joseph Priestley, Blair, Reid, and Alison.

Reynolds for whom "the 'Sublime' was in the main the 'Sublime' of Longinus, i.e., that quality . . . which gives distinction to works of literature and plastic art; and their typical procedure, like that of Longinus himself, consisted in viewing works in terms of the mental [?] powers – the genius, imagination, creative energy – of their authors and in determining their value by reference to the quality of the soul that shines through them or through particular passages or parts of them"[12] . . . with other writers like Hume, Akenside, Burke, and Reid, who "sought the 'Sublime' not primarily in works of literature or plastic art but in natural objects of one kind or another, and more particularly in the states of mind which such objects have the power to induce in human spectators" (pp. 165-6).

Crane's criticism is, on the whole, justified, for it is true that Monk treats the latter group of writers in the same narrative sequence as the writers of 'a more purely Longinian sort', but distinguished from them by being 'slightly more modern and progressive' (Crane's words). Crane is also quite correct for criticizing Monk's position that the psychological school emancipated criticism from rules, and the distinction of styles; Crane points out that the new school's speculations merely resulted in the substitution of a new decorum and set of styles (sublime, beautiful, picturesque).

Judicious as Crane's remarks are, they are also subject to certain qualifications. In the first place, the agreement between Longinus and Reynolds is more superficial than Crane indicates. (I go into this in more detail below.) In the second place, Crane is disposed to make 'pure' Longinianism both too rhetorical and too dependent on the Romantic concept of genius. As I have already stated, it is the thesis of this chapter that the most tenable estimate of Longinus lies between these extremes.

In the preface to the 1960 edition of *The Sublime*, Monk mentions the article by Ernest Tuveson, "Space, Deity, and the 'Natural Sublime'" (*Modern Language Quarterly*, XII [1951], 20-38) as one of the outstanding recent studies supplementing his own work. Actually Tuveson adds practically nothing to what Monk had to say about the natural sublime; he concentrates on the increase of sensitivity to bigness as such by discussing the background of Addison's *Spectator* essays on the

[12] In order to keep the long quotation from bogging down completely, I give here Crane's appraisal of this first group of writers. It occurs in the text at the point of my number for this footnote: "It was essentially a rhetorical approach, and in that respect it harmonized fundamentally with the approach implicit in most of the criticism which Monk calls 'neo-classical' . . .".

"Pleasures of the Imagination" which he regards as the first explicit statement of the theory of the natural sublime. The following quotation from Tuveson seems fair enough, but note how he, like Monk before him, moves between the poles of rhetoric and natural sublime.

> . . . it was natural that men should find in Longinus' definition of the "sublime" in rhetoric something highly congenial with the new feelings about the universe; but the symbol had emerged before the name came to be associated with it. (p. 38)

The Context will help us to ascertain whether the assertion that the word 'sublime' was not applied to the external world of nature until relatively late is supported by the evidence.

I will conclude our examination of the first group of scholars and critics by glancing at two translators of *On the Sublime.* Despite the intervention of 156 years there is very little difference in basic approach in the translations of William Smith and W. Rhys Roberts.[13] This can best be seen in the prefatory material.[14] Both scholars exhibit varying degrees of what we recognize by now as the traditional view of Longinus and the eighteenth-century sublime, basically rhetorical but with elements of the natural sublime. Taking them in chronological order I look first at the translation by Smith which Monk regards as the most representative of the eighteenth-century attitude toward Longinus. Consistent with the contextual nature of this study, direct quotations from Smith are not out of order. The question of Longinus' intent arises as early as the Dedication:

> His [Longinus'] Sense is faithfully represented, but whether this Translation has any of the original Spirit, is a Decision peculiar only to those, who can relish unaffected Grandeur and natural Sublimity, with the same judicious Taste, as Your Lordship [George Earl of Macclesfield].

Shortly thereafter in the Dedication Smith moves from the above intimation of the natural sublime to the rhetorical:

> I am sensible, that what I have done, might be done much better; but if I have the good Fortune to contribute a little, towards the fixing a true judicious Taste, and enabling my Readers to distinguish Sense from Sound,

[13] *Dionysius Longinus on the sublime: translated from the Greek, with notes and observations, and some account of the life, writings, and character of the author. By William Smith, A. M. Rector of Trinity in Chester . . . The Second Edition, Corrected and improved.* (London. . . . 1743) *Longinus on the Sublime. The Greek Text Edited After the Paris MS with Introduction, Translation, Facsimiles and Appendices by W. Rhys Roberts* (Cambridge, 1899).

[14] Below I collate the translations proper together with one by Einarson. See Appendix 1.

Grandeur from Pomp, and the Sublime from Fustian and Bombast, I shall think my Time well spent . . . (Preface)

However, it is notable that when Smith refers to Longinus' 'inward Grandeur and Elevation of the Soul', he does so in the context of Longinus' life, not his treatise (p. iii). This is most unfortunate because Smith unquestionably believes that his author is the third-century Longinus, a notion refuted by later scholars. Thus all of Smith's relation of biographical 'facts' about Longinus is irrelevant, which, in turn, vitiates to some extent Smith's critical appreciation because of its dependence on those supposed facts. (Monk never informs us, incidentally, of this matter. He probably should, considering the prominence of Smith among his source materials.) Bearing this caveat in mind, I quote a few additional passages from Smith.

He [Longinus] was, as I observed before, a perfect Master of the Stile and peculiar turn of thought of them all, and could discern every Beauty or Blemish in every Composition. ("Some Account of the Life and Writings of Longinus", p. vii)

"The Sublime," says Longinus, "is an Image reflected from the inward Greatness of the Soul." The Remark is refined and just; and who more deserving than he of its Application? Let his Sentiments be considered as Reflexions from his own Mind, let this Piece on the Sublime be regarded as the Picture of its Author. (*Ibid.*, p. xviii-xix)

These remarks are interesting because of their inclusion of the dichotomy, reiterated by Addison, of beauty and blemish, and because of the anticipation of the Romantic emphasis on the psyche, but the entire tenor of Smith's commentary stems from an earlier viewpoint. This is evident on page xx of "Some Account of the life, writings, and character of the author" where Smith eulogizes Longinus' style at great length, beginning with, "As his Sentiments are noble and lofty, so his Stile is masterly, enlivened by Variety, and flexible with Ease."

On pages xxvii-xxxiv of the same section Smith echoes the habit popular among critics of his day, of accounting for Longinus' status as a philosopher by attributing to him a short of quasi-Christianity. This supposedly enabled Longinus to form and deliver the maxims on conduct that are to be found in the treatise. There is no need to comment any further on such theorizing; at best it tells us more about Smith than Longinus. About all we can say is that there is no doubt that the eighteenth century yoked Longinus, Christianity, and the Bible together in order to serve its purposes. Monk has covered the ground quite thoroughly, which leaves it to me to observe merely that the school of thought which 'discovered' the origins of the sublime in the Old Testament only succeeded in begging the question of the true nature of the Longinian sublime. Not that they were aware of so doing, or, if they had been aware, would have cared very much! Each age finds what it wants to in the great literature and criticism of the past, as my subsequent discussion of additional modern critics will show. At any rate, William Smith is a faithful mirror of several of the leading critical tendencies of his day.

Apparently these tendencies were sufficiently ingrained upon the consciousness of Western critical thought to appear here and there in our own time. W. Rhys Roberts, whose translation of Longinus' treatise appeared just before the turn of the century, revives the bi-polarity of rhetoric and external phenomena that I noted in Smith. Roberts is, however, less sensitive than his predecessor, to the idea of transport in Longinus, as the following lines indicate:

> As to our author's own style we sometimes feel, as perhaps might be expected from his theme, that he fails to show that business-like directness [!] of exposition which is so effective when information or instruction is to be imparted, and which is so foreign to the atmosphere of a leisurely seclusion. (Introduction, pp. 33-34)

The foregoing is not only insensitive, it also fails to grasp the possibility, which I have said is one of my theses, that the further from poetic expression the critic goes, the harder it is for him to convey the idea of the sublime. In our second passage from Roberts' introduction he starts out well but ends up missing the point.

> Like the author of the "Dialogue on Oratory," he [Longinus] sees in literature not a convention, not a matter of form, but the reflection of a national life; a great style is evoked by great surroundings and great events. . . . He is himself a man of great moral endowments; the misfortune was that he had fallen upon evil days. (p. 34)

Here is another kind of emphasis on external events, as contrasted with Burke's, that can lead to specious conclusions. Roberts also makes the artist more subservient to his environment than Longinus does, if my reading of the latter is correct.

The passing of just seven years leads me to the second general group of critics I am surveying. It was in 1906 that A. O. Prickard's translation[15] of Longinus appeared. A great difference is immediately discernable between his approach to Longinus and his influence, and the approach of Smith and Roberts. Perhaps the best word for it is liber-

[15] *Longinus on the Sublime*, trans. A. O. Prickard (Oxford, 1906)

ality. Prickard is no captive of the party that would make Longinus primarily a rhetorician. Neither, on the other hand, does he get swept away by enthusiasm for the Burke-Kant complex of critical concepts. So far, so good. But Prickard's introductory remarks to his translation pay the price of catholicity without making the most of its potential advantage – blazing a trail to a constructive new critical outlook. Prickard eagerly lists the beneficiaries of Longinus' influence, but fails to differentiate one from another. He does not, for example, distinguish the different concepts of the sublime held by Addison, Reynolds, Lowth, and Burke. So while we thank Prickard for not forcing Longinus into uncomfortable positions, we cannot use his treatment of the Greek to increase our own understanding or ability to apply a Longinian critique to any given work of art with responsibility. In a word, Prickard is too general and indiscriminate.

Suffering from the same inadequacy is T. R. Henn, *Longinus and English Criticism* (Cambridge, 1934), one of the standard works on the subject since its publication. Apparently Henn's ruling assumption is that all great artists and critics from Plato to Eliot are likely to esteem the same general principles, though the names attached to them may differ. Taken in the most generous sense, Henn is probably right about this. Having stimulated his reader's interest along these lines, however, Henn merely appears to assume that he has said enough, and proceeds to analyze Longinus in terms of passages from all literary periods that he judges examples of Longinian principles, without subjecting the latter to close scrutiny. Hence, the reader soon senses a bit of circularity in Henn's presentation. In addition to this, Henn generally sees fit to omit specific documentation of Longinus' influence on a given author. (This is for the obvious reason that by his approach Henn cannot document the majority of these influences, the chief drawback of 'appreciative criticism', no matter how judicious and sensitive.)

To balance what I have just said, on the other hand, let us consider several passages from *Longinus and English Criticism* that intimate that better days were to lie ahead for critical assessment of Longinus and the sublime. Henn begins his book on an ironical note:

> A dozen quotations from modern critics will reveal the fact that the principles of Greek criticism must now be sifted very carefully before they can claim any validity in English . . . and it seems very likely that the analytic aspect of Greek criticism, with its emphasis on rhetoric and technique, is as definitely alien to the modern consciousness as it was acceptable to the Neo-Classic. (p. 1)

That Henn understands that the sublime is not fettered by rhetoric, natural objects or narrow morality is attested to by the following:

> So far, then, it appears that the term "sublime" is not necessarily limited to the terrible, the obscure, the calm, the solemn, but may be held to cover all literature of striking beauty and power. This may be corroborated by analysing the response to the sublime. (p. 12)

There are three passages in Henn that seem as fertile for developing deeper comprehension of *On the Sublime* as any in the book. I might add that they foreshadow some of the most exciting ideas that we will find in the critics of our third group. I give the three passages below, uninterrupted by further commentary on my part.

> If we once set aside the analytic method of the rhetoricians – and Longinus elsewhere gives abundant proof of his organic view of the sublime – the matter [use of figures] then becomes an explanation, together with a rationalization, rather than a prescription. Such and such effects are produced: the causes may be ascertained. Technical devices can be isolated; their failure can readily be seen. (p. 43)

> True to his principles, Longinus appeals not to the rhetoricians but to Demosthenes, and concludes that metaphors may be multiplied when passion is dominant, and this "screens the number of metaphors used." (p. 62)

> The importance of sentence-structure and rhythm, as conducing to "greatness," is repeatedly emphasized. Longinus is never quite free from the dominance of the rhetoricians: but it is to be noted that he realizes the possibility of a specious greatness through these methods. (p. 104)

Lest I allow Henn's superficiality, alluded to above, to escape being itemized, attention is invited to his discussion of Reynolds (pp. 114-116). Henn is, it seems, one of a rather large number of critics who are too quick to note the similarities between the famous painter and Longinus to see that there are fundamental differences too.

Henn states that the interpretation of 'ὕψους' narrowed steadily during the eighteenth century. It will be interesting to see if this is borne out by the Context.[16]

Elizabeth Nitchie merits attention on account of two articles that she published within the space of a year. With the later of these, "Longinus and the Theory of Poetic Imitation in 17th and 18th Century England" (*Studies in Philology*, XXXII [October 1935], 580-597), I will have little to do, except to observe that Prof. Nitchie traces therein the numerous seventeenth- and eighteenth-century English writers who were apparently influenced by Longinus' idea of imitation. She antici-

[16] See my Chapter XII, p. 209.

pates Godolphin's approach in her last sentence: "So liberal was the attitude of Longinus, that, on this matter as on many others, he proved to be 'all things to all men,' acceptable to the good and liberal critics of whatever school." As it turns out, you could not find in print anywhere a better statement of the credo of the liberal critic, the kind of critic that I am concerned with in this second group. It will be remembered, however, that I said above that there was possible a critical approach to Longinus that maintained the flexibility of a Nitchie, but without falling back on the somewhat lame 'all things to all men'.

Prof. Nitchie's second, and earlier, article is not only of some interest in its own right but includes in its scholarly apparatus a fascinating example of mutiple critical reaction to the problem of the sublime by a number of Nitchie's contemporaries. The article in question is "Longinus and Later Literary Criticism" (*The Classical Weekly*, 27, no. 16 [1934], 121-126, 129-136). Although one of her early statements has a familiar ring: "Although the title of the treatise is commonly translated by 'On the Sublime,' the work is really a discussion of good style, excellence in writing,[13] [sic]" Nitchie goes on in such fashion as to give lie to the above. She has a catholic, common sense approach that shows Longinus' many sides, and his direct or indirect influence on myriad English writers and critics right up to the twentieth century. (Though outside of the limits of this study, it is worth mentioning that Nitchie is one of the few critics you will come cross who see a sober Longinian strain in Pater.) Taken individually, however, Nitchie's remarks on Longinus and the sublime add little that is particularly interesting. Most of the interest lies in the contrast between her work and the body of footnote 13, to the article, indicated above, which illustrates the difference between Nitchie's liberal viewpoint and several more traditional positions. (Footnote 13 is very long and complicated, so in the interest of conciseness and clarity, I omit a few lines, and paraphrase others.) Nitchie introduces the footnote by observing that "the statements so often made about the influence of Longinus upon aesthetic theory are evidently based upon a wrong interpretation of the Greek title of the treatise". She then quotes Bernhard Bosanquet: "However philosophically incomplete, this work . . . [sic] is probably responsible for the exceedingly important part played by the theory of the Sublime in modern speculation."[17] Nitchie continues that "of those who wrote of the Sublime or of 'das Erhabene' (Burke, Kames, Kant,

[17] *A History of Aesthetic* (London, Sonnenschein, New York, Macmillan, 1910), p. 106.

Schiller) only Kames seems to have written with Longinus in mind". This statement supports the stand presented in this chapter on the degree of faithfulness of Burke and Kant to Longinus.

After saying that Bosanquet declares that Burke followed Longinus, Nitchie credits Rhys Roberts with greater accuracy, in his statement that "Burke's *Sublime and Beautiful* has no manner of connexion with the *De Sublimitate.*" Regarding the other three writers, Nitchie finds that Kant, as Burke, postulates terror as the basis for the sublime, that Schiller's treatment is almost wholly philosophical, and that although Kames constantly quotes and paraphrases Longinus he limits the sublime to the 'greatly elevated'. Nitchie's portion of the footnote concludes:

Several of the literary critics, such as Boileau and De Quincey, pointed out the real meaning of " ὕψους ," as Longinus himself defined it. But, although the writers on aesthetics show little of Longinus's influence, the popularity of the treatise in the neo-classic period certainly gave currency to the words "sublime", "bathos", "bombast", "frigidity", and to the pairing of the sublime and the pathetic, the sublime and the ridiculous, which are used well into the nineteenth century and by unexpected writers. Burns heard them up in Scotland, perhaps among the literary folk of Edinburgh, and wrote "To make a happy fireside clime/To weans and wife,/ That's the true pathos and sublime/Of human life." . . .

At this point in footnote 13 Charles Knapp, editor of *The Classical Weekly*, assumes command, as it were, and begins by remarking that he thinks it worthwhile to quote what Roberts wrote on the meaning of the title of Longinus' treatise:

The contents and character of the treatise will be found to be admirably indicated in the traditional Greek title " περι ὕψους " and in its accepted English equivalent *On the Sublime*, if only the words " ὕψους " and "Sublime" be correctly understood.

The English equivalent has, no doubt, often caused misconception. The treatise has been thought to be at once more ambitious in purpose, and more narrow in scope, than it really is. But the Greek title " περι ὕψους, " "Concerning Height or Elevation," does not convey that idea of abnormal altitude which is often associated with the word "sublime." [Even if this is true, it does not support Roberts' overall argument.] The object of the author rather is to indicate broadly the essentials of a noble and impressive STYLE [my emphasis]. In fact, if we were to describe the treatise as one on style, or even on literary criticism generally, we should be nearer the mark than if we connected it solely with the idea of "sublimity" in the narrower sense. [This sentence is not very edifying, because a treatise on style is quite different from one on literary criticism generally, and Roberts does not make clear just exactly what he means by sublimity in the narrower sense.]

The author's own words make this plain [!], for early in his book (i.3) he remarks that the friend whom he is addressing is too well versed in literary studies to need the reminder that sublimity is a certain distinction and excellence in expression and that it is from no other source than this that the greatest authors have derived their eminence and gained an immortality of renown. . . . [Apparently it never occurs to Roberts or Knapp that this concession by Longinus to Terentianus might be irony or a rhetorical figure of thought, or both!]

Knapp continues that it is also worthwhile to quote Professor Charles Sears Baldwin:[18]

. . . The Greek word [Knapp supplies " ὕψους."] is more general [than, says Knapp, the English word sublime]. Meaning literally height, it includes in this treatise all such effects of STYLE [my emphasis] as lift us, as move us beyond comprehension or assent to sympathy or resolve. But though the meaning is clear, an equivalent English term is still to seek. [Moot are the two points made about the word *hupsous* that it is more general than the word sublime, and that its meaning is clear.] "Elevation" has unfortunate suggestions of the rhetorical [Baldwin would be more consistent if he had used 'over-dependence on' instead of 'suggestions of', since he has already emphasized the centrality of style.]; "height" is too vague; "heightening," though nearer, is not generally used in this sense. Falling back on such a periphrasis as "heightening of style," we become aware that our word "style", as used generally and untechnically, is not far from the author's intention. Though in text-books and works of criticism it is often extended, in ordinary parlance it means that very heightening, or lift, which is discussed by the Great Unknown [Longinus]. So we shall convey his intention as fairly as seems feasible by translating his title "Style." [It seems that Baldwin is untidy in associating ordinary parlance with *On the Sublime*, which is, after all, literary criticism. However, to do him justice, Baldwin is correct in recognizing the nearly insurmountable semantic problem in moving between Greek and English in discussing the sublime. He is also on the right track in his obvious effort to relax and broaden the interpretation of Longinus' title, but it was for later critics to carry that search closer to fruition.]

Thus we have seen the interesting interaction within the confines of a single article of a liberal if somewhat imprecise view of the Longinian sublime and the attempts by three writers to be more precise resulting in an overliteral emphasis on style. To this point in the discussion of critical positions on the sublime we have seen champions of the rhetorical orientation, of the natural sublime, and of the intuitive commonality through the ages of the sublime, whatever it may be exactly. Still to seek is a critic who substantiates my thesis that Longinus' sub-

[18] *Ancient Rhetoric and Poetic* (New York, 1924)

lime is a phenomenon that exists where the demands of form, appropriate subject matter, and artistic inspiration are fused.

Turning next to F. R. B. Godolphin, "The Basic Critical Doctrine of Longinus 'On the Sublime'" (*Transaction and Proceedings of the American Philological Association*, LXVIII (1937), 172-183), we encounter an approach that in several ways advances beyond any treated above. For Godolphin sees that *On the Sublime* is not purely a treatise on rhetoric or a collection of random intuitions on literary art:

> The presentation of both explicit and implicit doctrines of Longinus as a part of a consistently held critical position involves certain dangers, especially since his purpose in writing led him to include much that was specifically practical in the field of rhetoric. However, a study of the whole seems to me to demonstrate beyond all doubt that it is neither a technical treatise on rhetoric* nor a collection of random observations and intuitions of literary values. Longinus conceives of skill and technique in rhetoric as means, not ends. The sublime consists of distinction and excellence in expression*, but more than this it demands a worthy conception of the divine power*. It exists, therefore, both as a definition of achievement and as a power or force. Elevation of mind*, then, is the most important element of the true sublime*.[19] (pp. 172-173)

Before quoting further from the body of Godolphin's article, it might be well to pause and observe that so far he is better on what Longinus is not than on what he is. The latter part of the passage is virtually a paraphrase of sections of the treatise. I pause also to render the footnotes to Godolphin's text because of the instructing reference made to two critics we have already discussed, and in the interest of affording the reader the exact sources in Longinus for Godolphin's interpretation.

The next two passages reveal the importance that Godolphin places on the religious element. He probably exaggerates its importance, but it is interesting to compare him on this score with William Smith.

[19] The asterisks represent Godolphin's footnotes 5, 6, 7, 8, and 9, whose contents are as follows:

5. The translation of Longinus 6.1 "χρίοις τῶν λόγων" as "judgment of style" in A. O. Prickard, *Longinus on the Sublime* (Oxford, Clarendon Press, 1906), p. 11 and Roberts, *Longinus on the Sublime* (Cambridge, 1907), p. 55 contributes to such an impression and is less in accord with the spirit of the whole than the translation of W. H. Fyfe, *Longinus on the Sublime* (London, Heinemann, 1927), p. 137, "judgment in literature." At 1.4 "ὑπερφυᾶ" is translated "elevated language" by Roberts but as "passages of extraordinary genius" by Prickard and "effect of genius" by Fyfe.

6. Longinus 1.3

7. Ibid. 9.9

8. Ibid. 9.1 "Τὸ μεγαλοφυές"

9. Longinus' fear that "Τὸ ὕψους" may be misunderstood leads him to use "γενναῖον" and "αληθές" frequently.

This basic position of Longinus is derived from the statement, "Nature has appointed us men to be no base or ignoble animals . . . she implants in our souls the unconquerable love of whatever is elevated and more divine than ourselves."* [Longinus 35.2] (p. 173)

If man is of a higher order of creation than the other animals, and if his aspirations are in the direction of that which is higher than himself, we have in Longinus not merely a humanist, but a humanist whose belief leads him toward a religious position for the ultimate sanction of his values. This view is emphatically reaffirmed in the last chapter of the work, where Longinus condemns those men who value that part of themselves which is mortal and transient, and neglect the development of that part of themselves which is immortal. Unless this is a mere figure of rhetoric, Longinus is here indicating an essential element in his view of the world and his faith in the worth of objects beyond those which may bring praise and pleasure in any material sense.*[20] [Longinus 44.8, 44.11] (p. 174)

I do not suppose that anyone would maintain that Godolphin has done violence to Longinus' feelings on matters spiritual, but the question remains as to how pertinent and enlightening Godolphin's stress is for furthering our understanding of the sublime. His problem seems to be that he cannot relate satisfactorily the concept of the sublime of a 'suprahuman world' and its requirement that it be kept firmly in check by the proprieties of conscious art. I quote:

In the first chapter Longinus has pointed out that " Τὰ ὑπερφνᾶ ", works of genius, lead the hearer not to persuasion, the proper object of rhetoric* [15 Aristotle, "Rhet." 1355 b 25.],[21] but " εις ἔμστασιν ," to transport. His conception of " Τὸ ὕψους " can only be understood in the light of a mystic experience which is the " ἔμστασις " that distinguishes the effect of the sublime from the effect of all merely technical skills. . . . Longinus, then, conceives a suprahuman realm to exist; the true sublime is that which enables the artist to convey his further vision, and transport is that effect of the sublime upon the reader which lifts him out of himself into a higher understanding. At the same time Longinus insists that nature is not without method and system* [17 *Ibid.* 2.2]. He stresses the fact that the sublime is not simply a matter of the intuition or mystic apprehension, but must be kept firmly in check by conscious art. Even in the "revels of the imagination" sobriety is required.* [18 *Ibid.* 16.4]. . . . Since the creation of a work of art requires art and nature to function in harmony, the effect of a work of art is related to both emotion and reason. (p. 175)

We follow Godolphin as he introduces some new ideas, which are valuable if still a little vague:

It is clear that Longinus is neither a subjective "aesthetic" critic nor a commonplace follower of the "rules."* [23 The repealed (sic) objections to

[20] Asterisks represent Godolphin's footnotes 10 and 12.

mechanical use of formulae should be noted, e.g. 16.3; 32.1] What we do find is a philosophic critic, an intelligent and sensitive man who shows at the heart of his interest in literature a truly Greek devotion to a law of balance and avoidance of excess. Art and nature* [[24] Longinus 36.4], intuition and reason, are extremes; and the creation and interpretation of literature lies in some form of reconciliation of both terms in each pair. (p. 176)

The reader may object at this point that Godolphin sticks so close to the text of the treatise that his discussion is little more than a paraphrase. So he does, but the significant point is the selection made for emphasis. Accordingly, I find it commendable that Godolphin appreciates Longinus' emphasis on a thorough understanding of an author by a critic, the necessity of particularity in criticism, and the use of comparative method for enlightenment instead of as a show of erudition:

The test suggested in Chapter 14 provides a valuable starting-point both for the creative artist and the critic. How would Homer, Plato, Demosthenes, or Thucydides have said this thing, or reacted to this way of saying it? The artist or critic who makes this imaginative test can obtain very definite human assistance toward the solution of a problem which from its nature precludes absolute certainty. (p. 178)

The use of concrete examples in the treatment of great art as compared with flawless art and indeed in the discussion of every critical generalization, is of the utmost importance to an understanding of Longinus. (p. 179)

The comparative method is another tool that Longinus uses, and here it should be noted that its purpose is enlightenment, not the accumulation of erudite details. Moses and Cicero provide him with materials not to be found in his own literature, and are not used for a mere parade of information.* [[32] *Ibid.* 9.9; 12.4] (p. 180)

Finally, Godolphin correctly interprets Longinus regarding the relatively little importance for the artist of the external world compared with the state of his own soul. And Godolphin comes close, without actually pinning it down, to the idea of literature as expression rather than description. Needless to say, this distinction is one of the central issues in the history of the eighteenth-century sublime.

Godolphin says that all his references are to the translation of Roberts, though with modifications, but he never identifies the latter. However, he is less influenced by the rhetorical possibilities of the treatise than Roberts. If this study has an abiding fault, it is Godol-

[21] All asterisks in the remaining passages of Godolphin indicate his footnotes, whose numbers and contents follow in brackets immediately after the asterisks.

phin's tendency to make Longinus the perfect critic – too good to be true. Maybe his staying so close to the treatise causes Godolphin to re-create the Greek critic in his own image through an overly indulgent reading.

In his review article on Walter J. Hipple, Jr., *The Beautiful, the Sublime, and the Picturesque in Eighteenth-Century British Aesthetic Theory* (Carbondale, 1957), Ralph Cohen presents two main criticisms.[22] He charges that Hipple is so concerned with the exposition of abstract philosophical systems that he neglects to offer the confused reader some concrete examples that illustrate the logic and methodology of those systems. Cohen further alleges that Hipple does not even accomplish what he set out to do because of the omission of certain important parts of several systems. This is no place to plead the case for either scholar. I will say, however, that although I am inclined to agree with Cohen in an overall estimation of the book, the latter nevertheless has pertinence for my investigation in a number of random comments.

The book is a systematic presentation of the esthetic credos of sixteen major critics. There is practically no discussion of minor figures. Somewhat surprisingly, Hipple has little to say about Longinus and his treatise. Indeed, he mentions them only fourteen times throughout. As a result, the main value for us of Hipple's work is its remarks corrective of Monk's earlier study. Three will suffice here. Hipple criticizes as invalid Monk's proposition "that the aesthetic speculations in the Britain of that age [eighteenth century] were an unconscious prolegomenon to Kant" (p. 284). And later (p. 371, n. 79) Hipple says, "This evaluation [the inability of the eighteenth century to deal imaginatively with the 'ultimates' in art] accords with the Kantian bias of Monk's study." (Significantly, Hipple has nothing to do with Kant.)

Nowhere does Hipple draw the lines of battle more distinctly than in the following passage:

> This program [Burke's method in his *Philosophical Enquiry*] is not, as some moderns [an obvious reference to Monk] have seen it, a step from the objectivism of the neo-classic to a psychological and subjective view; this whole dichotomy, applied to the aestheticians here examined, is an illusion – all the aestheticians from Addison to Kant and onwards conceive of the sublime as a feeling in the mind caused by certain properties in external objects. The real differences among these men are to be sought in the methods of argument and the causal principles which they employ. (p. 84)

[22] *Philological Quarterly*, XXXVII, no. 3 (July 1958), 291-4.

The last of the critics whom I have grouped together because of their broad view of Longinus is K. G. Hamilton. His *The Two Harmonies: Poetry and Prose in the Seventeenth Century* (Oxford, 1963) is one of the better recent studies of the causes of the divergence of the two major modes of verbal expression during the post-Renaissance era. In addition to one sustained discussion of Longinus and the eighteenth-century sublime (pp. 180-189), there are several other interesting comments made on the subject throughout the book. But primarily, Hamilton sees that the poetry, or language, of the passions of the early eighteenth century includes part of the development of the concept of the creative imagination (p. 42). Hamilton is probably correct in dating this earlier in the century than does Monk, but unfortunately he is, like Monk, entranced by the nineteenth-century idea of the 'creative imagination'. The twentieth century is inclined to look askance at a term such as this because of its attendant fuzziness and semantic pitfalls.

One of the cant opinions generally expressed whenever the subject arises of the differences between the sublime of Longinus and the sublime of the eighteenth century is that there was a shift from the Longinian sublime response in the artist to the eighteenth-century sublime response in the audience. This dictum is suspect on several counts. To begin with I have never seen anyone try to deal with the knotty problem of reconciling this supposed shift with the concomitant tendency to recognize the autonomy and original genius of the artist. To say that both phenomena existed simultaneously is surely to weaken the authority of each as a dominating concept. In the second place, certain modern readings of *On the Sublime*, as we shall see, remove the traditional emphasis on the artist. This sort of interpretation obviously precludes differentiating Longinus and the eighteenth-century sublime on the basis of response location. This study will offer enough examples of the sublime in the artist, in the natural sources of literary inspiration, and in the literary work itself to cause scepticism over the reality of a single dominating 'shift'.

Without discussing the problem in these terms, Hamilton finds that there was a shift in interest from the audience to the poet stemming from well before mid-century, if certain of his words on page 42 are taken at face value. However, on page 54 he seems to push the whole process further back in the century. Hamilton's exposition of this difficult matter is obfuscated by hazy chronology.

There is nothing vague, however, about the way in which Hamilton gives John Dennis his due as a critic influential on the course of poetry as it was to evolve during the eighteenth century (p. 138). Hamilton values Dennis for recognizing, with Longinus, the link between poetic experience and what Hamilton calls the unique language of poetry (p. 189).

I turn now to the third, and last, group of critics. It is hoped that treating their ideas will integrate the ideas of several recognized authorities with some of the questions that led to the undertaking of this context study in the beginning. In Caroline Bird Menuez, "Longinus on the Equivalence of the Arts" (*Classical Journal,* XXXVI, 1941, 346-353), we encounter an article that deals with the Greek in extra-literary matters. Menuez says that Longinus' appreciation of the art forms other than literature confronts him with the problem of a general esthetics, which, although he does not deal with as such, gives him a broader insight into literature (p. 346).

Although Menuez covers music, painting, and sculpture, it is in the discussion of the first of these that she makes her most telling points, and I will restrict myself thereto. She begins with musical accompaniment:

> He [Longinus] has made more than a chance simile, however, when he says that musical accompaniment is to melody what periphrasis is to thought ... (p. 347)

Menuez goes on to explain:

> This comparison of accompaniment to melody with periphrasis to thought gets at a principle of composition which holds both for patterns in words and patterns in sound. The consistency with which he [Longinus] applies the analogy shows that he almost conceives the nature of periphrasis in musical terms, a most natural conception in view of the assimilation of the function of musical accompaniment into the words themselves. ...
>
> In the course of warring against over-rhythmical writing he discovers another common principle between music and literature. ...
>
> In a striking passage on the effect of music he similarly equates the emotional excitement induced by music to that induced by literature, and implies that this effect is produced by the operation of identical principles in the respective media ... (p. 349)

Here Menuez quotes a long passage from *On the Sublime,* Ch. XXXIX in support of her thesis. Now it is well known that the classical rhetoricians were aware of the various elements, including rhythm, that served to persuade an audience – indeed, that was their job – but Menuez claims that Longinus transcends the rhetoricians in the sensitivity and profundity of his description of the psychological effect of rhythm in both music and literature. As she states, it is one thing to say that a great tragedy leaves you with the same feeling that an equally great symphony does, but quite another to describe as Longinus does this common reaction, and attempt to trace its source. She finds that Longinus starts with the response to rhythm and ultimately discovers that this response has a physical origin, producing an almost irresistible compulsion 'to move rhythmically in accordance therewith' (p. 350).

Menuez opines that Longinus recognizes the emotional effect of music without worrying about the ethical implications as Plato and Aristotle had earlier. The esthetic reaction has autonomous interest as the object of speculation. According to Menuez, Longinus, in speculating thus, refrains from splitting up sublimity into one half form and one half content. Instead, the building of phrase upon phrase erects a 'sublime and harmonious structure' (p. 351). I quote the conclusion of this passage from the article because it is at once a good rebuttal to Monk, and partial explanation, possibly, of the fact that the Context contains so much interesting material drawn from the one source that one would least suspect of harboring it, the rhetoric books of the seventeenth and eighteenth centuries. (Cf. Monk, p. 84)

> Here Longinus shows himself as one of the first to rate literature almost exclusively on style [but not straight rhetoric or imitation of nature in the sense of 'Mimesis'], as he is the first to recognize style as pattern of thought and emotion rather than a complex of word tricks [rhetorical tropes and figures]. He finds the origin of rhetorical figures psychologically in the mind's method of operation, and discovers that it is the subjugation of the object, whether real or ideal, to a pattern which pleases the mind, not merely its imitation [a most important point]: and if his love of music did not have something to do with leading his mind to the nature of these patterns in the beginning, he finds it at least illuminating to illustrate their operation from music, where they exist in abstract form. (p. 351)

An interesting thesis and a reasonable one at that. Olson is close to this particular kind of psychological orientation, as we shall see.

Our penultimate critic, Iris Murdoch, is not directly concerned with Longinus, but is included in this chapter because of her useful criticism of Kant as an esthetician of the sublime.[23] (As we have seen, at least one prominent scholar of the sublime relies heavily on this aspect of the great German philosopher!) Murdoch says that Kant distinguishes 'free' and 'dependent' beauty (as opposed to sublimity). 'Free' beauty is the simultaneous apprehension by the imagination and understand-

[23] "The Sublime and the Good", *Chicago Review*, XIII, iii (1959), 42-55.

ing of a sensuous object that is not brought under any particular concept and is verified in accordance with a rule we cannot formulate. It is pure form, devoid of external value. An example is a flower, or a bird's song. 'Dependent' beauty, on the other hand, is likely to involve a value judgment, and hence is less pure. Examples of this are a handsome person, and a song (with words) (p. 43). Murdoch, as I would, criticizes the Kantian dictum that art of 'free' beauty is non-significant. Where she turns to Kant on the sublime, I quote her directly:

> Whereas beauty is not connected with emotion, the sense of the sublime is. Strictly, whereas objects may be beautiful, no object is ever sublime. It is rather that certain aspects of nature occasion feelings of sublimity in us. Whereas beauty results from a harmony between imagination and understanding, sublimity results from a conflict between imagination and reason. . . . "It is an object (of nature) the representation of which determines the mind to regard the elevation of nature beyond our reach as equivalent to a presentation of ideas." (pp. 44-45) [Murdoch does not document her quotation from Kant.]

This sets up, of course, a tension between the completeness of the reason's apprehension of an object, and the incompleteness of the imagination's apprehension thereof. The experience of sublimity has a closer relation to morals than that of beauty, because reason – the moral will itself – is active in the experience. This theorizing by Kant is all very well when taken as part of a systematic whole, but I do not think it even necessary to point out that it tells us very little that we really want to know about esthetics.

Murdoch comments that, according to Kant, the sublime has nothing necessarily to do with art, in the sense that it is not restricted to art. The sublime can also be an uplifting emotion experienced in the Alps. Furthermore, for Kant the sublime is the failure of the imagination to embrace "an abstractly conceived non-historical, non-social, quasi-mathematical totality which is not *given* [sic] but only vaguely adumbrated by reason" (p. 49). Murdoch concludes that Kant associates sublimity with "the dream of an empty non-historical totality which is not given" (p. 50).

I would have to agree with Murdoch that the weaknesses in Kant's esthetics parallel those in his system of ethics. Instead of being involved in the particular art work, as, it seems to me, any esthetic must be to at least some degree, and instead of including history, as nearly all art does in at least a general way, Kant's esthetics would rise from the particular to the rational, timeless, and place-less. As I said above, Kant may have for many people a beauty born of pure thought, but he seems to be an unfortunate choice as the basis of a study of the eighteenth-century sublime with its proliferation of particularities.

Two pieces by Elder Olson complete my survey of modern studies of the sublime. The first to be written, and the most comprehensive, is "The Argument of Longinus 'On the Sublime'" (*Modern Philology,* XXXIX [1942], 225-258). The second is an introduction to the *University Classics* edition of Longinus' *On the Sublime* and Joshua Reynolds' *Discourses*, published in one volume (Chicago, 1945), pp. vii-xxi. Concerning Longinus' technique, this introduction is a simplified resume of the earlier article, but it contains other material of interest, which I will take up in due course.

One of Olson's main objectives in the article is the reconstruction of the lacunae in Longinus' treatise.[24] To this end Olson brings considerable ingenuity to bear on the analysis of the Greek's processes of composition. Olson finds that the basis of Longinus' argument is dialectics, using the triad, author-work-audience. There is no space here for recapitulating Olson's demonstration of the dialectic triad as the organizing principle of the treatise, but it suffices to say that Olson is very persuasive. Allowing for the excesses that inevitably result from the imposition of a disciplined exegesis on a rhapsodic original, we discover that Olson enables us to look at *On the Sublime* in a fresh way.

It will be remembered that Henn begins his book with an ironic reference to the supposed difficulty of validly transferring the principles of Greek literary criticism to English criticism because of the alien emphasis in the former on rhetoric and technique. Interestingly, Olson commences in the same general vein, but makes much more of it.

Lastly, for the "scholastic" rhetoricians of Greece and Rome, the question of sublimity is posed never as an end but as a question relevant to the various means – more specifically, to the different kinds of styles – of rhetoric; and, while for these rhetoricians the question would have been one of greater importance than for Plato or Aristotle [cf. Menuez], it would have been, nevertheless, specifically a rhetorical problem, and its solution would have consisted in the enumeration of stylistic devices – chiefly the

[24] Most commentators express great regret that the section of *On the Sublime* concerning the passions has never been recovered, if indeed Longinus ever did write it. Actually, the fact of the matter is that it probably would have been less interesting than the parts of the treatise that we have. There is every chance that Longinus had more insight into literature, and that more original, than he had into men's emotions taken of and by themselves. That is to say that while *On the Sublime* is a unique piece of literary criticism, Longinus' remarks on the passions would probably not have added anything to the extant corpus of Greek commentary thereon.

"figures" of rhetoric – which are constitutive of the elevated style. Whereas Plato draws a distinction between literary kinds and transcends it, whereas Aristotle discriminates among kinds of works and uses this discrimination as a principle of his treatment of them, and whereas the scholastic rhetoricians find their distinctions among rhetorical ends rather than among kinds of means, Longinus obliterates ultimately all such distinctions of kinds and end and makes the focal point of his inquiry a certain quality discriminated from among other qualities of composition. A treatise so ordered is distinct in method from these other treatments; and the statements which are employed in the prosecution of that method cannot be compared directly, without a precarious shift of meanings, to the statements which arise out of such variously opposed treatments as those of Plato, Aristotle, and, let us say, the author of the *Ad Herennium.* (pp. 229-30)

Olson continues his analysis by pointing out that Longinus, by analogizing back and forth across his dialectical triad, makes it impossible to base literary criticism on the distinctions of genre – at least, I am tempted to add, when sublimity is the underlying focus of that criticism. Olson emphasizes that such a dialectical approach precludes a theory of rhetoric just as surely as a theory of tragedy or comedy. Thus arguing, Olson concludes that one must admit that the foundations of the art must be stated in psychological terms. At this point he anticipates my objection (which I would surely make because of my reluctance to substitute another psychological approach to the sublime for the earlier eighteenth-century one, which I feel I have discredited) by saying that Longinus himself defines the sublime in terms of human character and faculties rather than in purely literary terms, and that the only way we can question Longinus' argument is to say that his terms mean something else than he says they do or that he is not really studying literature because he asks the wrong questions (pp. 234-5). I am least sympathetic to Olson's method at this juncture, which permits little flexibility, and seems to be more concerned with how Longinus thinks than with what he thinks. In addition, if Olson's close attention to the text of the treatise and the function of language causes me to group him with the 'quasi-Langerians', his emphasis on the artist's psyche at the expense of the art work qualifies his membership in the group.

After discussing the nature and role of passion, both from Longinus' explicit statements and from his own extension of Longinus' argument, Olson concludes his article:

It should appear from this discussion that the term "sublimity" can scarcely be taken as referring to a mere elevation of diction, for to take it in this sense is to regard a literary work as a mere arrangement of words and to collapse all the sources of sublimity into those which are merely ver-

> bal, and perhaps all of these, even, into synthesis alone. The treatise of Longinus affords every evidence that he sought to avoid such a reduction and that hence the word should not be taken in its merely stylistic sense but should receive its definition in terms of that communication of nobility which is made possible by the perfection of the human soul and of art, and which receives its answer in the wonder and admiration of all men. (p. 258)

Once again, it is interesting to observe here the result of Olson's highly disciplined approach. He correctly, according to my thesis, recognizes that *On the Sublime* is not a book on rhetoric, but then neglects the other possibilities of word arrangement (unlike Langer, who is most provocative on this matter) in favor of the artist's soul.

Olson's introduction to the *University Classics* edition of Longinus contains a number of interesting points, none of which is more worthy of attention than the comparison between Longinus and Edmund Burke. I quote Olson at some length, interspersing two comments of my own.

> Unlike Edmund Burke, who finds the sources of sublimity in qualities of the subject-matter of art, Longinus finds them in the faculties of the author. [Note how this statement makes Longinus appear to be more psychologically oriented than Burke, in the modern sense.] In each case the discovery results from the argument rather than from any other cause: if we differentiate the emotions of the audience, as Burke does, in terms which permit natural as well as artificial objects to be considered as their causes, the qualitative differentiations in the objects are responsible for the qualitative differentiations in the emotions; i.e., the source of the sublime is in the subject matter, not in the art [which is precisely the reason, I suspect, that Longinus virtually subsumes the term subject matter under the term artist in his argument; for Longinus is an artist (or at the least has the sensibilities of an artist) and a humanist, not, like Burke, a philosopher, and must therefore deny natural objects the power of by-passing the selective and discriminative faculties of the artist. This does not mean, however, that Longinus is necessarily less sensitive to the potential for sublimity in nature]; if, on the other hand, we are concerned like Longinus with an effort which, although it is similar to certain effects produced by natural objects, is itself a peculiar consequence of speech, the source must lie within the art and thus, given the other Longinian determinations, in the human faculties relative to discourse. (p. xii)

Olson goes on immediately to give his version of Longinus' five sources of the sublime. These include the elements that I have mentioned so often by now, but once again Olson comes close to Langer's appreciation of the semantic of language without quite attaining it (p. xiii).

As I promised above, Olson gives a penetrating insight into the differences between Longinus' and Reynolds' concept of the sublime. This commentary has added significance because of the traditional stand which sees closer agreement on the sublime by the two. Olson claims that for Longinus the source of the sublime dwells in the faculties of artist and audience, whereas for Reynolds it is the subject-matter, as constituted by the imagination, that transmits enthusiasm to both parties, and which guarantees 'the great effect' (pp. xvi-xvii). And then, in the following quotation, Olson makes what may be essentially the same observation, stood on its head, that I made in the long insertion in the passage concerning Burke just above:

> To make sublimity due chiefly to nature ['nature' apparently used here as human nature and external nature] is not to preclude the possibility of an art of the sublime [Reynolds'], but it is to assign to art the secondary role of insuring the efficacy of natural powers, or of imitating their efficacy in producing an effect which is the natural consequence of naturally great men employing a natural medium of communication. (p. xviii)

In summing up his comparison of Longinus and Reynolds, Olson states that they are not only dissimilar but completely unrelated to one another (in argumentative procedure, I think he means). Olson finds that they have neither the same critical problem nor similar assumptions:

> Longinus views the products of several arts in terms of a single effect; Reynolds views all the effects of a single art. Longinus conceives of the powers of the sublime speaker, including the "gift of expression" as natural; for Reynolds the "language," even, of painting is taught by art, and in general all the powers of the great artist are developed by art and are reducible to art. (p. xx)

If we feel that this peroration is a little too neat, and pushes the two critics too far asunder, we must also admit that he presents a strong case for eyeing Reynolds askance as any kind of pure Longinian.

In concluding this discussion of what are probably the most significant modern critiques of Longinus and the sublime, we are aware that none fully reckons with the implications to be found in a work like Mrs. Langer's. The three critics of the third group at times come close in various ways to her view of symbol and esthetic of non-discursive rationality, in a word, the complete fusion of man's mind, soul, and expression, but they never take the last step. Not that it really matters; in discussing the ideas of this and the two previous groups it would seem that practically every conceivable position *vis-à-vis* Longinus and the sublime has come to light. Some of our writers, like Langer and Murdoch, had only the most general connection with the eighteenth-century sublime, while others, like Monk, Godolphin, Nitchie, Henn, Hipple, and Olson, had the most specific kind of application thereto. Taken all in all, they should have provided us with a rich intellectual and esthetic background for the considerations to which I must presently turn.

II

POETS AND POETRY

In this chapter, which includes a number of extracts from poems and a larger number of critical remarks on poetry, I begin with an example of the former that stems from an early date in our period.

Hugh Crompton, *Pierides, or the muses mount* (1658):

1.

Give me the boul, the jolly boul
  Fill'd to the brim with Claret:
And since the Crown from th'head doth roll,
  Upon my nose Ile wear it,
Ile weare it there, and 'tis no crime
If I conceive my self sublime.
(From poem 5, "The Conceit")

1.

A Rout, a rout my fansie cries,
  If reason shall give way to't,
  I know not what to say to't.
Then wake sublimer thoughts, and rise,
    Help me quickly,
    I am sickly,
Despair is come, and pleasure dies . . .
(From poem 108, "The Exaltation")

The poems in this collection are in various stanzas and line lengths, but most of them are in iambic pentameter, and show the influence of Donne and Marvell. Crompton is definitely a minor talent, albeit an impassioned one. His use of 'sublime' is obviously closer to the sublime of the passions than the sublime of rhetoric, and the early date of the poems adds interest to this usage.

John Cotgrave, *Wits interpreter: the English Parnassus, Third Edition* (1671).

My advice to the Reader shall be this, to avoid the fore-mentioned Verbatim Imitations, which are altogether unprofitable: for, to deal clearly in this particular, none but the Intelligent, such as are the Muses friends, ought to ascend this our English Parnassus; let those of the lower form that are destinated to an Adoration of their fond old Authors, keep off, their shallow Conceptions can never reach to the Sublimities of this Composure: If a Spring of Wit, height of Eloquence, the Charms of Love, softer strains of Musical Songs, or the life and delight of new Inventions, are fitly designed for Ideots, then let their thick skulls adventure on this Volume.

(Preface)

Seen again here is an early usage of the sublime that is certainly not in a rhetorical frame of reference. On the other hand, the author's usage is so vague that I cannot say anything else about it for sure.

[T.W.], *The Poet's complaint, a poem* (1682).

This little volume consists of ten pages of poetry apparently original with 'T.W.', six pages of poetic quotations from well-known poets like Otway, Dryden, and Settle, and finally a four page piece in prose entitled "The Character of Poetry". The latter is an original piece of criticism, though only in the sense that 'T.W.' wrote it; it follows the Classical-Renaissance line throughout. 'T.W.' says of "The Character of Poetry":

And as for the Character of Poetry, it is a piece I had lying by me, which I think is a more correct and a seriouser thought, than is the Poem, most of which was writ Extempore, and too morrow being the day I take shipping I wanted leisure to transcribe it. Besides you know I never lov'd to take much pains.

("The Author's Epistle to a Person of Quality")

Poetry alone among all the Arts supplies Praise to Virtue, the Rampant Stile of Rhetorical Discourse, tho it borrow its fairest Flowers and square Periods from Poetry, being not comparable to it, which is far more sublime, and consequently more fit to immortalize the Memory of Heroic Actions. (pp. 19-20)

Notice the sharp division made between rhetoric and 'sublime' poetry.

[Wing attributes to] John Phillips, of Cambridge, *A reflection on our modern poesy. An essay* (1695).

The burden of the two page Epistle Dedicatory and the 220 line (approximately) poem is about the same as in John Dennis' criticism. The major fault of the poetry of the age is its irreligiosity. The only mention of the sublime occurs in the first verse paragraph:

If Poets be (as they pretend) inspir'd
With Head Divine, and Sacred Fury fir'd,
How comes it then, that each Poetick Piece
Gives now-a-days Encouragement to Vice?
Each Line (or else we think it will not do)
With wanton Love, and Flames unchaste must glow.
That scribling Fop that Would a Poet be,
First bids adieu to all his Modesty:
Invokes not Phoebus, but the God of Wine;
Crowns his hot Temples with th'inspiring Vine:
The Glas (Dull Sot!) must make his Thoughts sublime,
For in a Sober Mood what Bard can Rhime?
(p. 1, lines 1-12)

Another generalized usage.

William Coward, *The true test of poetry. Without which it is impossible to judge of, or compose, a correct English poem. To which are added, critical observations on the principal, antient and modern poets, viz. Homer, Horace, Virgil, Milton, Waller, Cowley, Dryden, etc. as frequently liable to just censure. A Poem.* (1709)

I found no reference to the sublime in the material comprising the 42 pages of prefatory and 25 pages of postscriptural sections of the text.

There is something more in Homer of the Greatness of the Design, as well as the frequent Loftiness of Expressions. 'Tis very well observ'd by a late Critic (to me unknown) that the Sublimity of a Miltonian Style is very improper and incongruous upon so mean a Subject, as the Praise of Cyder, being a late small Poem, wrote by an Ingenious Gentleman, tho' I think very much mistaken in the Choice of the Subject for such design'd Lines of Poetry. (p. 12, footnote)

See how the War-Horse paws the dusty Plains,
Chumps on his Bit, and shakes his shackling Reins,
Or with wide Nostrils snuffs the ambient Air,
Snorts with Distain, and smells impending War.
Nay even a Childish Top, describ'd by Him,
With such Pathetic Lines, and so sublime.
Seems the attentive Reader to enchant,
Nor does a natural Decorum want.
(p. 62)

Nor can I Dryden, Milton's Names omit
Both in their Age resplendent Lights of Wit.
Tho' Milton had th'Advantage above all,
If we Blank Lines True Poetry can call.
Because not fetter'd, neither cramp'd by Rhyme,
He'd room to make his Language more sublime.
(p.65)

The prose passage speaks for itself, as does the first poetry extract, which refers to Virgil in his *Aeneid*. The second group of lines uses the word sublime in the usual tradition with regard to Milton, but it is well to bear in mind that whenever we meet with the word sublime in poetry its usage may be accountable to one degree or another to the requirements of prosody, especially rhyming.

Giles Jacob, *The poetical register: or, the lives and characters of the English dramatick poets. With an account of their writings.* (1719)

The body of this book is comprised of the lives and characters of various poets (pp. 1-302) and some plays written by anonymous authors (pp. 303-332). I found only two references to the sublime throughout, and they are not interesting.

> To pass by Encomiums on the personal Merit of this great and modest Man; I proceed to his Talents. In the Writings of Mr. Addison there appears an uncommon Beauty; an Elegance of Style; an Improvement of Diction; a Strength of Reason; an Excellency of Wit; and a Nobleness and Sublimity of thought, equall'd by few, if any of our Modern Poets.
>
> (p. 2, on Joseph Addison)

> This Play [*Ibrahim the XII emperor of the Turks*][1] has not the Harmony of Numbers, nor a Sublimity of Expression; but the Distress of Morena is very moving.
>
> (p. 203, on Mrs. Mary Pix)

With regard to the first quotation, it is odd, but indeed the case, that Jacob uses 'sublime' in his section on Addison, but not in the sections on Milton and Shakespeare. Perhaps this is attributable simply to Addison's role around the time of Jacob's writing of popularizing the idea.

Notice that in the same passage 'Nobleness' and 'Sublimity' are placed together, as is so prevalent in Longinus. This corresponds, in a sense, with the curious substitution in William Mears' *A Catalogue of Modern Books* (London, 1722) of the word 'Sublime' in the place of the word 'Noble' where he lists the title of Edward Bysshe's *The Art of English Poetry* (1702). (For further detail see my Chapter XI, "Miscellaneous".)

Alexander Pennecuik, *Streams from Helicon: or poems on various subjects. In three parts. The second edition.* (1720)

I include the following passage in this Context because it is a notable example of a critic's having every imaginable opportunity to employ

[1] Throughout the text all interpolations within square brackets in quoted passages are mine.

the term sublime but not doing so. Perhaps Pennecuik serves to balance our view of the situation.

My Lord,
Tho the modern English Poets have display'd immortal Capacities, an Elation of Mind which Scales the Meridian of Poesy, delivered to Posterity massy Thoughts in a splendid Dress, chang'd its Complexion, and made it shine with a beautiful Visage, gain'd a miraculous Conquest over Ignorance, and left a perfect Pattern for Imitation; yet I think it ought not to deterr others, who have not so bright a Genuis, from intertaining the World with their Productions. Should all be mute because Addison, Pope and Garth have incomparably writ? We might as well infer no Man ought to fight for his dear Country, because the World hath been bless'd with an Engine and Marlburough [sic].

(Dedication to the Right Honourable Thomas Earl of Haddingtoun, Lord Binny and Byres . . .)

Joseph Spence, *An essay on Pope's Odyssey: in which some particular beauties and blemishes of that work are consider'd.* (1726)

This work is a set of three dialogues, *a la* Dryden, between Antiphaus and Philypsus. It might aid in interpreting their remarks if I quote what Spence says of their respective characters:

The enlarged Genius of Philypsus always led him to dwell upon the most beautiful Parts of a Poem with the greatest Pleasure; while Antiphaus, who has a very clear Head, and has given much into a strict way of thinking, is taken most with just Descriptions, and plain natural Ideas: The one was so possest with the Pleasure which he felt from fine Thoughts and warm Expressions, that He did not take a full Satisfaction in low Beauty, and simple Representations of Nature; the other, on the contrary, had such an aversion to glitterings and elevation, that he was distasted at any the least appearance of either. (p. 2)

I now come to the dialogue, which I quote at some length:

[Antiphaus] I will very readily allow what you say of that Great Man [Pope], return'd Antiphaus; and shall always pay a deference to your more lively taste of the Fine and Sublime in Poetry; but you must give me leave to dissent from you in some Particulars; if I do not agree with your Sentiments, in relation to several Lines and Passages of the Translation [Pope's of the "Odyssey"], 'tis perhaps bacause I fall so much short of you, in your inward sense of the high and elevated Beauties of Language.

("Evening the First", pp. 3-4)

[Philypsus] But how pardonable is it, for so exalted a Genius [Pope] to run sometimes into an excess of Ornament? And how admirable for such, to excell often in the just, handsome, natural Manner?

("Evening the Second", p. 42)

One of several references in Spence's essay to the Longinian idea of great genius' being permitted small blemishes.

[Phylipsus] On spiry volumes there a Dragon rides;
Here, from our strict embrace a Stream he glides:
And last, sublime his stately growth he rears
A Tree, and well-dissembled foliage wears.
("Evening the Second", p. 43)

These lines are quoted by Philypsus, of course, from Pope's *Odyssey*. A footnote identifies the passage "B. 4, 615 to 622". Pope's use of 'Sublime' appears to refer to the idea of pure elevation, certainly physical, perhaps spiritual also.

[Philypsus] "he speaks short, and in broken and interrupted Periods, which excellently represent the agony of his thoughts. – Afterwards we see he breaks out into Interrogations, which, as Longinus observes, give great motion, strength, and action to Discourse. If the Poet had proceeded simply, the Expression had not been equal to the occasion; but by these short Questions, he gives strength to it, and shews the disorder of the speaker, by the sudden starts and vehemence of the Periods." (*Ibid.*, p. 58)

Here Philypsus is quoting from Pope's notes on his *Odyssey*, and Pope in turn is quoting from Longinus, the section being identified in Spence's footnote as "De Subl. c. 17".

[Philypsus] These are the productions of a Sublime Genius, and speak an uncommon Spirit, together with a firm extensive Judgment, and an exact Sense of things. (*Ibid.*, p. 60)

Once again Philypsus is speaking of Pope.

[Philypsus] There are several masterly strokes of the Emphatical kind in the Odyssey. . . . This Manner is necessary in all Sententious passages, and moral reflections; 'tis often strong in expressing the passions: and peculiarly useful in the Sublime. (*Ibid.*, pp. 86-87)

[Philypsus] In the Sublime, nothing can be higher than the language of his [Pope's] Gods, Neptune and Jupiter:

If such thy Will – We will it, Jove replies,

This latter is that short full way of Expression, so frequent in Virgil and Homer, copied perhaps by both from the admired Example of it in Moses [footnote cites *The great Fiat*],[2] and grown since into an Axiom among the Criticks. (*Ibid.*, p. 88)

[2] Footnote to the above cites as the source for the one line quotation from Pope's *Odyssey*, "B. 13, 177. v, 154".

[Philypsus] But however great and handsome his performance is in the whole, I own with you that it has its faults, the common marks of Humanity: Yes, my Antiphaus, you convinc'd me the former Evening, that it is unavoidable for the greatest Genius not to fail sometimes [sic]. (*Ibid.*, p. 99)

A second example of the Longinian 'beauties and blemishes'.

[Antiphaus] The greatest Critick among the Roman Poets lays it down for a Rule, That where there are more Beauties than Faults in a Poem, that Piece is to be pronounced good: And one of the greatest Criticks among the Greek, carries it farther; He shews at large, That there is often a negligence, that is becoming; – That a greatness of Soul will carry a Man above the observation of little Circumstances; And That a Poet of a generous Spirit with faults, is greatly preferable to a low wary Writer without them.
("Evening the Third", pp. 144-145)

And yet another. It is a safe presumption that the Greek critic alluded to is Longinus.

James Ralph, *Sawney. An heroic poem. Occasion'd by the Dunciad. Together with a critique on that poem address'd to Mr. T---d, Mr. M---r, Mr. Eu---n, etc.* (1728)

Ralph's position is strongly anti-Pope. The sublime is not mentioned in the poem, but the Dedication contains the following two references:

Can any Lines [six lines from *The Dunciad*, beginning: Round him each Science by its modern Type] be more execrably dull? more stupidly nonsensical? the amount of the whole is this; that smoaking makes a Parson, and ragged Breeches a Philosopher; that English Musick is ridiculous for its dismal Score, and History remarkable for drinking Ale; which last thrice excellent Thought, I suppose, took its hint from the foregoing dismal Score, as well as the conceit of the Breeches from that sublime Aphorism, "He's a Heathen Philosopher, one may see his A – – e thro' his Pocket-holes.
(p. vi)

The above is one of a small number in this text of negative uses of the sublime, which helps to corroborate the existence, generally agreed upon by scholars of the period, of widespread mimicking of the satiric-sublime writings of major authors like Pope and Swift. Again in the passage to follow Ralph links the sublime with the ridiculous:

But 'tis not in the power of such malicious Scriblers [what the author calls "the authors of the Dunciad"] to derogate from the Merit and Character of Milton, and Addison, tho' they have so frequently attempted both; for even Mr. Addison's incomparable Simile of the Angel in the "Campaign" (a Poem which the best of the Fraternity could never equal) is sneer'd at in the following Lines, concluding a Rant of unintelligible Fustian, and most sublime Nonsense.

And proud his Mistress Orders to perform,
Rides in the Whirlwind, and directs the Storm.
(p. xiii)

James Miller, *Harlequin-Horace*: *or, The art of modern poetry*. (1731)

Both the Dedication and the poem are sardonically satirical towards contemporary London taste and art in general, and John Rich in particular. The sublime does not appear in the poem at all, and in the Dedication only once:

Well-judg'd therefore is it of you, Sir [Rich], to endeavour to engage 'em by such Diversions, as were never before seen, heard, or conceiv'd; and never can be judg'd of or understood. In which Attempt you have so wonderfully, and meritoriously succeeded, that whilst the Sublime of a Shakespear, the Tenderness of an Otway, and the Humour of a Vanbrugh, are represented by a Booth, a Wilks, and a Cibber, to empty Benches; you can by the single wave of a Harlequin's Wand, conjure the whole Town every Night into your Circle; where, like a true Cunning Man, you amuse 'em with a few Puppy's tricks while you juggle 'em of their Pelf, and then cry out with a Note of Triumph,

Si Mundus vult Decipi, Decipiatur.
(pp. vi-vii)

Miller's blast is interesting on two counts. First, there are not a great many references at this time to the sublimity of Shakespeare (as opposed to Milton), and second, the passage is a fascinating sidelight on the schemes of that phenomenal impressario, John Rich.

David Mallet, *Of verbal criticism*: *an epistle to Mr. Pope. Occasioned by Theobald's Shakespear, and Bentley's Milton.* (1733)

This poem of 224 lines in heroic couplets takes up Pope's side in the dispute with Theobald and Bentley. The only mention of the sublime is the following concerning the latter:

Such was his doom impos'd by Heaven's decree
With ears that hear not, eyes that shall not see,
The Low to raise, to level the Sublime,
To blast all Beauty, and beprose all Rhyme.
(p. 11)

James Dalacourt, *A prospect of poetry*: *Address'd to the Right Honourable John, Earl of Orrery, To which is added, A Poem to Mr. Thomson on his Seasons*. (Dublin, 1734) (Reprinted in London)

Dalacourt's *Prospect* is preceded in the volume by three other poems by different authors. They are shorter than the former, none running more than four pages, but address themselves to the same subject. My first quotation is from the third of these:

Lur'd by thy precepts, and inchanting tongue
As if by magic I too tempt the song;
While Orpheus' wonders are reviv'd by you,
And now, if ever, antient fable's true:
Sublim'd by music, here the rough rocks rise
A growing pile! behold it greets the skies! –
(R. Lloyd, A.B., "On the Prospect of Poetry", p. 10)

The remaining extracts come from Dalacourt:

First let your judgment for your fancy chuse,
Of all the nine the most unblemish'd muse:
Soft yet sublime, in love yet strictly coy,
Prone to be grave, yet not averse to joy;
Where taste and candour, wit and manners meet,
Bold without bombast, daring but discreet;
(p. 17)

Here Aegypt's Pyramids must heave sublime,
And blunt the teeth of all-decaying time;
(p. 34)

Rais'd by her hand Nile's daughter quits the ground,
Hardens her mummies, hears her Sistrum sound,
Tow'rs like her Pyramids, sublimely bold,
And almost rises half her height in gold.
(p. 44)

By architecture last he lays the scheme,*
And by some model bids his genius flame:
Works up the whole, and sees the building shine,
In all its parts with conduct and design:
The poem rais'd upon so fine a plan,
The test, the wonder, and delight of man,
Will stand the shocks, and injuries of time,
Built upon nature, and the true sublime.
(pp. 44-45)

*[Dalacourt's footnote tells us that Palladio lays down but five orders of architecture, and Longinus five fountains for the sublime.]

Aurelian's dead! endow'd with ev'ry art,
In which the two Minervas claim a part;
Whose character survives in the sublime,
As the best judge, and critic of his time.**
(p. 51)

**[Dalacourt indicates that he means Longinus]

Three of the above are the sublime of elevation, the last reference merely serves to place Longinus in his metier, and the first usage by Dalacourt is too vague to comment on. But the 'sublime' of "Built upon nature, and the true sublime" is very curious in its seeming anticipation of Langer's idea of each art form's own inherent laws. At the same time, Dalacourt's usage here does no violence to the intent of Longinus.

Thomas Hayward, *The British muse, or, A collection of thoughts, moral, natural, and sublime, of our English poets: who flourished in the sixteenth and seventeenth centuries.* (1738)

Like most of the commonplace books of poetry of our period, Hayward's is organized by topic. There is no topic of the sublime in this volume, nor, for that matter, in any of the dozen or so examples of this genre that I examined in the Folger Library. Hayward's Preface contains two references, albeit they are quite prosaic:

> Accordingly, at the end of his first volume [Gildon's *The Compleat Art of Poetry*], he gives us a collection, which he calls "Shakesperiana," but it consists of less than sixty pages; though, to have extracted only a part of the sublime images and sentiments of that divine and incomparable poet, would have filled a much larger volume than one, or perhaps both, of Mr. Gildon's. (p. xvii)

> Youth and age may improve equally by consulting it [*The British Muse*]: The one it directs, the other it admonishes: Whilst it amends the heart, it informs the head, and is, at the same time, the rule of virtue, and the standard of poetical eloquence; especially to those who can discern delicacy of wit, dignity of sentiment, and sublimity of thought, through antiquated modes of speech, and the language of an age ago. (p. xxiv)

It is worth remarking that the sublime of the second is closer by far to what I regard as the sublime of Longinus than to Monk's early eighteenth-century sublime of rhetoric.

Henry Pemberton, *Observations on poetry, especially the epic: occasioned by the late poem upon Leonidas.* (1738)

What Pemberton has to say in his chapter "Of the sublime" is very interesting. Thus it is the more remarkable that Monk merely mentions him in a footnote.[3] The pages cited there are indeed the most important,

[3] *The Sublime,* footnote number 62: "Of course all writings on the sublime were not typical of any orderly development. The rhetorical sublime occurs frequently, as for example . . . in Henry Pemberton's 'Observations on Poetry, Especially on the Epic' (London, 1738), pp. 151-155 . . ."

but Monk fails to tell us what they say. They turn out to be a good deal more than the same old tired rhetoric.

In the last place, after some notice of what is more peculiar to epic poetry, I shall conclude with a short examination, wherein truly consists that sublime, in which this kind of writing is expected to excell all others.
(Introduction, p. 2)

The gentle and polite character of Agis renders him in particular worthy the intimate friendship of the great Leonidas; in whom humanity and a genteel turn of mind distinguish themselves among his more sublime virtues.
(Section IV, "Of sentiment and character", p. 60)

The sublimity of this character [Demophilus] distinguishably appears by his behavior upon this occasion toward his kinsman Dithyrambus.
(*Ibid.*, p. 62)

Cold men have considered this sublime degree of that desire of praise, which is implanted in our nature, as a weakness: but it is certainly a part of Leonidas's character to hold it in high esteem ...
(*Ibid.*, p. 67)

Though orators do often expiate upon subjects suited to move the passions, and on those occasions make such an enumeration of particulars, whereby the image or picture of the thing described may break in upon the mind of the hearer with greater brightness and force; yet Longinus has judiciously distinguished between the design of poetic and oratorial imagery; that the scope of the first is ever to strike the imagination, whereas a greater degree of evidence is the proper intention of the latter.* [The footnote indicated cites section 14 of *On the Sublime*.]
(Section V, "Of the language of poetry", pp. 75-76)

The above extract prepares us for the important passages on page 151 f.

The fourth [kind of metaphor according to Quintilian] is the reverse of this, when actions of life and sense are ascribed to inanimate beings. This last Quintilian observes to be the boldest, and also the sublimest form of this figure.* [The footnote cites a passage from *Institut. orat.*] (*Ibid.*, p. 92)

Of writings, the sublime ode, and satyr admit of the boldest hyperboles; such exaggerations agreeing well with the impetuous warmth of that ode, and being also a very successful means of exposing follies, and exciting horror against vice, by representing either in their extremes. (*Ibid.*, p. 98)

Of all kinds of descriptive poetry the sublime ode requires the boldest diction; strength and a glaring brightness of expression being necessary to support this rapturous kind of verse. (*Ibid.*, p. 100)

There remains yet one topic more, upon which to examine the present poem [*Leonidas*]. For as this poem is of the kind, called heroic, it is not sufficient, that the fable or plan bear an exact resemblance to the real actions of men, and that the characters be a true picture of human nature;

but the action and the circumstances of it, as also the characters ought to be of so great and exalted a kind, as may constitute and support that sublime, which is required in this kind of poem.

Before we enquire farther into this particular, it is necessary to premise, that the sublime in writing requires no less a right cast of temper in the reader to perceive, than it does warmth and greatness of imagination in the writer to execute. For by such elevated objects and conceptions all men are not equally moved.

In general that faculty in the mind usually called taste, whereby we are touched with pleasure or disgust by objects presented before us, is not only seen in very different degrees in different men, but is also as various in the diversity of the objects, by which each man is principally affected.

In the course of human life we see some of low passions, who go on in an even attention to their affairs without being greatly moved by love or hatred, hope or fear; while others are strongly affected by the objects around them, some by quick resentment, others by warm emotions of good will, some disturbed by cares, and others excited by ambition. Philosophy undertakes to regulate these, and every other passion, and to direct each to its proper object. But though the enjoyment of life depends chiefly upon possessing a due degree of the good affections, yet no speculation or reflection can excite a lively sensibility in minds naturally cold and languid.

It is the same in taste: insomuch, that many of great understanding in the affairs of life, and even in the speculative sciences, are very moderately affected by the subjects, which are most usually considered as the objects of taste. Again, some are chiefly affected with mirth and humour, others with that unexpected comparison of distant things, which constitutes wit, others again with elegance and decorum; and all these tastes may be unaccompanied with any distinguished degree of that admiration, which impresses on the soul a solemn kind of delight at the view of what is great and uncommon, whether in the works of nature, such as boundless views, tempestuous seas, and stupendous mountains; or in the like actions of men, as great passion, high degrees of prowess and magnanimity, or sentiments raised beyond the ordinary temper of the human mind. But a disposition toward this kind of admiration is that, which disposes to a strong relish for the sublime in writing or actions.

Longinus, as necessary to constitute the sublime in writing, requires for the subject suitable conceptions and passions, and in the language, whether prose or verse, a happy choice of words, with an appropriate figurativeness of phrase, and to complete the rest such a harmony and cadence as may improve the dignity of the expression.

A happy choice of distinct and comprehensive words, that may convey the sense with brevity, evidence, and force, is doubtless the principal character, which constitutes the sublime of language. Of this Longinus has given an eminent instance in that passionate ode of Sappho, which he produces.

(Section VIII, "Of the sublime", pp. 151-153)

That pomp of sound has force to aid the sublime by giving additional energy to the expression, the powerful effects of music abundantly prove:

and figurative forms of speech promote the same design, whenever they render the expression more close, or more comprehensive.

In relation to the subjects most conducive to excite this admiration, wherein we have placed the sublime, besides vehement and enthusiastic passion, not only exalted sentiments, but also such images and actions, as are marvelous, conduce to this end. Hence we find, that writers have at all times made choice of such representations to warm, and fill the imaginations of their readers. (*Ibid.*, p. 154)

But sublimity of sentiment is the supreme excellence of a work of this kind: for without controversy this constitutes the truest, and the highest degree of the sublime. Whatever pleasure we may feel from great and uncommon images, we must acknowledge, that every thing of that kind has the strongest effect upon young and tender minds; whereas sublimity of sentiment will not only warm the heart of youth, but rivet itself more firmly in the soul, as the judgment is matured by time and experience; in short, will ever be considered as the last perfection of the human mind, as long as manliness and public spirit shall have a name in the world. (*Ibid.*, p. 166)

One of the clearest indications that Pemberton is not basically concerned with rhetoric is his statement from page 152, "But though the enjoyment of life depends chiefly upon possessing a due degree of the good affections, yet no speculation or reflection can excite a lively sensibility in minds naturally cold and languid." I think that the rhetorician would beg the *raison d'être* of his function if he made such an assertion; his task is to persuade ALL minds, regardless of their make-up.

It will be noticed further, that Pemberton recognizes the sublime of rhetoric and external nature, but seeks a rapprochement between them by emphasizing the sublime of sentiment. All of which makes him a man of his age – of the age of sensibility – in a different sense than that attributed to him by Monk.

Thomas Hayward, *The Quintessence of English poetry: or, a collection of all the beautiful passages in our poems and plays: from the celebrated Spencer to 1688. The whole instructive, moral, and humourous: and adapted to all degrees of mankind: alphabetically digested under proper heads, in chronological order of time. Collected from some hundred volumes, by the ingenious Tho. Hayward, and other gentlemen. To which is prefix'd, an alphabetical catalogue of authors, poems, and plays quoted in the collection: also an historical and critical review of this and all the essays of the kind hitherto published. By Mr. Oldys. In three volumes.* (1740)

The Preface of this work contains exactly the same two passages on the sublime that I quoted under the head of Hayward's *The British Muse* (1738).

[Anon.], *An essay on tragedy, with a critical examen of Mahomet and Irene.* (1749)

In a footnote to page 12, the editor says that the author did not observe the title page of the play in question closely, or he would have noticed that the name of the play is "Irene". The author, however, mentions Samuel Johnson's name, and discusses the play in such a way as to leave little doubt that it is his.

And, of the many species of dramatic Writings, there is none so noble in its nature, so useful in its end, as tragedy; 'tis this that gives the sublimest lessons of virtue and morality; 'tis this that forms the hero and the patriot: 'Tis tragedy that instructs us to moderate our passions (from whence all the evils in the moral world arise) curb their impetuous sallies, and reduce them to hearken to the precepts of enlightening reason. 'Tis this that polishes and refines our manners, teaches us to support every situation in life with due dignity and decorum, calls off our attention from the low groveling pursuits of folly, and directs its flight to the sublime regions of real wisdom. (p. 3)

But as I despair of finding any expressions sublime enough to do justice to so curious a [plot] device [in *Irene*], I must beg leave to give it you in his own. . . . Having thus far consider'd the conduct of the fable and characters, it is now time to speak to the diction and sentiments, which may not improperly be called the colouring and drapery of the piece. And here our author triumphs over almost every opponent. Never do any strain'd metaphors, unmeaning epithets, turgid elocution, high sounding rants, disgrace his scenes. He is sensible, that the true sublime does not consist in smooth rounding periods, and the pomp of verse, but in just and noble sentiments [sic lack of punctuation] strong and lively images of nature: And to this for the most part he closely adheres . . . (pp. 24-25)

The usage of sublime here is not very precise, but it is obvious that it does not mean either the rhetorical or natural sublime.

[Anon.], *An ode on the powers of poetry*: *To which are prefixed Observations on Taste, and on the present state of poetry and criticism in England.* (1751)

The word sublime does not appear in this insignificant poem, but does occur in the following passage through an allusion to Longinus. The locus of the extract is a section preceding the poem called "Continuation of the Discourse before the Ode on Martial Virtue".

No Critic, which I have seen, has spoke of the Excellences and Imperfections of "Paradise Lost" as if he had made a perfect Discovery of either: but this is sayed with great Difference to Mr. Addison when compared with the Rest: he had Taste; of which the other are as insensible as Blocks of Marble. The Critics (pardon me ye Shades of Aristotle, Longinus, Horace, and Quintilian, for calling them by that venerable Name!) which swarm in the last Edition of "Paradise Lost," like Flies and other Insects in the Mid-summer Sun at Noon, affect me with a sorrowful Concern: the Addition of their Injudicious and ridiculous Observations, (with an Exception to some of the explanatory Notes,) and in a Stile suitable to the worthless Matter which it cloaths, makes the whole like a superb Palace and Gardens surrounded with a filthy Mote of Mud and rank offensive Weeds: I speak of them all from the grave and profound Prelate to the most boisterous and flashy Brawler that ever mistook his Talents; who with the insipid Editor of the Work may be justly deemed as despicable Quarry for a fine Writer as an Ant or a Wasp would be for an Eagle: one of these illicit Dealers in Criticism, who may be literally sayed to plunge on without Fear or Wit, has been already well handled by some ingenious Gentlemen.

John Armstrong, *Taste: an epistle to a young critic.* (1753)

Monk also quotes the first of the following extracts as an example of the mid-century's satiric treatment of the sublime.[4] My second quotation would seem to fall into the same category.

> But hear their Raptures o'er some specious Rhime
> Dub'd by the musk'd and greasy Mob sublime.
> For Spleen's dear sake hear how a Coxcomb prates
> As clam'rous o'er his Joys as Fifty Cats;
> (p. 9)

> Judge for yourself; nor wait with timid Phlegm
> 'Till some illustrious Pedant hum or hem.
> The Lords who starv'd old Ben were learndly fond
> Of Chaucer, whom with bungling Toil they conn'd.
> Their Sons, whose Ears bold Milton could not seize,
> Would laugh o'er Ben like mad, and snuff and sneeze,
> And swear, and seem as tickled as you please.
> Their Spawn, the Pride of this sublimer Age,
> Feel to the Toes and Horns grave Milton's Rage.
> (p. 15)

Nathaniel Weekes, *On the abuse of poetry. A satire. Second edition.* (1754)

This poem of about 450 lines is a pretty conventional protest against the taste of the times. Perhaps the most striking thing about its use of the sublime is its frequency.

Milton's Paradise Lost, I am apt to think, would still have lain unregarded by some Thousands, had not Mr. Addison taught us how to admire it, which we cannot sufficiently do. I wish some learned and judicious Divine would

[4] *The Sublime*, p. 63.

in the same manner illustrate the several Excellencies of the sacred History: We have already innumerable Critiques on Shakespear and other Poets; and it would be more decent and becoming in Some to exert their Talents in the Defence of the Doctrine of Christianity, than in correcting the Errors of the Drama. Besides, it would be a means of bringing Religion into some Reputation, which it has at present almost lost. The Writings of St. Paul would furnish the Undertaker of such a Task with the noblest Sentiments and sublimest Eloquence; he might not only there shine as a divine Critic, but induce even Deists Themselves to read, honour, and admire the sacred Historian. (Preface, p. iv)

No little Rhimer in these modern Days,
But sets his Nothings at immortal Praise;
Will his melodious Trifles sweet pour forth,
And wonder in himself at their vast Worth!
If in Description he can make a Rhime,
He calls his Genius great, his Wit sublime!
(p. 5)

Some too must imitate great Milton's Stile,
Tho' weak their Genius, and tho' vain their Toil;
At his sublime and lofty Sense they aim,
Creep when he soars, and sink involv'd with Shame.
(p. 7)

If you must write, and have a Knack to Rhime,
Embrace some Subject worthy of your Time;
Your Genius, Strength, and Parts examine well,
And on what Theme your Wit can most excel:
These Talks perform'd, proceed with Caution on,
For much is to be lost, and little won!
Let Nature dictate, and let Art refine,
And by the Test of Judgment prove each Line.
Be easy, delicate, concise, and plain,
Tho' free, sublime; tho' learned, yet not vain:
Your Words well plac'd, and with right Judgment chose,
Are certain Rules which true sublime compose.
(*Ibid.*)

Still make your Language to your Subject fit,
For what's most natural is most like Wit.
A clear Idea, perfectly exprest,
To bear the strongest Marks of Truth confest;
Whose Sense and Beauty Proofs sublime impress,
And most expressive in the plainest Dress.
(p. 8)

Accept, O sacred Shade! accept this Praise,
From one who honours and adores thy Lays.

To thee alone I dedicate my Time.
Explore new Truths, and study arts sublime.
(p. 10)

The above presumably refers to Addison, who is mentioned a few lines previously.

Nor shall immortal Young neglected lie;
While I can sing, his Praise shall never die.
Sententious Bard! to Virtue ever dear;
Sublime in Wisdom, and to Truth severe!
(*Ibid.*)

See – who in Ink will dabble still,
And says a Nation's Fate demands his Quill!
Fond of his Trash he styles himself the Wise;
Some few assent, but Numbers more despise.
No nervous Lines his languid Diction grace,
Far-fetch'd Conceits rise up in ev'ry Place;
No Wit to charm, no soothing Numbers roll,
Nor Thoughts sublime to touch the rapt'rous Soul.
(p. 16)

Shall Britain be reproach'd in after Times,
For wretched Authors, and as wretched Rhymes,
When she has flourish'd in sublimest Arts?
(p. 19)

In England, let some Bard, ye Pow'rs! arise,
Sublime as Plato, and like Homer wise;
(*Ibid.*)

We will not often see Plato called sublime!

Daniel Webb, *Remarks on the beauties of poetry*. (1762)

Monk tells us (p. 108) that Webb "wrote much, but said little, on the arts of painting, poetry, and music", and goes on to discuss him mainly in connection with the last-named. He omits, however, a passage in which Webb makes a rather nice distinction in connection with the object of the poetic image:

If the Pathetic, as should seem from these proofs, must owe its effect to the occasion which produced it; the same may be affirmed, in part, of the sublime: I say in part, because though great sentiments, when produced in the Drama, must, in common with the pathetic, derive a particular and specific beauty from a happiness in their application; yet there will be this difference between them, that if a pathetic sentiment be considered independent of the occasion which produced it, it loses its pathetic force. On the other hand, if a sublime sentiment be considered in the same light, it loses the advantage it received from a happiness in its application, but retains its intrinsic greatness. (pp. 100-101)

John Brown, *A dissertation on the rise, union, and power, the progressions, separations, and corruptions, of poetry and music. To which is prefixed, The curse of Saul, a sacred ode. Written by Dr. Brown.* (1763)

Brown's work has extensive references to the sublime, which I include *in toto* because of my belief that they are nowhere else summarized. *A Dissertation* also includes an unusually fine discussion of the opera in England in the 1760's.

But his [Saul's] Despair returning, David calls on his attendant Choir to raise a more sublime and affecting Strain . . .

(The Argument of the Ode, p. iv)

> Ye Planets, and each circling Constellation,
> In Songs harmonious your Generation!
> Oh, while yon radiant Seraph turns the Spheres,
> And on the sted-fast Pole-Star stands sublime;
>   Wheel your Rounds
>   To heav'nly Sounds;
> And sooth his Song-inchanted Ears,
>   With your celestial Chime.

("The Ode", Sixth stanza, p. 8)

Odes, or Hymns, would naturally make a Part of their [primitive tribes'] domestic Entertainments: and the Chiefs would be proud to signalize themselves by their Skill in Melody and Song. For their Songs being enriched with all the great and important Subjects relative to the public State; nothing could be more suitable to a high Station in the Commonwealth, than a Proficiency in this sublime and legislative Art. (Section IV, p. 44)

It is remarkable that Plutarch, after labouring in vain through many Pages, to prove that the Principles of all the Virtues are to be found in Homer, is forced at length to conclude; "It is true, indeed, that *bad* Actions and Principles are intermixed and described in the same Manner; which was necessary, for the Introduction of the Sublime and Wonderful: But this only makes the Contrast the stronger; so that the Reader is necessarily led to *select* the *Good* and *reject* the *Bad* (u) [Footnote "u" reads: "In Vita" Homeri.]." (Section V, p. 80)

The next great legislative Bard whom I shall now mention, was Pindar. At the Period when He flourished, the Fortune and Glory of Greece were riding to their Meridian: The legislative Arts had now obtained a higher Degree of Perfection: And accordingly we find, in his sublime Songs, the fullest and most perfect Union of salutary Principles, thrown out in Maxims religious, political, and moral. (*Ibid.*, p. 82)

Eschylus, who stands first in Order of Time, partakes much of the rude Genius of the early Periods. His Imagery and Sentiments are great; his Style rugged and abrupt; and of a Cast so totally different from that of Homer, that it is astonishing to hear the Critics, one after another, affirming that Homer was his Model. His Writings present to us all the Characters of a sublime, original, and uncultivated Genius, which scorned any other Tutoress than Nature. (*Ibid.*, p. 84)

The noble Writer [Lord Shaftesbury in his *Characteristics*, Vol. 1], next, seems to attribute the late Cultivation of Comedy to "the Spirit of literary Criticism, which in the Nature of things could not arise, till it had Materials to work on;" and This he supposeth to have been the false Sublime of their Tragedies, which were often parodied in the old Comedy [Greek].

(Section VII, pp. 148-9)

In a succeeding Period, when the Distractions of our Country, had driven the native Britons into Wales, an English King still felt their Power, admist the Mountains and Poverty of that barren Region. He was so highly exasperated by the Influence of their Songs, which breathed the Spirit of Liberty and War, and retarded his Conquest over a hardy People, that he basely ordered them to be slain: An Event, which hath lately given Birth to an elegant and sublime Strain of Poetry. (f) [Footnote "f" reads: An Ode, by Mr. Gray.]. (Section VIII, p. 158)

The Song, in the Days of this sublime and original Bard [Ossian], appears evidently to have worn the inartificial and mixed Forms of Composition, which we have found generally and of Course to prevail in the early Periods. (*Ibid.*, p. 159)

The Book of Psalms, the Lamentations, the Songs of Moses, David, Isaiah, and other Prophets, all written in Measure, and sung by those who composed them, are so many striking Instances of the true and unequaled Sublime. . . .

It may be regarded as an extraordinary Circumstance, that this first *mixed* Form of Composition [hymn, ode, narration, dialogue, etc.] should have continued unchanged for a Period of at least a thousand Years; and that from first to last it should never move forward, so as to produce the Epic and Dramatic Species: But on Examination it will appear, that the same Cause (the Worship of the one God) which produced the highest Degree of Sublime in the hymnal Species, naturally checked the Course of Poetry among the Jews; and prevented that Progression which we have found to arise from the natural State of Things, in Pagan Countries.

(Section, X, p. 176)

But the common Genius of their [Italian] modern Church Music or Motets is altogether different; It is infected with the same Puerility of Stile with their Opera Airs: An unbounded Compass, extravagant Divisions on single

Syllables, a Play upon particular Words to the Neglect of the general Tenor of the Song, form its general Character. How can it be otherwise? When the same Musicians, (and these seldom much interested in the subject, or acquainted with the Language of their sacred Poetry) generally compose both for the Opera and the Church. Some noble Exceptions, however, may be found to this general Remark . . . But the most eminent Instance is in Benedetto Marcello a noble Venetian; many of whose Psalms, if we consider their Expression either as sublime, tender, graceful, or joyous, clearly excel the vocal Compositions of all his Countrymen, in Variety, Simplicity, and Truth (y) [Footnote "y" reads: It must be observed, that Marcello's Compositions are not set to the Latin Translation; but to an Italian Paraphrase of the Psalms.]. (Section XII, p. 210)

Note the grouping of sublime in the above passage with words like 'tender' and 'graceful'.

Of this Species of Poem [Oratorio] the Italians have some fine ones, written by Metastasio. They cannot perhaps be ranked in the first Class, either for Sublimity or Pathos. But Elegance of Style, Simplicity of Plan and Conduct, animated by a noble Spirit of Devotion, prevails throughout these Compositions. (*Ibid.*, pp. 216-17)

It would be enlightening to have more from Brown on the difference between sublimity and pathos. Does he hold with Longinus, for example, that they are generally coexistent, but not necessarily so?

That this Representation of sacred Subjects [sacred story told in epic ode] is the highest and most interesting Union of Poetry and Music, needs no elaborate Proof: It stands intimately connected with all the sublime Truths, the great and affecting Events of our Religion, which, when thus exhibited by the united Powers of Poem and Song, call forth all the noblest Emotions of the human Soul; and exalt it to the highest Pitch of Elevation that our mortal Condition will admit. (Section XIII, p. 238)

Thus Brown stands at the end of a school of thought popularized among some critics by John Dennis two generations earlier.

The Selection of the Anthem from the sacred Scriptures might receive the public Approbation of the Society [Brown's proposed Poetic and Musical Academy for the more effectual reunion of these two arts in the species song, anthem, hymn, and tragic choir (chorus)]: And the Hymn, controuled by the same sober Judgments, would assume that pathetic Sublimity and Simplicity of Style, which tends to elevate the Soul to the Contemplation and Love of divine Things. . . . The Epic Ode, directed by the Taste and Wisdom of this Academy, would obtain its Completion. The greatest and most affecting Subjects, drawn from the History of our own or other Countries, would rise before us; while the sublimest and most interesting Events recorded in the sacred Scriptures, thus recommended and adorned, would make their Way through the nobler Passions of the Heart.

(Section XIV, p. 239)

The relatively loose usage of words like 'sublimity' and 'pathetic' can be seen as late as the 1760's in a writer like John Brown. Compare the distinction made between the two words in the extract from page 217 with their incorporation into one term, 'pathetic Sublimity', in the last quotation.

III

ORATORY AND RHETORIC

This chapter is particularly significant by virtue of its length and richness of eighteenth-century material, much of the latter being a telling challenge to Monk's summary description and dismissal of the century's treatises on oratory and rhetoric.[1] In connection with this matter there are several questions that might profitably be kept in mind while perusing the quoted passages. For instance, must we admit that the sublime in classical oratory, designed to persuade rather than to transport, is necessarily devoid of interest and influence on future literatures? Is Longinus foremost a rhetorician?[2] Do these same authors always conceive of contemporary oratory in the same terms as they do classical oratory?

In the pages that follow we should discover at least some partial answers to these questions. I will have occasion to query Monk, on methodological grounds, concerning the rhetoric-Longinus-Boileau triangle, and will present some passages whose tenor seems distant, indeed, from the province of rhetoric narrowly defined.

The works written originally in French find their place in this chapter by virtue of the fact that they received English translations and were rather widely disseminated in Britain. In one case the contents are as much the contribution of the translator as the French author. The number of French rhetorics in English translations, along with some of their remarks, will cause us to wonder about the truth of the commonplace that between the years 1660 and 1760 French literary theory was nearly strangled by the rules, while England looked on, smug in her freedom and individuality.[3]

John Smith, *The mysterie of rhetorique unveil'd* . . . (1665)

[1] See *The Sublime*, pp. 84 and 107 particularly.

[2] See Chapter I, *passim*.

[3] See comments on Henri Peyre below, p. 89.

Object. But it may be you will say, there were several books extant before, that much illustrate the Tropes and Figures of Rhetorick.

Answ. It is very true, that many learned Worthies have done exceeding well herein; yet to use the expression of one of them: That a child upon a Gyant shoulders can see further then the Gyant: So I, having the help of their labours, and of other Books, have by Divine assistance (without ostentation be it mentioned) used a more distinct and easie method throughout the whole current of my Discourse, then any other upon this subject yet extant; whereby matters of high and excellent sublimity are bowed down to the weakest capacities.

(The Author to the Reader)

Lastly, For that the holy Scripture is not barren of, but abounds with tropes and figures of all sorts, as containing the most excellent and sublimest eloquence, and is like a pleasant garden, bedecked with flowers, or a fruitful field, full of precious treasures, I apprehended it a work worthy the undertaking, to dig into those sacred Minerals for the better finding out the Metaphors, Metonymies, Synecdoches, etc. which lie hid there, and have given Scriptural Examples pertinent to each of the Tropes and Figures ... (*Ibid.*, pp. 3-4)

Bernard Lamy, *The art of speaking: written in French by Messieurs du Port Royal: In pursuance of a former Treatise, Intituled, The Art of Thinking.* (1676)[4]

[4] The subject of the Messieurs, or 'solitaries' of the Little Schools of Port-Royal is, in itself, quite interesting. Reference to David C. Cabeen and Jules Brody, general editors, *A Critical Bibliography of French Literature* (Syracuse University Press, 1961), III: *The Seventeenth Century*, ed. Nathan Edelman, Johns Hopkins University, reveals a large corpus of contemporary writings on both the Messieurs and the institution in which they served.

According to *A Critical Bibliography* and Howard C. Barnard, *The Little Schools of Port-Royal* (Cambridge, 1913) *passim*, there is no reason to suppose that Bernard Lamy was closely associated with Port-Royal. Barnard tells us (p. 34) that after the dispersal of the Little Schools of Port-Royal in 1656 (largely through the efforts of the Jesuits), several of the solitaries wrote treatises on education, based partly on the theories of the one-time director Saint Cyran and partly on their own classroom experience. These treatises enjoyed rather wide dissemination, which could account for Lamy's knowledge of *The Art of Thinking*.

Because of the prominence of Port-Royal as a source for several documents in this chapter, it might be useful to recapitulate here Barnard's most salient descriptive remarks concerning this Jansenist abbey school. The boys' school at the abbey, and the solitaries (who were under no formal vows) both began their existence in 1637 or 1638 (p. 14). By this date the term 'little schools' designated coeducational elementary schools, as distinguished from the 'colleges' of the University of Paris, which were really secondary schools. On the other hand, 'Little Schools' was really a misnomer, as several pupils attended Port-Royal until the age of sixteen (p. 29). There was no room in Saint-Cyran's theories for the education of the masses (p. 42). The Little Schools were destroyed in 1660, after exist-

The art of speaking is divided into four parts dealing with how speech is formed, the role of art in speech, pronunciation and versification, and the differences between styles, respectively. There is also subjoined to this a treatise on the *Art of persuasion*. Only part four of the main treatise offers an appreciable number of references to the sublime. These lean toward the rhetorical orientation that we would expect, but to some extent also embrace sublimity of all subject matter. There is no information in the volume by which we can definitely determine the translator of the French original. All of the following passages are taken from part four.

The Matter is to direct in the Election of our Style. Noble Expressions that render a Style Magnificent; great Words that fill up the mouth, represent things great, and argue strength of judgment in the person who speaks in so sublime a way: but if the matter it self be unworthy, if it be great only in the Imagination of the Author, his Magnificence turns to his prejudice, and shows the weakness of his judgment, in putting a value upon that is only worthy of Contempt. (Chapter II, p. 22)

The Art of Speaking having no peculiar matter, every thing subject to our thoughts, being matter for Discourse, there are Infinite diversity of Styles, as the sorts of things of which we may speak are Infinite: Yet the Masters of that Art have reduced the peculiar matter for Writing under three kinds: Sublime, Mean, or Indifferent. There are three Kinds of Styles answerable to these three Kinds of Matters; the Lofty, the Plain, and the Moderate. Sometimes these Styles are called Characters, because they denote the quality of the matter that is the subject of the discourse. (*Ibid.*, p. 23)

We must likewise be careful not to say any thing in one place that may contradict or interfere with what we have said in another. We have an Example of this Fault in Hesiode, who in his Poem called the Buckler, speaking of Prosepine, says that she had "a filthy humour running at her Nose": Longinus observes well, that Hesiod's design being to make her terrible, this expression did not suit, but made her rather odious and contemptible. (*Ibid.*, p. 26)

---

ing for fourteen years. They never had more than fifty pupils at once, and not more than 250 all together (p. 44). "The aim of education at Port-Royal was and continued to be moral and religious ... As a result of this, mere knowledge always held a subordinant place in the Little Schools of Port-Royal ..." (p. 62) Saint-Cyran's "onslaught on secular studies was stoutly resisted by the Jesuits and notably by Father Bouhours [see below, pp. 201-203], who has left us in his *Entre-tiens d'Ariste d'Eugene* a vigorous criticism of the style of many of the Port-Royal writers" (pp. 64-65). (Certain of the latter were capable apparently of somewhat complicated syntax.) Barnard sums up his appraisal of the teaching of the solitaries by saying that it was based on love rather than fear, emphasized the vernacular, fastened on the content (albeit expurgated) of the Classics, and extended the curriculum to new fields like geography and history (p. 238).

This sublime Character is hard to attain: 'tis not every one can raise himself above the common pitch, at least continue his flight: It is easy to fly out into great expressions, but then if those great Expressions be not sustained by greatness of matter, and replete with solid and serious things, they are but like Stilts, that show the smallness and defect of the Party at the same time they exalt him. (*Ibid.*, p. 30)

I shall say little of this middle Character, because it is sufficient to know that it consists in a Mediocrity that ought to participate of the grandeur of the sublime Character, and of the simplicity of the plain Character. Virgil has given us examples of all these three Characters; his Aenead's are in the sublime Character, where he speaks of nothing but Combats, Sieges, Wars, Princes, and Hero's: In them all is magnificent, both sentiments and words. (*Ibid.*, p. 34)

His [Virgil's] Georgicks are of the middle Character: The matter of which they treat is not so sublime as the matter of his Aenead's, he speaks not there of Wars and Combats, and the establishment of the Roman Empire, which are the subject of his Aenead's; nor are his Georgicks so plain and simple as his Eclogues. (*Ibid.*, p. 35)

Nevertheless upon reflexion we shall find the pleasure we conceive in a well-composed Discourse, proceeds only from the resemblance betwixt the Image form'd by the words in our mind, and the things whose Image they bear; so that it is either the truth that pleases, or the conformity betwixt the words and the things. That which is called Great and Sublime, is nothing but that conformity in its perfection and excellence. Longinus in his Book of this Sublimity, has given us an example of a sublime expression taken out of the First Chapter of Genesis, where Moses speaking of the Creation, uses these words; And God said let there be light, and there was light; an expression that gives a strong Idea of the power of God over his Creatures, which was the thing that Moses designed. (Chapter V, p. 60)

That which makes their [men who think that that which is rare is therefore great] stupidity the more remarkable is, that they admire what they do not understand, Mirantur quae non intelligunt; because obscurity has some appearance of grandeur, sublime and exalted things being for the most part obscure and difficult. (*Ibid.*, p. 64)

As I said above, Lamy's underlying interest is rhetoric, but many of his descriptions of the sublime are faithful to Longinus. It is probable that Lamy is indebted to Boileau's translation of just two years before. Thus in the second document of this chapter we see evidence of a phenomenon that makes it so hazardous for Monk to dismiss the eighteenth-century books on rhetoric and oratory as being of the slightest interest in the development of the sublime during the century. This phenomenon is, of course, the existence in such treatises of concepts of sublimity that range widely from the rhetorical sublime.

Jean Le Clerc, *Parrhasiana: or, thoughts upon several subjects; as criticism, history, morality, and politics. By Monsieur Le Clerc, under the feigned name of Theodorus Parrhasi. Done into English by ***.* (1700)

Monk mentions Le Clerc very briefly in three places in *The Sublime* (p. 79, 84n., 177n.), but really dismisses him as just another in a long line of dreary rhetoric writers. The fact of the matter is, however, that Le Clerc has a sceptical and perspicacious mind. The first chapter of *Parrhasiana* is particularly interesting in its denial of the long tradition that the ancient poets of epic and drama were primarily concerned with moral instruction. Le Clerc says that this was little more than a desirable side effect as far as the ancients were concerned. His remarks on the sublime impress the modern reader as sensible, perhaps too sensible.

If we imitate the false Thoughts of the Poets, only by being conversant in their Writings, we must certainly much more spoil ourselves by their Stile, but especially when we are young. That which is not too swelling for Verse, is insupportable in Prose: and after we have been accustom'd to the Bumbast of the Poets, we are apt to think we crawl on the ground, when we deliver ourselves in a plain natural manner, and the most elevated Language of Prose seems dull and insipid. Thus while we endeavour to write sublimely in Prose, we fall into a poetical Affectation, which is condemned by all the Masters of Eloquence.

(Chapter I, Of Poets and Poetry, pp. 7-8)

The third thing that makes us take so much pleasure in reading the Poets is their Stile, wherein two things are to be observed: The first is the Expression considered in itself, and the other the cadence or the harmony of their Verse. Their Expression pleases when it is according to the Rules of Art, because it is pure, proper, and simple, when it ought to be so, and figurative when it ought to be otherwise. The Figures above all are frequently employ'd in their Compositions, drawn from the most elevated and beautiful things, so that they fill the Mind with nothing but noble and sublime Ideas. (*Ibid.*, p. 14)

The liveliness of their [the Poets] Colours strikes our Eyes so strongly, that we forget with them the Rules of good Sense, if we are not very much upon our Guard all the while we read them. The irregular Imagination of the Poet expresses itself in so noble and sublime a manner, that it easily overpowers ours, and gives it the same Movements, by which itself is agitated, and this makes all its Irregularities to disappear. (*Ibid.*, p. 16)

The Interpreters of the Code have taken a world of pains to find out the Reason of this Law [Emperor Justinian's, by which a poet did not enjoy the 'Privilege of any Immunity'], as I have observ'd in those whom I have consulted, but have miss'd it in my Opinion. However several good Reasons may be assigned: The first is, That the public Masters of other Sciences are serviceable to the State, by instructing the Youth in useful Knowledg; but a Poet whose chief Business it is to spend his time in composing Romances in Verse, (for Epic Poems are the sublimest Productions of Poetry) what such mighty Service does he do the State, as to deserve a public Recompense? No Roman Emperour ever believed it, and for that Reason they wou'd not grant the Poets any Immunities. (*Ibid.*, p. 39)

The above passage is ambiguous. We cannot be sure whether Le Clerc is applying a sort of utilitarian or practical standard to poetry (he seems to do this in other passages), or whether his emphasis is on the contrast between the frivolousness of verse romances and the sublimity of the epic poem.

We propose to ourselves three Things in Speaking or Writing, or at least one or two of them; that is, to instruct, to give pleasure, and to move the Passions. We may likewise reduce to three sorts of Things, all that we undertake to talk about: The first is of that which regards common Life, or things of pure Speculation, which of themselves are not proper to excite any Movement in the Mind of those that hear them; The second is of that which is a little more elevated, tho' for all that it has nothing extraordinary nor great: The third is of great Things that are not common in Good and Evil. The first require a simple and proper Stile; the second an Elocution somewhat more raised, and the third a sublime Stile. We ought to look upon it as an inviolable Law, always to suit our Stile to our Matter and Design.

(Chapter II, Of True and False Eloquence, pp. 76-77)

They that dont't [sic] know what it is to write in pure and proper Terms, and to express themselves with Perspicuity, imagine that there's nothing so easie as this, and that 'tis much more difficult to speak in a more elevated Manner. These People are of Opinion, that a stronger Genius is required to describe some tragical Accident in a pompous magnificent manner than to discourse of the ordinary things of Human Life, in a clear familiar way: But in this they are extremely mistaken. 'Tis much easier, for instance, to imitate the Hydropic Sublimity of Seneca or Lucan, than the unaffected simplicity of Terence, and some Epigrams of Martial. I dare affirm that those that are capable of writing like Terence, may reach Lucan's Grandeur, if they please: but I defie a Man who has always used himself to a swelling Stile, ever to imitate Terence happily. To speak of a modern Language, I am perswaded that Brebeuf, who, as every one knows, has translated the Pharsalia in Verse as bloated, as those of the Original, wou'd never have been able to compose two or three Pages of Moliere's Misanthrope; and that Moliere on the contrary, if he had thought it worth his while, cou'd have soared as high as Brebeuf. We have several pieces of La Fontaine written in as good an Heroic Stile as any by those that have always practis'd the elevated Stile, but there is not one of these sublime Genius's that cou'd ever come near his Fables.

What I have here maintain'd may seem a Paradox to those that have not sufficiently reflected upon it: However, to convince these Gentlemen I wou'd only desire them to try how they can imitate any Author that has written in a proper and simple Stile, and is esteem'd in his kind, and afterwards to imitate the sublime Stile of any of our most elevated writers. They will then be convinced by experience that the ancient Masters of this Art had reason to judge the first more difficult than the second, altho' the first does not seem to be so at first sight. (*Ibid.*, pp. 79-81)

The Reason of this [Horace's statement in the *Art of Poetry* that "even the Tragic Poets sometimes express Grief in common Language" (Le Clerc's translation)] is because we cannot be touched but by the natural representation of a Passion, and that all Affectation shocks us. I am perswaded that a simple plain Discourse, provided it be naturally delivered, moves those Auditors that have a true Taste, more feelingly than the tallest Metaphor; and that even upon Paper it is much more affecting than one that is penn'd in a more sublime Stile. (*Ibid.*, pp. 84-85)

In this passage Le Clerc uses the word sublime in a negative manner in order to make his point about the 'affect' of simple style. Compared with Fenelon's remarks on the sublime of simplicity (see below, p. 94), which seem to sound an uncommon note for his time, Le Clerc's view regarding simplicity in literature is evidently in agreement with that of a number of critics who appear soon after the turn of the century in France and England. Their espousal of the affective power of plain, natural discourse is probably not 'pre-romantic', but rather a neoclassical insistence on the simplicity to be found in the Ancients. In Addison, for instance, the regard for simplicity is even applied to champion the merits of certain English ballads, a form of expression far removed from the more formal genres of the period.[5]

[5] So apposite to this point is Albert B. Friedman, *The Ballad Revival: Studies in the Influence of Popular on Sophisticated Poetry* (University of Chicago Press, 1961), that I quote a number of passages therefrom. Friedman, be it noted, does not find that the writers and critics of the early eighteenth century in England and France are rule-bound, a position supported by several of the excerpts in this chapter of the Context.

"I think it can be shown that the ballad revival in the first half of the eighteenth century was actually sponsored by neoclassicism. . . . Ballad criticism began in England with Addison's *Chevy Chase* papers. Before him there had been Sidney's testimonial and a few brief, scornful notices, but there had been no sustained piece of writing, in fact no reasoned criticism of any length, until Mr. Spectator spoke in the ballad's behalf. Papers Nos. 70 and 74, much too well known to need summarizing, demonstrate the 'extreme natural and poetical' sentiment, the 'majestic simplicity' of the old song of 'Chevy Chase' to all such readers as are not 'unqualified for such entertainment by their affectation or their ignorance.' " (p. 87)

"Addison's major point is that the ballads illustrate that a poem can succeed,

The following extract occurs immediately after a passage in which Le Clerc declares that there are occasions on which the auditor expects to be moved by loftier rhetoric, and despises the poet if he does not use appropriate ornaments. Then:

> When the Occasion is extraordinary, or when the Subject is naturally sublime, we expect a Stile of the same Dignity, that transports, that ravishes, that governs and turns our Souls about as it pleases. This is the sublime Stile, concerning which Longinus has written a Treatise, which is in every Body's Hands, especially since it has been [by Boileau presumably] translated into French. I will not dwell any longer upon these two latter sorts of Stiles, which are or ought to be properly the Stile of Sermons; if we except those places in them, where we only explain the Matter before us, without drawing any Consequences from it, or making any application to the Auditors. 'Tis sufficient to say, that those that aspire to this Eloquence cannot too often read over those Passages in the celebrated Masters of this Art where 'tis handled. An infinite number of People confound the sublime Stile with Fustian, and think they ravish all the World with Admiration, when they lose themselves in the Clouds, and are laugh'd and ridicul'd by all Men of a true Palat. The reason of this is, because they don't enough consider the Rules of this Art, and don't know that we ought to express ourselves in magnificent Terms only about those things that are Sublime in their own [sic] Nature. (*Ibid.*, pp. 85-86)

Perhaps it is worth mentioning here that some modern critics who make such a dramatic distinction between the French subservience to the rules and the English scepticism of the rules in the period 1650-1700 fail to appreciate how the former can, as Le Clerc above, advocate

---

indeed best succeeds, by virtue of simplicity of style and thought. Needlessly complicated thought and excessive or overly ingenious ornamentation please only the literary dandies. His unconventional use of the ballads by way of illustration commits Addison to a secondary proposition: any work which, like the two ballads [*Chevy Chase* and *The Two Children in the Wood*], has pleased many generations of readers and readers of all strata of society, from Sir Philip Sidney to the humblest tinker, must have great, if recondite, merit." [By their very nature, the theories of Longinus and Langer are also independent of epoch and social stratifications.] (pp. 90-91).

For the same phenomenon in seventeenth-century France, Friedman cites Moliere: "Even if he had not left a record of it, we might have taken it for certain that Addison had read and was impressed by Alceste's argument [in *Le Misanthrope*, I, ii, of the superiority of an old folksong to a certain sonnet which is only a pastiche of precious amorous trivia]. But the excerpt need not be accepted as one of Addison's sources to serve our purpose: it does well enough simply as a parallel. For Moliere is not merely praising the *vieille chanson*; nor is he using the scene simply to express through a convenient *porte-parole* an unusual, personal taste for such poetry. His character compares the old song with the refinements of precious thinking and phrasing as an instructive example of the neo-classic ideals of simplicity and naturalness." (pp. 103-104)

deference to the rules in a way that allows considerable freedom to the artist, while reminding him of the needs of decorum. In other words, Le Clerc would have the writer attend precedent mainly in order to avoid excesses of expression. This can hardly be thought of as artistically stifling.

Antoine Arnauld, *The art of speaking: Written in French by Messieurs Du Port Royal: In persuance of a former Treatise, Intituled, The Art of Thinking. Rendred into English. The Second Edition, Corrected.* (1708)[6]

Arnauld's work reproduces verbatim many of the passages to be found in Lamy's version of the Messieurs du Port Royal above. For the record, Arnauld presents unchanged the passages we have quoted from Lamy, pages 218, 219, 221, 224, 227, 246, 249. The following quotations from Arnauld are brief and not interesting:

> There is nothing so subtil and sublime, but may be made intelligible to the weakest Understanding, if among the things which they know, or are capable of knowing, we can find out ingeniously such as have resemblance or similitude with those which we would explain to them. (p. 107)

> 'Tis true, the Art of working upon an Auditory is much above the reach of a young Scholar, for whom the antient Rhetoricks were properly made. This Art is acquir'd by sublime Speculations, by reflections upon the nature of our Mind, upon our Inclinations, and motions of our Will. 'Tis the fruit of Experience and long Observation of the manner wherewith Men act and govern themselves; in a word, this Art is no where to be caught so methodically as in the precepts of Morality. (p. 284)

Samuel Werenfels, *A discourse of logomachys, or controversys about words, so common among learned men. To which is added a dissertation concerning meteors of stile, or false sublimity . . . translated into English.* (1711)

[6] Barnard, *op. cit.*, informs us that almost from the beginning various members of the Arnauld family were closely associated with Port-Royal, starting with the appointment in 1602 of Jacqueline-Marie Arnauld as abbess (p. 7). And "... eventually she became the instrument whereby twenty-one other members of the Arnauld family entered Port-Royal, either as nuns or as solitaries" (p. 8). On his part, Saint-Cyran persuaded Dr. Antoine Arnauld "to ally himself with Port-Royal and ultimately to enter the priesthood" (p. 16).

Barnard quotes Sainte-Beuve as stating that "the whole quarrel of Jansenism can be simply defined as the quarrel between the Arnauld family and the Society of Jesus" (p. 47).

Wing gives two editions of *The art of speaking* that appeared in England earlier than the edition used for my Context: a 1676 edition printed for Moses Pitt, and a 1696 edition for T. Bennet.

The excerpts from Werenfels that follow form the largest contribution to the entire Context by any one author, and for two reasons. First, Werenfels' writings are particularly esoteric as far as the general student of the eighteenth century is concerned. Second, and more importantly, Werenfels' remarks have the kind of interest that justifies the prolixity of my borrowings from them. The title page identifies the author as a native of Basel, Switzerland, and tells us that the *Discourse* was originally written in Latin and later translated into English, but does not say by whom. As a group, the passages I will examine reflect a certain strength of mind.

. . . Nor was it at all improper, I thought, to join these two Treatises [see title above] together: for as it is a common Error in Logical Disputes, to confound a mere Verbal Difference with a Real; so in Rhetorick, they who affect Sublimity, are frequently betray'd into Meteors of Stile, or Fustian. If I have any where offended against my own Rules, in either of these Respects, it may serve to inform the Reader what strict Precaution is necessary against those Faults, which they, who write concerning them, cannot even at the same time avoid. (Preface, p. x)

Let there be undeniable Indications of Ingenuity and Candor in all your Writings, and always aim at Clearness in expressing your self: Bring the Reader to an understanding of your Opinion by the same way, the same train of Arguments and Method of thinking, by which you was brought to the Belief of it your self: Be inquisitive after the most significant words, such as will make the most lasting Impression on the Minds of the Reader; and see that by no hard Words, nor confus'd Method, you perplex and tire him: Be persuaded of this Truth, that People may talk too rhetorically, with too much subtilty, too sublimely, too copiously, too briefly, too quaintly, but never too clearly: Look upon your self as writing not only for the Learned and Ingenious, but for the Ignorant and Dull; for Readers who will not be attentive, who will read you with Prejudice; who, if they can't espy Faults in your Writings, will, with the help of a good Invention, make them, or at least fancy and affirm them to be there; and who wou'd be better pleas'd to find one error in your Writings than twenty Truths.

("A Discourse of Logomachys", Ch. X, p. 180)

Not to deceive the Reader with a doubtful Expression, by the Meteors of Stile is meant Phrases, which seem to be sublime, but are indeed trifling and vicious. The term is borrow'd from Longinus the Rhetorician, who by ὔψηλά Orationis, understands a Diction truly sublime, and by μετέωρα one which has only a vain appearance of Elevation. . . . And hence the word [μετεωρολεσχί] has always imply'd something of Reproach; and not only the Pretending and Vainglorious were signify'd by μετεωρολο, but all vicious Sublimity in Stile was also call'd μετέωρα : as from the Abuse of the word Phoebus, a Man who makes extravagant Flights in a Discourse, is said in French, parler Phoebus.

To understand what is a Meteor in Stile, 'tis necessary that we understand what is true Sublimity, which is therefore first to be explain'd. . . . 'Tis at every man's Pleasure to judg, as he sees fit: for I am not going to construe Rhetoricians Terms, but to give Precepts of Stile.

To a Great and a Sublime Stile, by which I mean the same thing, 'tis requir'd, First, that the Subject it self be great and sublime. Some things are more valu'd among Men, and others less: the former, being more esteem'd, are call'd the Greater; and those, which are regarded in an inferior degree, the Less: and such as excel among the first are term'd, in an eminent manner, sublime, and produce Admiration in us; as those which are little, move our Contempt.

All those things therefore are great and sublime, which we admire for excelling among them, to which Mankind give the Preference: Thus Kings are great, because they are of a distinguish'd Rank among Men of Dignity and Figure, and they are still greater who excel among Kings; and he is greatest who is King of Kings, and Lord of Lords: and upon the same account Actions and things are also call'd Great.

Nor are only those things great which are good, but also the bad, because they beget Admiration by excelling in their Kind: Thus we say, great Cruelty, Great Villany, great Misery, and the like. And these things generally impress us more strongly, and appear greater to us than those which excel in Goodness; for they raise the Passions of Anger, Indignation, Fear, Sorrow, Terror and Despair, which are apt to magnify an Object, because these Affections are as much more violent in Men, than those which relate to Good. . . .

Now it is not always necessary that an Orator's Subject shou'd be great in the Judgment of Philosophers, or wise men, who estimate not the Value of Things by the vulgar Standard: 'Tis sufficient if it is great in the common Opinion of Mankind, or of those to whom we address our selves. Thus a General, tho above so base a Regard himself, may yet make a noble Speech to the Soldiers about Plunder, in order to animate them to Battle, by the Hope of Booty; and an Orator may declaim warmly on an Injury or Affront, as an important Matter, tho Socrates or Diogenes wou'd have thought it a Trifle. But if a thing, which is great in it self, shou'd not appear so to an Audience, we must first prove it such in a simpler Stile, and by force of Reason, rather than Magnificence of Words: And when by clear Tokens we perceive we have succeeded in this Point, then, and not before, we may raise our Stile into the Sublime, and give it a Majesty. For this reason, the Beginning of a Discourse ought to be plain and natural; because 'tis improper to speak pompously on a Subject, before we have made its Dignity to be understood, since a Hearer may have far meaner Thoughts of it than we.

But to select a lofty Subject, is not alone sufficient to render a Diction sublime; we must also have a Genius equal to the Argument, and be able to discern its several Beautys, and form an Idea of it, which shall comprehend all its Excellence.

This we may call a Capacity and Vigour of Imagination: That is a capacious Imagination, which can at once, or in a very short time, present to it self a Multitude of Things without Confusion, which surveys an illustrious

Subject on every side with wonderful Celerity, and examines it, and distinguishes what are the bright Parts of it, and to what it may properly be compar'd, or oppos'd.

("A Discourse of the Meteors of Stile", pp. 187-189)

In the above Werenfels offers one of the strongest early eighteenth-century anticipations of Burke's sublime of terror that are to be found. Interesting also is his distinction between the types of people in the audience *vis-à-vis* the nature of the sublime, another anticipation – this time of the various theorizers, 1730-1760, who plumb the psychological possibilities of the sublime.

But Imagination is not the sole, nor the chief thing in a Stile; the Judgment must preside over the whole, for* [*Here Werenfels quotes from the *Art of Poetry* of Horace.] good Sense and Understanding is the Foundation of writing well. If all that a hasty and luxuriant Fancy suggests, is not fit to pass in a Poem, how much greater Caution must be had in Prose, the Gravity of which allows far less Liberty to the Fancy? . . . Let the Imagination view and review its Idea on every side, till it pleases the Judgment, and a true Critick pronounces; "This Part of it is admirable, this is to be display'd to the Audience."

After the Image of a noble Subject is finish'd in the Mind, and approv'd by the Judgment, the next care is concerning the Words, which are as it were the Colouring, that we paint it out to others; so that it may seem as lofty to them as it does to us. Words, therefore, shou'd be equal to the Image, and the Image to the Thing; and consequently in a sublime Stile, they shou'd also be sublime, which they are three ways; By the Authority of the Persons who use them, by their Sound, and by their Signification.

Words are sublime by the Authority of such as use them, which are not taken from Places where the Rabble and baser People resort, but from the conversation of Persons of good Breeding, and honourable Birth and Employment. A polite Taste will easily distinguish these in any Language, from those which are render'd coarse and sordid, by being in the Mouths of the Vulgar. When I speak of Words, I understand also the Phrases, call'd Proverbs, and the like.

Words are great in Sound, and Periods and Sentences (which have also a relation to the Sound of Words) if they fill the Ear, and are but just remov'd from oppressing it; like these in Virgil, "Venti ex Cavernis erumpunt;" The Winds burst out of their Caverns: And these

> – – – – – Crines effusa Sacerdos
> Tercentum tonat ore Deos, Erebumq; Chaosq;
> Tergeminamque Hecatem.

And those of Claudian, when he says, "Ceres", upon the loss of her Daughter, "Toto bacchatur Olympo". But of this the Ear must judg, which is more elegant in some than in others.

But the greatest Sublimity of Words consists in the Signification; for every man knows some are more significant than others, as in Latin, "amare" signifies more than "diligere", "flagitare" than "petere", "erumpere" than "evadere" (and in English to "loathe" than to "dislike", and to "shock" than to "move", etc.) It conduces therefore to the Elevation of Stile, not only to use Words which signify great Things, but also to select those which carry the fullest Sense. Thus, "Fury furnishes Arms", is loftier than if the Poet had said "Anger" instead of "fury".

Besides the more known and the principal significations of any Word, there are innumerable others affix'd by common Use, which some call a secondary Sense. . . .

There are few Words which have not a Variety of these Significations, which are to be observ'd in every sort of Stile, and especially in the Sublime; not only that nothing may be signify'd by a Word contrary to what we design, but also that these Significations may serve to increase the Sublimity of the Discourse. . . . Nay, I may affirm, that nothing imparts greater Majesty to a Discourse, than Words which have many Significations of this this kind: For here a noble Sense lies conceal'd in few Words, and those the most simple, than which there cannot be any thing more sublime.

(*Ibid.*, pp. 192-195)

Werenfels' three sources of the sublime style correspond rather closely with Longinus' five sources of the sublime. Though the former uses the word 'style' in his discussion, it is apparent that he actually transcends that term's ordinary limitations.

Tropes also, and especially Metaphors, heighten a Stile, when justly imploy'd; but they cannot find place in a sublime one, unless they are render'd necessary, either by the variety of the Discourse, or because the proper Words seem not fully to answer the Greatness of the Subject: 'tis then we are to borrow others, which are of a more lofty Sense. But in the Doctrine of the Tropes, too many convince the World they can play the Rhetorician.

Most Readers will think what has been already laid down, sufficient to Sublimity of Stile; but one thing, in my Opinion, is still behind, and which, for ought I know, may be the chief. An Orator not only paints out his Subjects in his Oration, but also himself; for, as Demetrius truly says, "The Writer's Image is to be seen in every Word he uses." In the sublime Stile, therefore, we shou'd not only make the Subject, but even our Mind appear sublime; I say the Mind, not the Wit, which may sometimes be spritely and great, where the Mind is base and little.

He has a great and noble Mind, who is so wholly mov'd by Things which are important and great, as to be delighted only with them, and to regard them so entirely, as to despise those which meaner Minds esteem, as of no Consequence to him; who is of one Tenor in every Condition of Life, always Master of himself, true, sincere, open-hearted, and tenacious of the Right; and who so preserves his Dignity, as not to be overborn by Fear or Hope, or any other Perturbation, to commit an unworthy Action.

Let an Orator paint himself thus, if he wou'd obtain a Majesty to his Speech.

And thus he will always draw himself thro the whole Discourse, who does not labor it with a servile Diligence and Care, nor follow the trifling Rules of Rhetoricians, which is the Mark of a narrow Mind; but whose Eloquence shines with a masculine Vigour, and is simple and correct. This is to be found in him who speaks as he thinks, and who is more careful what he says, than how he says it; and who, in short, speaks well, not because he endeavours to do so, but because he cannot speak otherwise: Such a Man delivers himself with a certain noble Boldness and Liberty of Speech; and as he has nothing unmanner'd and rude, so he is far from a childish Bashfulness and Awe, and a fulsom and prostituted Flattery.

(*Ibid.*, pp. 196-198)

Any doubts that Werenfels is independent of the rhetorical sublime are dispelled by the last three paragraphs of the above extract. He is, again, quite close to Longinus, here on the importance of the character of the orator (artist).

From what has been said, it appears how extraordinary a thing it is, not to strike out one sublime saying or two, but to make a whole Discourse so. Briefly to comprise what I have said; he who would perform this, must form a great Idea from a noble Subject, and express also a Sublimity of Mind in Words so significant, as to TRANSPORT [my emphasis] a Man into an admiration both of that and his Subject. . . . But in the Sublime very few write tolerably . . . while they pursue Sublimity, they only write Fustian, and by soaring, catch nothing but an empty Cloud, a Meteor of Stile; which is the inseparable Consequence of injudiciously affecting to the sublime.

The Meteors of Stile may all be reduc'd under these three Heads: 1. When a Diction truly sublime is employ'd on a trivial Subject. 2. When the Subject is great, but the Stile is not truly so. 3. When neither the Subject, nor the Stile is truly sublime. The Cause of the first is, that either we estimate indifferent Things above their real Value, or else imagine we can't handle a Subject elegantly, unless we treat it magnificently: the former argues a little Mind, and both of them a Weakness of Judgment.

(*Ibid.*, pp. 199-200)

There is another sort of Meteor, which consists not in using a magnificent Stile on a mean Subject, but in using a vicious Sublimity on a Subject truly great. I call all that vicious Sublimity, which seems to be sublime to some Persons, but is not really so. They offend in this kind, who think every thing sublime, which is obscure.

(*Ibid.*, p. 206)

But a Man need not take Pains to be obscure, since, as Examples of many of the First-rate Writers testify, 'tis scarcely possible for us to avoid it, especially in the sublime Stile, when we endeavour to say lofty Things in lofty Words: for when we labour to form a great Image of a Thing in our Mind, we often croud so many Ideas together, that the Imagination is confounded and perplex'd; and we can't tell what it is we are conceiving, which necessarily renders the Expression dark and involv'd. Sometimes the Image is form'd distinctly in the Mind, but we are at a loss for Words equal to it; and while we seek too far for them, we become unintelligible. And sometimes we strive to comprize a great Thought in few Words, to increase the Force of the Expression; which, if rarely us'd, and with Perspicuity, makes a Stile very sublime: but how readily we slide from hence into Obscurity, the Instance of Tacitus declares. This is to be excus'd in great Writers, and not to be imitated, especially by those who can only imitate their Faults.

(*Ibid.*, p. 209)

They also mistake Meteors for Sublimity, who think every thing to be sublime which is rare and extraordinary. They despise Words and Phrases of common use, and observe nothing in an Author as they read him, but what is seldom to be found.

(*Ibid.*, p. 209)

And thus Figurative Words, tho more rare than proper, are not therefore always more sublime: But we are so far from being Gainers, by changing the last for the former, that it is frequently a Disadvantage to us.

(*Ibid.*, p. 212)

Neither do they distinguish a Meteor from Sublimity, who affect too exquisite an Ornament in the sublime Stile, and always hunt after measur'd Periods, Stops and Pauses, and Antitheses, and Comparisons, exactly answering one another; and contrive to repeat Words and Sounds in equal time, to begin and end alike; and to have round Sentences, unexpected Clauses, and a smart playing with Similitudes, Oppositions, and Ambiguitys of Words; to rehearse Sayings and Actions of the Antients; and to bring, I will not say to haul, everything in the World, by an ingenious Allegory, into their Subject. If some of these Particulars are sparingly us'd in a pleasant Discourse, they pass well enough; if they are thick sown, they are abominable, even in a ludicrous Argument; but in a serious and sublime one they are monstrous, and not to be endur'd, and are as indecent as if a grave Man shou'd go to dance a Jig in a publick Assembly.

(*Ibid.*, p. 213)

. . . Many of the Fathers have stuff'd their Writings with these Foolerys, and propagated them to our Age; and so heartily are they embrac'd by some of our Preachers, that Posterity, I question not, will inherit them.

(*Ibid.*, p. 214)

A sublime Stile will admit a more sparing Ornament, sometimes, but not always; for if the Image we form in our Mind is truly great, it will appear the greater, the more simply 'tis express'd . . . And if some Parts in a sublime Discourse are to have the Ornament of Words, we shou'd be careful that the Ornament shew it self as little as possible.

(*Ibid.*, p. 215)

We must also observe a Mean in our Ornaments, lest we divert a Reader from the Passions we intend to excite in him, to admire the Delicacys of the Stile, and other mechanical Graces . . .

(*Ibid.*, p. 216)

Farther; they do not distinguish a Meteor from Sublimity, who think Sublimity consists in highsounding Words, that promise somewhat considerable under them, but signify nothing extraordinary . . .

(*Ibid.*, p. 217)

But of all Meteors, none have a greater appearance of Sublimity, than those which Quintilian calls Praecipitia, and others tumida, turgida, and inflata; which are swollen, and flatulent, and full of Tumor. A Tumor in Stile, is a certain Excess of Elevation, into which all are betray'd, who possess a Strength of Imagination rather than of Judgment; and whenever they would speak magnificently, make use of every thing that serves to exalt a Stile, but observe no Decency or Moderation.

If these Persons wou'd form a great Image, they form a vast one; instead of a sublime one, they make one which is enormous; and for an admirable one, they invent one wholly incredible and prodigious. They can't think of a tall Man, but they make him a Giant, and they magnify a valiant Man into a perfect Romance-Hero.

(*Ibid.*, p. 220)

If they happen to strike us with some appearance of Sublimity, when uttered boldly, and with a confident Air, it is, because we are all proud Creatures, and are not only pleas'd to see ourselves lifted above inferior things, which wou'd not be a Fault; but at the same time that we debase our selves beneath things really mean and vile, we haughtily elevate us above those which are truly excellent, as it were in revenge, to recover the Dignity we shamefully gave away to the other.

(*Ibid.*, p. 229)

Thus, from the large number of passages given, it is easily seen that Werenfels is much nearer the spirit of Longinus than he is to Classical rhetoricians, and this in spite of the fact that his book is intended to deal with problems of words and style, and largely for the benefit of the public speaker. To summarize Werenfels' leading ideas with respect to the sublime, in the order that they occur in the extracts above, we find that he believes that the sublimity of a man's expression is first of all determined by his own character, that the effect of a word's sound on the ear is vital, and that there is a basic distinction between the sublime on the one hand, and wit on the other. (Addison makes much the same point in the *Spectator*, Nos. 58-63, which appeared within the same year as *A Discourse of Logomachys*.) Further, Werenfels agrees with Longinus in identifying transport as the base element of the sublime and in warning against the use of obscurity to achieve sublime effects. In the face of the balanced prose style so much in evidence during the early years of the century, Werenfels declares that antithesis and servile imitation of the Ancient writers are inimical to the sublime. And perhaps most significantly of all, Werenfels is one of the most adamant of all of the writers here included who find simplicity at the heart of the sublime; to ignore simplicity is to incur the danger of raising a meteor.

Werenfels, as the author of a book on style, is so close to the spirit and letter of Longinus that he impels one to hesitate in dismissing eighteenth-century rhetoric books out of hand as *jejune* reiterations of the Classical rhetoricians or as perversions of *On the Sublime*.

John Brightland, *A grammar of the English tongue, with the arts of logick, rhetorick, poetry, etc.* (1714)

This work has not the interest of original thinking, but rather of an important trend in the rhetoric books of our period. This trend is the lower position assigned to diction as such in the expressions of language calculated to move or persuade. We have just seen evidence of this emphasis in Werenfels; Brightland continues the strain, if less strikingly so.

Nay, we may without Vanity say, that no Public School in Europe has any Course of Poetry equal to what we give here. We have seen all that have been taught, and not one of them proceeds any farther, than the art of Versifying, by teaching the several Quantities of Words, and what each sort of Verse requires. But this is the Art of making Poetasters, not Poets; of giving a Taste of Numbers, but not of the sublimer Beauties of the Authors they read, which are of the first magnitude; by which means we often find, that those who have spent many Years in teaching Schools, are the worst Judges in the World of the very Authors they teach.

(Preface)

Then say what Thanks, what Praises must attend
The gen'rous Wits, who thus could condescend!
Skill, that to Arts' sublimest Orb can reach,
Employ'd its humble Elements to teach!
Yet worthily esteem'd, because we know
To raise Their Country's Fame, they stooped so low.

(To Mr. Brightland, Upon his Excellent Design of an English Education, 4th stanza)

The Style [of the pastoral] ought to be natural, clear and elegant, but nothing sublime or lofty, or set off with such Ornaments as are not at all agreeable to the Humility of the Subject. (p. 142)

> There is no Action that do's not proceed
> From Manners, and the Sentiments indeed.
> And therefore these, in this sublimer Art
> Of Tragedy, must claim essential Part.
> (Chapter IV, "Of Tragedy", p. 153)

The Diction, or Language of Tragedy, can demand but the fourth Place in the essential Parts, and is of the least importance of any of them; yet must peculiar Care be likewise taken of this, that every Passion speak in such Words and Expression as is natural to it.

(*Ibid.*, p. 155)

The above is a clear statement of an early eighteenth-century weakening of the role of diction as rhetoric in exalted expression.

The Reasons of Poets and Orators are the same when they would make Things appear worthy of Pity, or terrible, or great, or probable; tho some Things are rendered so by Art, and some by their own nature.

(*Ibid.*, p. 166)

I quote the above passage, even though it does not mention the sublime, because it helps to support our growing suspicion that by and large the eighteenth century is not interested in making a sharp distinction between rhetoric, oratory, and art.

We need say no more of this Poem [any epic poem], the Rules at large would be too extensive for this Treatise, and but of little Use; the Poem being not to be undertaken but by a Master, and by a Genius that does not appear once in a Thousand Years.

(*Ibid.*, p. 168)

Note the prominent usage of the idea of genius in this, a grammar book.

The Subjects of Discourse being extreamly various in the Nature, it follows, that there must be as great a Variety in the Style: But the Masters of this Art have reduc'd them all to three Kinds, which they call the Sublime, the Mean, or the Indifferent.

Let the Subjects of which we design a lofty Idea be never so noble, its Nobleness will never be seen, unless we have Skill enough to present the best of its Faces to the View. The Best of Things have their Imperfections, the least of which discover'd, may lessen our Esteem, if not extinguish it quite: We must therefore take Care not to say any thing in one place, which may contradict what we have said in another: We ought to pick out all that is most great and noble in our Subject, and put that in its best light, and then our Expression must be noble and sublime, capable of raising lofty Ideas: And 'tis our Duty to observe a certain Uniformity in our Style; tho all we say have not an equal Magnificence, so far at least as to make all the Parts of a piece, and bear a Correspondence with the whole.

("Rhetoric; or, The Art of Persuasion", pp. 189-190)

The mean or middle Style consists of a participation of the sublime on one side, and of simplicity or the Plain, on the other. Virgil furnishes us with Examples of all the three; of the Sublime in his Aeneids, the Plain in his Pastorals, and the Mean (or Middle) in his Georgics.

(*Ibid.*, p. 190)

These final two extracts conform to both Classical and eighteenth-century statements that are generally considered orthodox. Yet we notice again that, so stated, there is enough flexibility to admit most of the tenets of pure Longinianism.

Francois de Callieres, *Characters and criticisms upon the ancient and modern orators, poets, painters, musicians, statuaries, & other arts and sciences. With an Heroic poem (in Blank Verse) intituled The Age of Lewis the Great. Written originally in French by the Arch-Bishop of Cambray, and made English by F.G.* (1714)[7]

Characters and criticisms is a 180-page raillery, cast in the form of a military romance, on the subject of the war between the ancients and moderns. It is rather tiresome and unimaginative. The allusions to the sublime are very generalized and add nothing new to our study, but I offer them for the sake of completeness.

Nor were the Italians less jealous to see a Spaniard at their Head. A certain Critick amongst 'em, who was known to be the famous Castelvetro, loudly declared, during the March, they were going to be dishonour'd amongst all Nations, and all Future Ages, since their Country was so destitute of an Orator Sublime and Eloquent enough to be their General, that they were obliged to acknowledge a Mean and Foreign Author of Comical Romance; that the Latins would have very good Reason to use them like Barbarians, and no longer acknowledge the Italians for their Lawful Issue . . .

(Third Book, p. 39)

He [Apollo, who makes this and the following decrees at the close of the war] confirms to Homer the possession of those glorious Titles he has so justly acquired of the greatest Poet, and most sublime Genius that ever lived.

(Eleventh Book, p. 164)

[7] The Archbishop of Cambray is Francois Fenelon, whose *Dialogues* follow immediately below.

In relation to the Orators, Apollo declares, that Demosthenes is the most Sublime, Lively, Pathetic, and Eloquent of any that ever yet spoke in Publick: He continues to him the Title of Thundering Orator, who cuts to pieces, bears down, and dissipates all that oppose his victorious Eloquence.
(*Ibid.*, p. 170)

He maintains Aristotle in the Reputation he has so justly acquired, for one of the most immense and sublime Genius's that ever lived.
(*Ibid.*, p. 172)

He declares the Stile of Calprenede to be truly Heroical, Noble, and Sublime, as it ought to be for Romance, which is a piece of Poetry in Prose. He places therefore the Works of this Author in the first Rank of serious and Heroick Romances; commending him particularly for having known how to bestow great and beautiful Characters upon all his Hero's.
(*Ibid.*, p. 174)

Francois Fenelon, *Dialogues concerning eloquence in general*; *And particularly, that kind which is fit for the pulpit*: *By the late Archbishop of Cambray. With his letter to the French academy, concerning rhetoric, poetry, history, and a comparison betwixt the antients and moderns. Translated from the French, and illustrated with notes and quotations*; *by William Stevenson, M.A. Rector of Morningthorp in Norfolk.* (1722)

Monk merely cites the *Dialogues* in a footnote (*The Sublime,* 84 n.). Perhaps his reasoning in doing so is that the work purports to treat of pulpit oratory, Longinus is essentially a rhetorician, and thus any mention in the *Dialogues* of Longinus or the sublime is bound to be in an exclusively rhetorical context. How mistakenly this argument is applied to Fenelon's book will become obvious in the excerpts that follow; they both support our thesis that the eighteenth century tended to fuse rhetoric and art, and provide commentary of considerable interest in their own right.[8]

[8] See E. B. O. Borgerhoff, *The Freedom of French Classicism* (Princeton, 1950), "Le je ne sais quoi: Le P. Bouhours" (pp. 186-200). In Cabeen and Brody, *op. cit.*, Brody calls (p. 285) Borgerhoff's chapter brilliant in the manner that it "sees in the 'je ne sais quoi' only the most obvious symptom of a concern for the ineffable expressed in a variety of other ways by writers from Balzac to Fenelon. [It] uncovers in this reputedly intellectual century a widespread willingness not to understand. Especially useful is the notion that the urge for independence and vitality and the instinct for order formed not an antagonism but a balanced tension."

In further support of my contention, I add what Brody has to say of Henri Peyre, *Le Classicisme Français* (New York, 1942): "Of outstanding interest: [is the] distinction between rationalisme, as it is commonly understood, and intellectualité, a passionate urge to uncover and communicate through art the secrets of the human heart" (p. 88).

A. . . . One cannot but see that he [Demosthenes] has the Good of the Republick entirely at heart; and that Nature itself speaks in all his Transports: for his artful Address is so masterly, that it never appears. Nothing ever equal'd the Force and Vehemence of his Discourses. Have you never read the Remarks that Longinus made on them, in his Treatise of the Sublime?

B. No: Is not that the Treatise that Mr. Boileau translated? Do you think it fine?

A. I am not afraid to tell you that I think it surpasses Aristotle's "Rhetorick"; which, though it be a very solid Tract, is yet clogg'd with many dry Precepts, that are rather curious, than fit for Practice; so that it is more proper to point out the Rules of Art to such as are already eloquent, than to give us a just Taste of Rhetorick, and to form true Orators. But Longinus, in his Discourse of the Sublime, intersperses among his Precepts, many fine Examples from the greatest Authors, to illustrate them. [Here there is an asterisk in the text calling attention to a footnote, which is the famous eulogy of Longinus from Pope's *Essay on Criticism*.] He treats of the Sublime in a lofty manner, as his Translator has judiciously observ'd: He warms our Fancy, and exalts our Mind; he forms our Taste; and teaches us to distinguish what is either fine, or faulty, in the most famous ancient Writers.

B. Is Longinus such a wonderful Author? Did he not live in the days of Zenobia, and the Emperor Aurelian? [No, probably not.]

A. Yes; you cannot but know their history.

B. Did not those Days fall vastly short of the Politeness of former Ages? And can you imagine that an Author who flourish'd in the Declension of Learning and Eloquence had a better Taste than Isocrates? I cannot believe it.

A. I was surpriz'd myself, to find it so: but you need only read him, to be convinc'd of it. Tho' he liv'd in a very corrupted Age, he form'd his Judgment upon the ancient Models; and has avoided almost all the reigning Faults of his own Time; I say almost all, for I must own he study'd rather what is admirable, than what is useful; and did not consider Eloquence as subservient to Morality; nor apply it to direct the Conduct of Life. And in this he does not seem to have had such solid Views as the antient Greeks, and especially some of their Philosophers. But we ought to forgive him a Failing, for which Isocrates was far more remarkable, tho' he liv'd in a more refin'd Age. And this Defect ought the rather to be overlook'd in a particular Discourse, where Longinus does not treat of what is proper to instruct Men, but of what is apt to move and seize their Passions. I chuse to

---

Thus it is quite possible that the French neo-classical period could formulate a concept of the sublime, embracing formal and spontaneously subjective elements, that would be received enthusiastically across the Channel.

recommend this Author, Sir, because he will help to explain my Meaning to you. You will see what a glorious Character he gives of Demosthenes, from whom he quotes several Passages that are most sublime: He will likewise shew you those Faults of Isocrates that I mention'd. If you be unwilling to take the trouble of becoming acquainted with these Authors, by reading their Words; you may get a very just Notion of them by consulting Longinus.

("Dialogues concerning Eloquence; The First Dialogue, between A., B., and C."; pp. 14-17)

This long passage contains three items worthy of comment. To begin with, the first exchange between 'A' and 'B' illustrates the way in which rhetorical and literary matters are fused, if not muddled, by our period's writers. In quick succession we are presented with the ideas of Longinus' commentary in his treatise on the orator Demosthenes, Boileau as translator of Longinus, and the comparison of the latter with Aristotle's *Rhetoric*. These lead, in turn, to two further ideas: Monk argues that Boileau, at the cost of doing some violence to the intention of *On the Sublime*, reinterprets Longinus in a vein that inspires ultimately a new esthetic of the sublime for the eighteenth century (see above, Chapter I, p. 23, f.n. 7). Now whether or not Monk is correct in this, it should behoove him to discuss Fenelon, even if it is a book on rhetoric, when it is so plainly established near the beginning of the work that it is Boileau's version of the sublime that underlies the entire treatment of the term. And second, it is notable that Aristotle's *Rhetoric*, and not his *Poetics*, is the foil to *On the Sublime*.

The second interesting item in the passage is the fact that the *Dialogues* commits the same biographical error with regard to the identity of the historical Longinus as I noted in my discussion of William Smith in Chapter I. The resultant fallacy is less damaging to Fenelon's treatment of Longinus than to Smith's, however, because of the many subsequent non-biographically inspired remarks.

Finally, the third item of significance in the passage is the comment of 'A' that Longinus is faulty for studying what is admirable rather than what is useful, that he does not consider eloquence subservient to morality. The test of utility we have already noticed as a prominent tendency of the period. There are also others who underestimate the broad moral implications of *On the Sublime*, but I would say that Fenelon has somewhat less company on this score.

C. But if true Orators be Poets; I shou'd think that Poets are Orators too: For Poetry is very proper to perswade.

A. Yes; they have the very same End. All the difference betwixt them consists in what I have told you. Orators are not possest with that Enthusiasm which fires the Poet's Breast, and renders him more lively, more sublime, and bolder in Expression. You remember the Passage I quoted from Cicero.

C. Which? Is it not -----

A. That an Orator ought to have the Stile almost of a Poet; that *almost* [sic] points out the difference between them.

(Ibid.; "The Second Dialogue"; p. 80)

A. ... In such Passages [transports of grief], one ought studiously to avoid all refin'd uncommon Thoughts; and even neglect Connection and Order; otherwise the Passion describ'd has no appearance of Truth, or Nature, in it. Nothing is more shocking than a Passion express't in beautiful Figures, pompous Language, and well-turn'd Periods. On this head, I must recommend [here footnote tells reader to see *Peri Hupsous*, sections xviii, xix, xx, xxi] Longinus to you, who quotes many sublime Examples from Demosthenes, and others.

(*Ibid.*, p. 85)

A. ... For, besides his possessing many excellent Qualities, the Fault we complain of, is the natural Effect of his Stile. [Here 'A' is discussing a preacher whom he and 'B' have recently heard.] We have already agreed that the Modulation of the Voice shou'd be exactly suitable to the Words. Now his Stile is even, and uniform, without the least Variety. On the other hand, it is not familiar, insinuating, and popular: and on the other, it has nothing in it that is lively, figurative, and sublime: but it consists of a constant flow of Words, that press one after the other, containing a close and well-connected Chain of Reasoning, on clear Ideas. ... He is very capable of convincing People: but I know few Preachers who perswade and move them less than he doth.

(*Ibid.*, p. 96)

The complexity of the problem is illustrated thus: Longinus distinguishes between the power of the orator to persuade and the poet to transport; Fenelon in the above speech of 'A' distinguishes between the preacher's ability to convince on the one hand, and persuade and move on the other.

B. What! do you think that Demosthenes and Tully did not learn by-heart those finish'd Orations they have left us?

A. We know very well that they compos'd and wrote their Harangues, before they spake in publick: but we have several Reasons to believe that they did not get them by-heart, word for word. Even the Orations of Demosthenes, as we have them, shew rather the Sublimity and Vehemence of a great Genius that was accustom'd to speak powerfully of publick Affairs; than the Accuracy and Politeness of an Author.

(*Ibid.*, p. 110)

B. Seeing you condemn the florid swelling Stile; what kind do you reckon fittest for publick Use?

A. There ought to be a Variety of Stile in every Discourse. We shou'd rise in our Expression when we speak of lofty Subjects; and be [here a footnote quotes in Greek a passage from Longinus, section xxxi.] familiar, on common ones, without being coarse, or grovelling. In most Cases, an easy Simplicity and Exactness is sufficient: tho' some Things require Vehemence, and Sublimity. If a Painter shou'd draw nothing but magnificent Palaces, he cou'd not follow Truth; but must paint his own Fancies; and by that means, soon cloy us.

(*Ibid.*, pp. 130-131)

A. . . . But the Stile of a true Orator has nothing in it that is swelling or ostentatious: he always adapts it to the Subject he treats of, and the Persons he instructs: and manages it so judiciously that he never aims at being sublime and lofty, but when he ought to be so.

(*Ibid.*, p. 132)

A. . . . I forgot to tell you that he [St. Austin] quotes that Passage of the Prophet Amos which begins thus [marginal note identifies quotation as coming from ch. vi.] "Wo to them that are at ease in Zion, and trust in the mountain of Samaria – – – –": and assures us that in this Place the Prophet has surpass't every thing that is sublime in the Heathen Orators.

C. But how do you understand these Words of St. Paul; [marginal notes cite I Cor.] "My speech and my preaching was not with the enticing (perswasive) words of man's wisdom – – –?" Does he not tell the Corinthians that he came not to preach Christ to them, with the Sublimity of Discourse and of Wisdom: that he "knew nothing among them but Jesus, and him crucify'd:" that his preaching was founded not upon the perswasive Language of human Wisdom, and Learning, but upon the sensible Effects of the Spirit and Power of God . . .

(*Ibid.*, p. 139)

A. . . . Every thing is painted in such a lively manner as strikes the Imagination. The Prophet [Nahum] far out-does Homer. Read likewise [note cites ch. v] Daniel denouncing to Belshazzar the divine Vengeance ready to overwhelm him: and try if you can find any thing in the most sublime Originals of Antiquity that can be compar'd to those Passages of sacred Writ.

(*Ibid.*, p. 155)

As for the sublime and vehement kind [of speaking], he [St. Austin] wou'd not have it florid; "nor [note cites Aug. de Doct. Chr. 1, IV.] embellish't with the Ornaments of Speech: but rather full of the most pathetick Emotions . . . For the Speaker following the impulse of his Thoughts, does not industriously study the Beauties of Elocution; but naturally uses such as rise from the Subject itself."

(*A Letter to the French Academy*, pp. 217-218)

The other Occasion wherein he [St. Austin] powerfully sway'd the Minds of his Audience, is thus related by himself: "We must not imagine that a Man has spoken in a lofty sublime Manner, when he receives many Acclamations, and great Applause. These are sometimes given to the lowest Turns of Wit, and the Ornaments of the moderate sort of Eloquence. But the sublime Strain ofttimes overwhelms People's Minds with its Vehemence: it renders them speechless: it melts them into Tears. . . ."

(*Ibid.*, p. 219)

Before I conclude this Head, I must add a few Words concerning the Eloquence of the Fathers: for, some learn'd Men judge of them too unfavourably . . . But they shou'd consider the corrupted Taste of the Times in which the Fathers liv'd. Rome began to lose its Taste soon after Augustus's Reign . . . The Fathers being train'd up under the weak Declaimers of their Times were led away by the common Prejudices; which the wisest Men scarce ever resist. It was not thought tolerable then to speak in an easy natural way . . . But if we had the Patience to examine the Works of the Fathers, we shou'd find many valuable Things in them. S. Cyprian has a Grandure and Vehemence that somewhat resembles Demosthenes. In S. Chrysostom we find an exact Judgment, noble Images, and a solid Morality explain'd in the most obvious agreeable Manner. S. Austin is at once sublime and popular. He leads us to the highest Notions, by the most familiar Turns of Expression. He asks Questions; he puts Questions to himself; he answers them. His Dicourse is a sort of Conversation between him, and his Audience. He uses pertinent Comparisons to clear every Doubt. We see him sometimes condescend to the lowest and coarsest Apprehensions of the People, in order to reclaim them.

(*Ibid.*, pp. 239-241)

[After telling how 'an Author that has too much Wit' exhausts him, Fenelon proceeds:] I love a gentle Light that refreshes my weak Eyes. I chuse an agreeable Poet that adapts himself to common Capacitys: who does every thing for their sakes; and nothing for his own. I wou'd have a SUBLIME [sic] so familiar, so sweet, and so simple, that at first every Reader wou'd be apt to think he cou'd easily have hit on it himself; tho' very few are really capable of it. I prefer what is amiable, to what is surprizing and wonderful. I wou'd have a Man that makes me forget he is an Author; and seems to converse with me upon the level. I wou'd have him set before my Eyes, a labourer who is concern'd for his Crop; a Shepherd that knows nothing beyond his Flock and his Village; a Nurse tenderly anxious for her Infant. I wou'd have him turn my attention, not on himself, but on the Shepherds whom he makes to speak.

(*Ibid.*, p. 255)

In light of the relatively early date of the book, this passage is extremely interesting. In the first place, for a French work it is surprisingly free of the supposedly rigid neo-classicism of that nation's theorizers on art.

In addition, the passage is a striking early example of the eighteenth-century shift of the location of the sublime response from the author to the subject itself, and yet, be it noted, not in the kind of subject matter that was to appeal to the proponents of the natural sublime. Fenelon speaks not of raging seas, brooding crags, or terrifying abysses, but rather of the spiritual quality that permeates, if you will, the more homely objects of the sublime poet's perception. In a word, this passage impresses as being much closer related to the Wordsworthian 'rural sublime' of the end of the century than to the natural sublime of mid-century. Thus, we observe that the well-established development of the concept of the sublime in the eighteenth century from being word- or language-oriented to being involved in man's psychological response to the immensities and terrors of the natural world is not the only development to be found.

'Tis true the Academy wou'd frequently happen to be divided upon these Questions. The Esteem that some have for the Antients; and others, for the Moderns, might hinder them from agreeing in their Judgments. But I apprehend no ill Effects from a Contest so calm, so polite, and so moderate as that wou'd prove. For in this Case, Everyone might freely follow his own Taste, and his own Notions. Such an Emulation might improve Learning. May I presume here to offer my Thoughts on the Subject?

1. I begin with wishing that the Moderns might surpass the Antients. I wou'd rejoyce to see in our Age, and our Nation, more vehement Orators than Demosthenes, and sublimer Poets than Homer. The World, instead of losing, wou'd certainly gain much by it. The Antients wou'd not be less valuable than they have always been; and the Moderns wou'd add a new Ornament to human Nature. The Antients must still retain the Glory of having begun, and shewn the way to others; and of furnishing them with the Means to excel themselves.

(*Ibid.*, pp. 302-303)

On the other hand we ought to consider what may be said in favour of the Antients. Now, besides their having furnisht our modern Authors with almost all the best Thoughts they have; we ought to set a Value even on those Parts of the Antient's Works that are not faultless. Longinus observes that [note cites Long. section xxxiii.] "a Discourse too much polish't and refin'd is in danger of being mean." [Fenelon goes on in the next 14 lines quoting from this familiar idea of Longinus.]

(*Ibid.*, pp. 314-315)

Virgil, who had a full View of all the Roman Magnificence, has yet given a Beauty to King Evander's Poverty; and made it an Ornament to his Poem. [Here follow ten lines cited in the margin as "AEn. viii. v. 359 – – –".] The shameful Corruption of our Manners hinders us from raising our Views to

admire the Sublimity of these Words, "Aude hospes contemnere opes – – –."
(*Ibid.*, p. 319)

At the end of Fenelon's volume is an index, which contains the following entries:

Sublime, explain'd and exemplify'd by Longinus, p. 16
Character of the true Sublime, p. 255
See Scripture: Antients
[under Scripture;]
it excels all other Books in Sublimity, Grandure, and natural Representations, pp. 129, 150.
[under Antients the word sublime is not mentioned.]

It seems beyond dispute that the *Dialogues* deserves a better fate than being relegated to a footnote citation in a lengthy study of the sublime.

[Anon.], *The Many Advantages of a Good Language to any Nation: with An Examination of the present State of our own: As also, An Essay towards correcting some Things that are wrong in it.* (1724)

Since a fair share of the contents of this book is a discussion of style, there is ample opportunity for the author to use the sublime, but he never does until just a few pages from the end. Up to that point, it appears that he uses the word 'grave' to mean sublime, there being at least four instances of such usage.

If you think any Argument upon the Grammatical Enquiries must be low, and had rather have something more sublime, shew how impossible it is that a Language should reach to the exalted Subjects of God and the Creation, and draw forth Passions equal to those noble Themes, unless the Language it self be stored with Words as sublime as they: Or if you had rather exersise your Talent in Satyr, ridicule the Faults and Defects of our Language that want mending. Collect our deep Gutturals, our comical Abbreviations, our twenty Diphthongs; and run a Prong into the Backside of our Schoolmasters, that keep their Schollers seven Years under their Rods and Axes, and then send them home without being able to write English. That is a Subject that will bear Satyr, and deserves it: Do but cure that Evil, and you will be Benefactor to Thousands.
(A Letter to a Friend, pp. 83-84)

From the context of this passage, brief as it is, we can easily see that the author applies the concept of the sublime to both subject matter and words of an exalted kind.

[Anon.], *The art of speaking in public: or an essay on the action of an orator; as to his pronunciation and gesture. The Second Edition cor-*

rected. With an Introduction relating to the famous Mr. Henly's present Oratory. (1727)

The author of this 217-page treatise is very niggardly in his use of the word sublime. The examples that came to light show, however, that he is perfectly capable in this book on oratory of using the word in a non-oratorical sense.

Therefore to prevent the Growth of such Censures for the Time to come, it will not be amiss, if every young Student, that has the least Hopes or Prospect of appearing in a public Capacity, read over the following Treatise, which is very exactly and justly extracted from the best Authors, Ancient and Modern; and, when he has carefully perused and well digested the Contents hereof, He may with the greater Pleasure, and Satisfaction, both consult and understand the Ancient Orators and Critics; such as Demosthenes, Cicero, Longinus, and Quintilian, who have, without Doubt, writ the best Pieces, that ever appear'd in Print, concerning Eloquence, Elocution and their Beauties.

(Introduction, p. xxi)

They [certain 'whimsical people'] say in the first place, with a regard to Preachers; that Action is unworthy of their Ministry, and that it is a scandalous thing for those God hath honoured with so serious and sublime a Function, to be studying in the very Exercise of it, how to frame their Voice and move their Body, when they should think of nothing but his Glory . . .

(Chapter II, p. 14)

He [the effective preacher] must also lay more Stress upon Words of Quantity; as, grand, high, sublime, profound, long, large, innumerable, eternal . . .

(Chapter XI, p. 167)

John Oldmixon, *The arts of logick and rhetorick, illustrated by examples taken out of the best authors, antient and modern, in all the polite languages. Interpreted and explain'd by that learned and judicious critick, Father Bouhours. To which are added, parallel quotations out of the most eminent English authors in verse and prose: wherein the like observations are made on their beauties and blemishes, in all the various kinds of thought and expression.* (1728)

I must initially offer a caveat: This work is virtually a melange of the criticism of Bouhours and Oldmixon.[9] Thus it is often difficult to distinguish where the original author ends and his translator begins. By

[9] For an interesting sketch, with numerous bibliographical references, of Bouhours' importance, in his own right, in the history of taste see V. M. Hamm, *Father Dominic Bouhours and Neo-Classical Criticism* (*Jesuit Thinkers of the Renaissance*; *Essays Presented to John F. McCormick, S.J.* (Milwaukee, Marquette University Press, 1939), pp. 63-75.

the same token, the reader soon comes to realize that Oldmixon's volume, although entitled *The arts of logick and rhetorick*, has practically nothing to do with logic, as it had been understood for so many centuries. Herein logic becomes little more than decorum and appropriateness of thought. In effect, we find that in this work logic and rhetoric are the same thing. An outstanding fact about *The arts of logick and rhetorick* is the prevalence of the word sublime. I make no attempt to give an exhaustive listing of the passages in which it occurs, but concentrate instead on the more interesting ones, merely citing the others by general usage at the end of this section.

Being sensible how difficult it was to succeed in such parallel Quotations [French and English], I cannot but be as sensible of the Caution I shou'd have taken in addressing them to you [George Dodington, a Lord of the Treasury]; tho' if there is not that scrupulous Equality in all of them, which may be expected in Things of this Delicacy, there will be found the Sublime, the Grand, the Fine, the Agreeable, and all the various Kinds of Thought, which are so finely spun in the French Critick's [Bouhours'] Explanation of them.

(Dedication, p. xii)

There is no Book among the Ancients which instructs, and at the same time delights, more than Longinus's Treatise of the Sublime, and the Pleasure chiefly arises from the Examples he produces of the various Kinds of Thinking out of the Greek Poets and Orators. Bouhours refines upon Longinus; and, without penetrating so far as the latter has done in Argument, he proves what he asserts by Citations out of the best Authors, whether it is for Reproof or Applause. I have endeavor'd to do the like in my Quotations out of the English Writers.

(The Preface, p. xviii)

The Discourse which seems to be most artless is most beautiful: Quintilian says, Nothing is harder than what every one imagines he could do himself, which is the Simplicity so much commended by Longinus, Bouhours, and the best Criticks, and so much decry'd by the Translator of Homer, who assures us, in the notes he took from the Dutch and French Commentators, that Simplicity is a Word of Disguise for a shameful unpoetical Neglect of Expression; wherein he shews us that he does not really understand what is meant by Simplicity, which he confines to Language, though a Thought is much more likely to be simple, as coming immediately from Nature, than Expression, which owes much of its very Being to Art.

(*Ibid.*, p. xxii)

There is no need to elaborate on the anti-rhetorical tendency of the above. The translator of Homer referred to is presumably Pope.

But where the fabulous System does not support him, Truth should be the Rule of Thinking, in Verse as well as Prose. I do not by this intend to deprive Poetry of the Marvellous, which distinguishes it from the most noble and sublime Prose. I mean no more than that the Poets should not destroy the Essence of Things, by endeavouring to raise and embellish them.

(Part I; "Of False Thoughts, and True Thoughts; and in what the Difference between them consists"; p. 7)

When I read the holy Scripture, which is at the same Time so simple and so sublime, is it the Conceit of my own Dignity, or the Corruption of my Heart, which causes the Delight I take in it? Is it not rather the Simplicity and Majesty of the divine Word, which makes an Impression; and may we not in some wise say the same of the great Masters in Poetry and Eloquence?

(*Ibid.*, p. 39)

Here is another of our many examples of the sublime being found in the simple expression of the Bible.

In Dr. Echard's Book before-mentioned, we have a great Number of such Instances, of such Kind of Pulpit Oratory; in some of which we find the Sublime of Nonsense, and in some the Grimace of Buffoonry; as these, "it is Goodness by which we must ascend to Heaven; Goodness is the milky Way to Jupiter's Palace; to strengthen us in our Journey we must not take the Morning Milk, but some Morning Meditations."

(*Ibid.*, p. 48)

The very learned and polite Dr. Burnet, in the Dedication of the Theory of the Earth, begins his Address to the King thus; "New found Lands and Countries accrue to the Prince whose Subject makes the first Discovery, and having retrieved a World that had been lost for some Thousands of Years out of the Memory of Man, and the Records of Time; I thought it my Duty to lay it at your Majesty's Feet." This Thought is very Fine and Just, if you look on it as a just Theory, as which the Author presents it to the King; for tho' he does not throw the Globe at his Majesty's Feet; yet he lays there the Description of it, and such a Description as has triumph'd over the Cavils and Criticisms of other Theorists and Philosophers; and as much as I respect the Names of Woodward, Keil, Whiston, who have objected against Dr. Burnet's Theory; I am satisfy'd his beautiful Imagination and sublime Stile, will preserve that Work, when all other Theories, and Criticisms upon Theories, shall be as much in the State of Oblivion as the Chaos out of which the eloquent Doctor raises the fair Creation.

(*Ibid.*, p. 56)

Men of the best Taste, delight most in Thoughts that have Elevation and Sublimity. Grandeur in a Thought is what transports and ravishes, provided it is agreeable to the Subject; for it is a standing Rule to think as the Subject requires; and nothing is more out of Reason, than to have sublime

Thoughts on a Subject which demands ordinary Ones: 'Tis better to have ordinary Thoughts on a Subject which demands sublime Ones. Longinus says . . . [Here Oldmixon cites several arguments of Longinus to support his argument.]

(Part II; "That the Justness of a Thought is not of it self sufficient to render it good"; p. 69)

The French Jesuit [Bouhours] commends Tasso for an infinite Number of sublime Thoughts, which in Comparison with Milton's are of no more Value than Tinsel compar'd with Gold, as Boileau calls it the Cliuquant de Tasso & l'Or de Virgil. If Virgil's Gold is so much preferable to Tasso's Tinsel, what must Milton's be, who for the Sublime excels Virgil more than Virgil excels Tasso.

(*Ibid.*, p. 81)

In what follows, is contain'd the utmost Strength and Beauty of the English Tongue. It cannot be translated into French, and has nothing equal to it, for the Sublime in Demosthenes or Cicero; "Where are now the Great Empires of the World, and their great Imperial Cities? Their Pillars, Trophies and Monuments of Glory! Shew me where they stood, read the Inscription, tell me the Victor's Name;" What an Insult is this on the Vanity of Humane Greatness!

(*Ibid.*, p. 91)

Thoughts equally just and noble; tho' to be truly noble, Thoughts must be just, yet they may be just on a Supposition, that they are founded on Fact, and false when the Fact being examin'd, the Foundation appears to be ill. Such are the Sentiments in the Panegyricks on the French King, quoted by Pere Bouhours; had the Facts been true, the Thoughts would have been noble, and the Expression sublime; but for want of that Truth, they are like the Meteor in Mr. Prior's Verses of the French King's Plume of Feathers,

That did but blaze, and rove, and dye.

(*Ibid.*, p. 111)

We sense here that Bouhours has added an Enlightenment drive for fact to Longinus' requirement for justness in attributing sublimity to someone or something.[10]

We return now to Pere Bouhours, who tells us, that Comparisons well chosen, and taken from what is great in Nature, form always very noble Thoughts. Longinus, who wrote Rules for the Sublime, not only in Expression, but in Thought, thinks nobly himself, when he compares Demosthenes to a Storm of Lightning, that ravages and bears down all before it; and Cicero to a Fire that never goes out, and as it advances still, encreases in Strength.

(*Ibid.*, p. 119)

[10] On the other hand, Chandler B. Beall points out Bouhours' conciousness of the value of the half-understood, the secret, and the hidden (*A Critical Bibliography of French Literature*, p. 289).

In the above passage Bouhours' recognition of the sublime of expression and thought is explicit.

I [Oldmixon] must own I am pleas'd when I meet with any Instance of sublime or fine Thoughts in Foreigners, that we can't parallel in our own Tongue; for without Partiality the Advantage is almost always on our Side, as in this Example of Trivulci and Earl Syward. [The examples given are not particularly interesting, nor do they alone prove Oldmixon's somewhat chauvinistic point.]

(*Ibid.*, p. 143)

As one must have good Eyes, and even artificial ones, Telescopes and Microscopes, to have a just View of the Works of Nature; so none but Persons of very good Understanding can find out the entire Sense of a delicate Thought. This little Mystery is the Soul of such Delicacy, insomuch, that if a Thought has nothing in it mysterious, neither in the Substance nor in the Turn, and shews it self entire at the first View, it is not delicate, tho' otherwise it may be witty; from whence we may conclude, that Delicacy is a Sort of Improvement of the Sublime and the Agreeable.

(*Ibid.*, p. 156)

This is a thought-provoking passage. It is quite clear that Oldmixon is referring to a kind of obscurity that is neither purely psychological nor the result of the phenomena of external nature. He calls it a mystery. Without being dogmatic on the point I suggest that this mystery of 'the entire Sense of a delicate Thought' is essentially the intrinsic logic, organization, or semantic, call it what you will, that is perceptible only to those few persons who have the nervous make-up that apprehends such matters. If my hypothesis is correct, we can see that the eighteenth century might be expected to have the same proportion of people capable of responding to each art's organization as our own era, though even less knowledgeable than we in the fields of psychology and esthetics, and in a vocabulary thereof.

Another result, of course, of my theory is that the line separating oratory and rhetoric from purely literary expressions becomes somewhat blurred, the difference being now mainly what the listener can perceive in spoken expression as compared with what the reader can apprehend. This is a very real and important difference, but it invites a re-evaluation of our traditional distinctions between rhetoric and literature.

Thoughts may surprise, elevate, or touch, by Delicacy, Sublimity, or Agreeableness, and yet be vicious, because they are not natural: as those of

Crassius were, which we have spoken of before, and which Pere Bouhours made the Model of right thinking.

(*Ibid.*, p. 208)

Thus Bouhours and Oldmixon do not invariably see eye to eye.[11] This and other disagreements between the two critics give an indication of the difficulty of keeping their ideas separate throughout the volume.

The Fault of the Bombast Stile is, that it would go beyond the Sublime, and 'tis in Thought the same as in Expression. . . .

Is it not a great Pity that so much of the Sublime, so much of the Noble, the Grand, and the Delicate, should be all spoil'd by a Campaign or two of the Duke of Marlborough's, and so many great and grave Things become Ridicule and Mirth.

(Part III; "How the Sublime, in the Way of Thinking, becomes Bombast; the Agreeable, Affectation; and the Delicate, Subtlety". p. 230)

The reference to the Duke of Marlborough is intended to criticize the deplorable contemporaneous custom of exaggerating the feats of modern heroes at the expense of the heroes of antiquity. The key is the element of exaggeration.

Malherb is not often guilty of such Rants, nor does he often forget himself as he does here, tho' the Sublime may be carried farther in Verse than in Prose; and Poetry admits of bolder Thoughts than Eloquence, but that Boldness ought to have its Bounds, and even the Marvellous in an Epick Poem, becomes ridiculous as soon as it exceeds Verisimility.

(*Ibid.*, p. 248)

Oldmixon does not make it clear in the environs of the above passage, unfortunately, as to whether he is applying the Aristotelian verisimility of 'probability', or a more literal eighteenth-century variety.

I have not always Mr. Pope's Homer by me, or I would have compar'd this Translation of a Passage in him after Boileau, with his Version, after the Original, if it was so, to have seen whether there had been any Thing lost in the French, or, that Rhime was wanting to keep up the Sublime. Tho' Father Bouhours does not quote this Passage as an Example of the Sublime, propos'd for Imitation; yet Longinus introduces it with crying out, "How sublime is that where he says,"

L'enfer s'émeut, etc. Hell at the Noise, etc.

[11] To keep this in perspective, however, see A. F. B. Clark, *Boileau and the French Classical Critics in England* (Champion, 1925), pp. 262-74. Clark sketches Bouhours' considerable influence among English critics.

Tho' it is not directly to the present Purpose, I cannot forbear repeating what Longinus quotes out of the "Ilias" immediately before it.

> What Space a Man can from a lofty Rock,
> On the Seas Margin in the Air behold
> Th' intrepid Coursers of th' Immortal Gods
> Leap at a Bound, etc.
>
> Ilias 5.

"He measures the Extent of their Leap," says the Greek Critick, "by that of the Universe. Who is there, that when he sees the Magnificence of this Hyperbole, does not cry out, If the Horses of the Gods were to have taken a second Leap, there had not been Space enough in the World for them?" How many Images still greater than this do we meet with in Milton?

(*Ibid.*, p. 261)

The preceding extract is one of the relatively rare examples we have wherein both Longinus and Milton are mentioned in the context of the sublime of celestial space. I would be taxed to the utmost to state, on the evidence of this passage at least, that there is a profound difference between the concepts of the sublime of the two writers, yet a large portion of modern criticism so finds.[12]

There is no Swelling in that Sublime [a passage from Corneille]; and if, as Longinus teaches us, such Swelling is vicious in Tragedy, which is naturally pompous and magnificent, what must it be in common Discourse; and can it be avoided too carefully?

(*Ibid.*, p. 265)

The merry Poem, "Hudibras," is full of Allegories, which, as laughable as they are, may, for Justness, serve for an Example to the sublime Writers [to avoid diffuseness], Butler almost always keeping within Bounds.

(*Ibid.*, p. 291)

All Thoughts, in the Words of the Ingenious, ought not only to be True, in Proportion to their Subject, to be Noble without Bombast, Agreeable without Affectation, and Delicate without Subtlety. They should be also plain, clear, and intelligible. Without that, the Sublime and the Marvellous are ridiculous.

(Part IV; "Thoughts ought to be Plain, Clear, and Intelligible"; p. 357)

To form sublime Images, our Poets need only remember, or read, the glorious Actions of the Duke of Marlborough, which have more of the Hero in them than all the Heroes of the latter Ages; and they would, I doubt, find the Subject too grand for them. We have not met with any Images yet equal to his Victories, to his sedate Course and rapid Conquests.

(*Ibid.*, p. 410)

12 Marjorie Nicolson is an example of this critical position.

This second reference to the Duke comes close to violating the very principle that Oldmixon discusses in the first. (See p. 102 above.) I thought it might be interesting to compare the listing for 'sublime' that Oldmixon gives in his *Index* with the supplemental citations that I promised at the start. First Oldmixon:[13]

Sublime in Scripture, 122, 123. Agrees with Simplicity, 123. How it becomes Bombast, 225. Requires Care, 240. Examples 260, 262.

My list:

Sublime of Panegyric

xv (Dedication)
95 (Part II)
101 (Part II)

Sublime of Nonsense

49 (Part I)

Simplicity in the Sublime

113 (Part II)

Sublime in Scripture

122 (Part II)

Sublime, Agreeable, Delicate

231 (Part II)

Sublime and Bombast

252 (Part III)
274 (Part III)
276 (Part III)

Sublimity in Milton & *Paradise Lost*

261 (Part III)

English Chauvinism *vis-à-vis* the Sublime

283 (Part III)

[Anon.], *Rhetoric; or The principles of oratory delineated.* (1736)

This work is probably the best example in the present chapter of Longinus turned to the purposes of an eighteenth-century treatise on rhetoric and oratory. As such it serves as a foil to its more interesting companions.

Cicero and Quintilian have been particularly consulted, who have left us in their works the Precepts, and Models of the sublimest Eloquence. They indeed ascribed its force more to Nature than Art; but at the same time were apprehensive of the advantages of Art, by the pains they have taken to digest their own Observations and practice into a regular System.

(Dedication)

Comparison beautifully sets off one thing by comparing it to another, which

[13] These headings are rendered exactly as they appear in Oldmixon's *Index*.

bears some good likeness to it, as Laocoon's roaring, when he felt the bite and poison of those hideous Serpents, is thus resembled . . . [Here follows the quotation from Aen. 2. 223.] Thus Longinus compares Demosthenes to thunder and lightning, which bears down all before it . . .

("Of Particular Figures", p. 26)

From the evidence here, we gather that the above Longinian comparison of Demosthenes to thunder and lightning was especially popular with eighteenth-century commentators.

As there are three principal qualifications required in an Orator, to Instruct, to Please, and Move the passions; so three kinds of Eloquence correspond to them, namely the Plain or Simple, the Sublime, and the Mixt.

("Some Extracts; Relating to the Subject of Eloquence, from Mr. Rollin's Method of Teaching and Studying the Belles Lettres. 1. Of Style". p. 37)

The sublime is another species quite different from the former [the plain style], and comprizes in it whatever is great and noble. The plain Stile, though perfect in its kind, and full of inimitable beauties, produces none of those important effects, without which Cicero thought Eloquence to be trifling. In this the Orator is serene and calm, and the equality of Stile in it does not warm and raise the Soul: But the sublime produces admiration, mingled with some degree of astonishment and surprize. [Here follows a Greek quotation of five lines that is probably from Longinus but which is not identified.] The Sublime ravishes by that grand and majestic tone; by those quick and lively emotions; that force and vehemence, which prevails, and leaves the hearer as it were struck down, and darted with its thunder and lightning. Longinus has given a treatise on this subject, which is alone sufficient to form a true taste of the Sublime. He gives as its obvious character . . . [quotation from *On the Sublime*]

(*Ibid.*, pp. 41-42)

Figures are not the least part of the Sublime serving to give a vivacity to the Discourse. Cicero imputes the death of Clodius to a just anger of the Gods, who at length reveng'd their temples and altars profaned by his crimes. He does it after a sublime manner, by appealing to those very altars, and Gods themselves . . . [another quotation from Longinus] . . . We must admit, as contributing to the Sublime, what we call amplification; which consists in a multitude of words drawn from the particular circumstances of things. The Sublime may appear in this, as well as a simple thought, and herein lies the Difference between Demosthenes and Cicero. Demosthenes is sublime, in that he is close and concise; Cicero, in that he is diffused and extensive. And Plato's Stile is justly esteemed lofty, though it flows gently, and without any Noise.

(*Ibid.*, pp. 43-44)

I must concede that if all the eighteenth-century treatises on oratory and rhetoric were as dull and unoriginal as this one, no scholar of the period could be very much impugned for dismissing the entire genre in a single sentence.

John Lawson, *Lectures concerning oratory. Delivered in Trinity College, Dublin.* (Dublin, 1759)

Of Lawson's *Lectures* Monk says only that the fact that it was published and sold "bears witness to the interest of the age in rhetoric and to the apparently infinite capacity of the eighteenth-century reader to endure repetition" (*The Sublime*, p. 107) because Lawson says nothing that had not been said before. I make no claims for great originality on the part of Lawson, and acknowledge that much of his commentary is merely repetition of the tried and (supposedly) true, but I submit the following extracts in the belief that they contain some interesting views of the sublime.

Lectures concerning oratory is notable for the emphasis throughout on genius (though not necessarily ORIGINAL genius), and for its denial of the seventeenth and early eighteenth-centuries' custom of dividing up into categories the various passions, the understanding, soul, etc. (See especially p. 154 in the text.) Perhaps the work reflects its late date, in our period, in its negative criticism of Swift's style for lacking elevation (pp. 79, 85, 86). Certainly as far as Lawson is concerned, satire is out of style.

. . . What comick Wit and Humour [in Boccaccio's *Decameron*]! What Delicacy, yet Simplicity of Style and Sentiment! He is a Model in this Kind: It was his Genius. Milton's Sublimity transports, astonishes; his Attempts of Humour move Pity.

(Lecture 1, p. 12)

About the same Time, History, which had hitherto appeared in a mean Dress, arrayed herself in all the Charms that Eloquence could bestow; pure, easy, flowing in Herodotus; in Thucydides, elaborate, deep, sublime. This latter, beside the extraordinary Spirit of his Narration, hath interwoven many admirable Speeches, written with the utmost Brevity and Force, which render his Work peculiarly fit for the Study of one who would speak in publick . . .

(Lecture 2, p. 31)

. . . Demosthenes, raised Eloquence to the Summit of Perfection: Uniting the Elevation and Majesty of the Philosopher, to the deep Sense and Conciseness of the Historian, he added to both, the Fire and Vehemence of Pericles, thus equally fitted to instruct, to affect, to convince. Examine his Orations attentively; you find nothing superfluous, nothing idle, no glittering

Points, no affected Turns, no false Sublime, no studied Pathetick; but all seemingly artless, plain and simple; yet under that apparent Simplicity, Energy, Vehemence, Sublimity, [:] Passion irresistable.

(*Ibid.*, pp. 32-33)

In the mean Time, O Mortal admitted to the View of Secrets, hidden from all others of the human Race, fail not in applying this Knowledge to thy own Advantage, since thou can'st not at present to the Publick; --- for the Fates forbid as yet the Conversion of a deluded World. First and principally, seek after Wisdom and Virtue; For Elevation of Soul can alone support Sublimity of Genius. Next, Be unwearied in tracing back Eloquence to its true Source, the Monuments of pure Antiquity of those Heroes whom you have lately seen. Imitate their Solidity, their Method, their Justness, their Purity, their Force, their Sublimity. Hope not however though you should succeed well in this noble Ambition, to obtain the Applause of your Fellow-Citizens; neither be discouraged by their Censures: Leave them to their own depraved degenerate Taste.

(Lecture, 4, p. 71)

Dante flourished about the End of the 13th Century, when as yet there were no Writings of Note in Prose. Although the Plan of his Poem be faulty, and many of his Expressions are now become obsolete, yet for Sublimity of Thought, for lively Description, for Strength and poetick Fire, he hath not been excelled by any, who followed him.

(Lecture 5, p. 74)

Conformably to what we have taken Notice of in other Countries, here also, Conceit and Epigram have had their Turn of reigning; happy, if it were yet ended. One sees in many late Productions a Similitude of that Manner for which Dr. Sprat was distinguished in Prose, and more lately an eminent Satirist in Verse, short, sententious, and pointed; in the former, mingled with the florid and declamatory: In which latter Way particularly, many ingenious Persons, who profess themselves Imitators of Milton, have contributed to hurt the Language, soaring beyond the Bounds of Propriety, and tumid where they should be sublime.

(*Ibid.*, pp. 79-80)

The above passage incorporates further evidence of the fact that Lawson is a man of his time. For him, metaphysical poetry and poetic satires are things to be gotten over. If he is so far from being a reactionary in this area, perhaps his use of the sublime should be attended with an attitude other than boredom with what is taken to be merely tiresome reiteration of the past.

Next after the Poets, this Treasure [the works of Homer, whom Lawson calls an original genius] was most useful to the Orators, who found here an inexhaustible Store and noble of lofty Images and to none was it more use than to Demosthenes, who having applied himself from the Beginning to acquire a Resemblance of this Poet and of Thucydides, hath happily united the Clearness, Abundance, and Elevation of the one, to the Weight, Nerves, and Brevity of the other; thus sublime without swelling, and close without Dryness.

(Lecture 7, p. 111)

The same Principles shew likewise the Truth of a Rule often repeated; "That an Orator ought to be esteemed a good Man." You cannot be much affected by what he says, if you do not look upon him to be a Man of Probity, who is in earnest, and doth himself believe what he endeavoureth to make out as credible to you.

Is it not from hence, that there have been Times, in which the Words publick Spirit, Good of the Community, Love of one's Country occurring often in a Discourse, however used, have yet been treated with some Degree of Scorn or Ridicule? Why? Because these Terms, naturally representing very noble Ideas and sublime Springs of Action, had been sullied, contaminated, as it were profaned by Tongues, where the Heart was governed by corrupt, base, and mercenary Principles.

(Lecture 11, pp. 172-173)

Thus, in contradiction to his opinion of certain earlier kinds of poetry, the idea of sublimity springing in large part from the nobility of the writer has not gone out of fashion in Lawson's estimation. Instead of saying that this is just repetition of the past, I might better remark that the persistence of this Longinian element of the sublime is weighty testimony to its vitality.

A former Observation leads to a fourth Rule: "In speaking to the Passions, as much as possible conceal your doing so." It should be perceived only by the Effects, otherwise it appears like a Design to deceive, and puts your Hearer on his Guard. To this Purpose a Greek Critick [footnote cites Longinus] recommends the Use of the Sublime, as hiding the other in its superior Brightness.

But there is nothing more carefully to be avoided, more destructive of the End proposed in speaking to the Affections, than Elegancies and Prettiness, fine turned Periods and glittering Conceits.

(*Ibid.*, pp. 183-184)

The last Figure I shall mention as frequently ill-conducted, is Irony, where the Speaker means differently from what his Words literally understood, import. This Figure is useful not only in Comedy and Satire, its most usual Province; but hath Place also in the Pathetick and Sublime: As in this spirited Irony of Dido,

> "Go, follow Italy thro' Tempests, haste,
> Seek flying Kingdoms o'er the watry Waste (a)."[14]

[14] Lawson's footnote cites *Aeneid*, p. iv.

And this of Satan,

> "Or have ye chos'n this Place,
> After the Toil of Battle to repose
> You weary Virtue, for the Ease you find
> To slumber here, as in the Vales of Heav'n?"

The Dangers attending this Figure are these three; one is ever apt to break in upon it. Your real Sense is ready to burst out, and mingle itself with the ironical, which makes an odd incoherent Mixture. This Fault, in long continued Irony, seemeth scarcely avoidable, since it is laid to the Charge of Lucian, Cervantes, and Swift, the three great Masters of this Figure.

(Lecture 15, pp. 266-267)

I quote the preceding because of the manner in which the categories of the sublime and irony are brought into such close proximity, a rare occurrence in the Context, and, presumably, outside of it.

Eub. [Eubulus, who along with Philemon debates the matters that make up this Lecture] . . .

Concerning the first of these lofty Sentiments [Vehemence], there is no Difficulty in shewing that the Poets excel peculiarly in them.

An unanswerable Proof of which is, that they who have written upon Sublimity of Sentiment have drawn the Examples they cite, chiefly from Poets: And this, it is plain, must be the Case, both from the Nature of the Thing, and from the Fact. By a lofty Sentiment is meant, as I suppose, whatever conveys to the Mind an Idea of somewhat noble and grand, whether it strike more immediately the Understanding, or, as some love to speak, the moral Taste or Sense; or whether it strike the Imagination. Of the former Kinds are moral Sentiments, such as bespeak Greatness of Soul; a sublime disinterested Virtue; or undaunted Courage, unbounded Ambition.

(Lecture 17, pp. 294-295)

Perhaps the Poets on the new Settlement of the Stage after the Restoration, mistook in the Manner they established, and might with better Judgment, even Success, have retained that of Beaumont and Fletcher so far as relates to Style. Comedies, in easy well composed Measures might, it seems, admit Familiarity without Meanness; and Seriousness, and, on fit Occasions, even Sublimity, without Dryness or Bombast. This was the antient Model; and is still followed by the best Writers among our Neighbours.

(*Ibid.*, p. 310)

Regardless of the validity of Lawson's conjecture, this passage has an obviously non-rhetorical application, showing once again the danger of ignoring an entire group of treatises on the superficial assumption that because of their titles their contents are predictable and uninteresting. The above passage refutes such thinking.

Style is, "An Assemblage of Words considered with regard to Propriety of Signification, and Arrangement in Sound." As the Methods of expressing

Thoughts are various, and these Expressions may be differently ordered, there must be great Diversities of Style. The most antient Division, that of Homer, is perhaps the best: It is threefold; the Concise and Nervous; the Copious and Sweet; the Vehement and Sublime; which several Kinds he hath exemplified in three of his Heroes; preserving to each his distinctive Character of Eloquence through the whole Poem.

(Lecture 18, p. 325)

For what it is worth let us compare the definition of style placed within the quotation marks in the above excerpt with the quotation in Chapter I (p. 19) from Donovan by way of Langer, remembering that the former is supposedly true to the context of a rhetoric book, and the latter a suggested modern approach to discovering the true intent of Longinus. Surely Donovan's 'aural absorption trying to make its way among syllables which have been fixed by significance' is virtually identical with the unidentified quotation given by Lawson! Each definition consists of two terms: sound and signification. Our conclusion? Another indication that we had better be wary in placing as poles apart the entities of rhetoric and literary art. Adding further to the play of eras and contrasts evoked by the above passage is the fact that, just as it foreshadows, in a sense, a modern school of thought on esthetics, the excerpt also reveals an obeisance to the great Ancient, Homer, that we might well find surprising at as late a date as 1759. All of this is enough to make a neo-classicist out of almost anyone!

With respect to this last Kind [the Vehement and Sublime], some modern Criticks have been at much Pains in distinguishing the Sublime from sublime Style; a Distinction according to my Judgment imaginary. For this I take to be the Truth. If a Passage consist but of one grand Thought or Image, the more simple the Expression, the more Sublime; because it renders a grand Thought with Precision: As in this,

His dantem fura Catonem. Virg.

If there be a Course of lofty Sentiments connected together, the Expression must be continued, must have Length, and be supported by suitable Harmony and Strength, as in these Lines of the Iliad (a) [footnote cites Book XXIII]:

Hell felt the Shock, and her astounded King
Leap'd yelling from his Throne, afraid lest Earth
Should yawn, by Neptune riven, and disclose
To Gods and Men his dreary Realms, in Smoke
And Stench involv'd, and dreadful ev'n to Gods.

In both Cases, the Style, though in Appearance different, is alike sublime, being in both, the most proper Expression of sublime Conception.

From these Observations may be drawn useful Consequences. Some of which I will briefly mention.

First, Style is truly a Part of Genius, and so far depends upon Nature. For being determined to Thought, and this Power of Thinking arising from the Frame of the Soul, Style must in this respect be the Product of a natural Talent; so that without this Foundation, this Talent, no Degree of Art or Care can bestow a fine one; the utmost which these can do, is to preserve from gross Errors; and thus advance to Mediocrity.

Hence Secondly; the first Endeavour of all Teachers should be, by forming the Judgment to assist the Genius. A young Person who is capable of thinking well, may be trained up to think better, to know what is right, to chuse among his own Thoughts the best, and range them to Advantage: The Consequence whereof will be, that he shall of Course form to himself a good Style, for Thoughts make Words and mould them to their own Size. Whereas the usual Method is opposite hereto; to lay out much Time and Pains upon Words, to overwhelm the Memory with Rules concerning Tropes, Figures, Periods, Harmony; with little Care to form the Understanding, to settle distinct Notions of what is right and wrong, true and false; which is to begin at the wrong End: Style cannot bestow Judgment; perfect the Judgment, it will create a Stile.

Thirdly, We may from hence learn how to answer a Question often asked, and much disputed about, "Is a good Style valuable, and why?"

As it is really a Part of Genius, inseparable from, and not to be acquired without that, it is like every other Branch of Genius, valuable. But the Question is, "In what Respect is it such Part, being so far only of Value?" I answer, Entirely as a proper Cloathing of Thought: For fine Words without suitable Conceptions are ridiculous Sound; and the Cloathing of good Conceptions in mean Language is disguising and debasing them: Of which latter the Hazard is much less, as it can happen from peculiar Circumstances only:
For,

Fourthly. In general; clear, strong, lofty Ideas paint themselves in conformable Words; but the following Conditions are supposed in the Speaker: That the Language he employs hath arrived at some tolerable Degree of Perfection, otherwise Instruments for Genius to work with are wanting: That the Speaker hath a good Knowledge of this Language: And that by Exercise he hath acquired a Facility of expressing himself therein. To which may be added, that he should have regard to the Age, to Custom, to the Mode of Pronunciation, so as not to use Terms obsolete or low, nor depart from the received Tone or Idiom: Minuteness, however easy, by no Means to be disregarded: In these Particulars Style dependeth not at all upon Genius, but on Conversation and Knowledge of the World; accordingly, the Observance of them merits not Praise, but the Ignorance or Neglect of them is unpardonable.

(*Ibid.*, pp. 326-329)

The reason for citing this passage, probably the most important for my purposes in the entire work, should be apparent. Lawson explicitly denies the validity of separating the sublime and the sublime style. He reiterates the central importance of genius, and the necessity that the great style be formed by great thoughts. The latter anticipates the besetting problem of the entire nineteenth century in English literature: the creation of a modern Grand Style. Thus Lawson looks back to Longinus and forward to the development of his own national literature, and all of this in a volume of lectures concerning oratory. We should perhaps take leave of Lawson at this high point, but instead give a final excerpt in the interest of completeness:

> So much for the general Attempt to address the Passions: Particular Observations are these.
>
> Occasions often occur in every Part of your Discourse, in the Explanatory, in the Argumentative, where the Pathetic may be proper: But in those Places, it ought to be merely a Stroke, a Flash, rapid and instantly disappearing. Insist upon, lengthen such Passages: You soon offend, or fatigue.
>
> The Situation most fit for, I may say, peculiar to this Kind, is the "Application." Here it is, that you are to unfurl all the sails, or to raise the Metaphor, that you are to pour forth the whole Storm of your Eloquence; to move, to exhort, to comfort, to terrify, to inflame, to melt. Your Thoughts, your Language, your Voice, your whole Form should be animated. You cannot be too soft, too insinuating, too rapid, too various, too sublime.
>
> (Lecture 21, pp. 401-402)

As mentioned briefly above, the most significant thing about Lawson's *Lectures* is probably its proximity in so many particulars to the treatise of Longinus. In the excerpts given here alone there are at least seven major points of agreement between the two writers: The sublime is closely connected with the passions; elevation of soul is a *sine qua non* for the orator or author who would produce the sublime; the achievement of the sublime can be abetted by the imitation of proper models; the sublime style and the sublime are really indistinguishable; simplicity of conception and expression can often lead to sublimity; style is not a separate, external entity, which can be obtained automatically by the writer by exercise or method; and no matter to what heights the sublime may carry the artist in the frenzy of inspiration, there must always be a place for judgment to play its role as a sort of grand arbiter of good taste.

When the implications of Chapter I of this study are fully brought into play, it is perhaps not so surprising that a document like Lawson's can be found in apparently popular usage well past the middle of the eighteenth century. If it contains little that intrigues by its novelty, it at least rests on ideas of timeless appeal. And in it the spirit of Longinus appears alive and vibrant.

As in the case of Oldmixon's treatise, the *Lectures concerning oratory* includes a number of allusions to the sublime that I can only cite for the record:

Quotation from Longinus on the point that sublimity can have minor blemishes. (pp. 66-67)

The same principle *vis-à-vis* the sermon of Archbishop Tillotson. (pp. 98-99)

The sublime in Milton and *Paradise Lost.* (pp. 259, 265, 296)

The necessity of the sublime to passionate expression, as opposed to the plain sense of logic, geometry, etc. (p. 283)

The sublime in Martial. (p. 302)

The sublime eloquence in the dialogue between Augustus and Cinna in *Cinna* by Corneille. (p. 309)

The sublime in Socrates. (p. 330)

The sublime in Plato. (p. 336)

The sublime in St. Augustine. (p. 357)

John Ward, *A System of oratory, delivered in a course of lectures publicly read at Gresham College, London: To which is prefixed an inaugural oration, spoken in Latin, before the commencement of the lectures, according to the usual custom. Two volumes.* (1759)

Monk groups Ward's work in the same category as Lawson's, and has exactly the same comment on it (*The Sublime*, p. 107). To the extent that Ward is far less provocative than Lawson, Monk is perhaps partly justified, but even in Ward's observance of Classical precedent, we notice the way in which rhetoric reveals a richer frame of reference than Monk and others are wont to allow.

He [the orator Gorgias] wrote, as Cicero informs us, in the demonstrative or laudatory way [marginal note cites *De clar. orat.* c. 12.]; which requires most of the sublime, and makes what Diodorus Siculus said of him the more probable, that, "He first introduced the strongest figures, members of periods opposite in sense, of an equal length, or ending with a like sound, and other ornaments of that nature."

(Lecture I, pp. 6-7)

Nor have there been wanting some eminent writers of this kind [on oratory] among the Greeks since the time of Quintilian; two of whom I cannot omit to mention, Hermogenes, and Longinus, the author of the incomparable treatise "Of the Sublime", a book which can scarcely be too much commended, or too often read.

(*Ibid.*, p. 10)

And tho the word Stile, in its proper sense, respects only what is written; yet it is applied to speech, and so I shall sometimes use it. Now there are usually reckoned three sorts of stile, called the low, middle, and sublime.

(Lecture II, p. 23)

Indeed as the florid and sublime characters more especially relate to the orator's province, who has the greatest occasion for them; the Name of Eloquence has been more peculiarly appropriated to those characters.

(Lecture III, p. 34)

An appeal to heaven, or any part of inanimate nature, has something very sublime and solemn in it, which we often meet with in sacred writ.

(Lecture XXXIV, p. 104)[15]

But the greatest advantage of the Greeks lies in their plenty and variety of words; for which reason they have less occasion for tropes or circumlocutions, which when used from necessity, have generally less force, and weaken the stile.

(Lecture, XXXV, p. 124)

But under these disadvantages, Quintilian seems to give his countrymen the best advice the case will admit of. That what they cannot do in words, they should make up in sense. If their expressions are not so soft and tender, they should excede in strength; if they are less subtle, they should be more sublime; and if they have fewer proper words, they should excell in the beauty, as well as number of their figures. [marginal note cites *Inst. orat. Lib.* xii. c. 10].

(Lecture XXXV, p. 125)

The like may also be said of figures; either of words or sentences, in reference to this character; which admits of the finest descriptions, most lively images, and brightest figures, that serve either for delight, or to influence the passions, without transport or extasy, which is the property of the sublime.

(Lecture XXXVII, pp. 157-158)

In my two last discourses I treated upon the low and middle stile, and shall now procede to treat on the sublime; which being the most noble, as well as the most difficult part of our orator's province, it may not be improper to consider it somewhat more largely and distinctly.

(Lecture XXXVIII, p. 163)

But the justest propriety, joined with the greatest strength and highest elevation of thought, are required to complete the true sublime.

(*Ibid.*, pp. 163-164)

Greatness of mind, and elevation of thought, are indeed in a great measure the gift of nature; but yet they may be improved by study, and frequent converse with noble subjects. Besides, a sublime thought may sometimes be obscured or depressed by an ill manner of expressing it.

(Lecture XXXIX, p. 178)

The next thing to be considered is composition. The force of which, as

[15] This and the remaining passages occur in Volume II.

Longinus observes, is so great, that sometimes it creates a kind of sublime, where the thoughts themselves are but mean, and gives a certain appearance of grandeur to that, which otherwise would seem but common [marginal note cites Sect. 39].

(*Ibid.*, p. 180)

The more solemn and important the subject is, the less room it leaves for the speaker to appear witty. While the mind is employed upon solid and weighty affairs, it cannot well attend to the lesser beauties of wit and humour; and if it could, they would be wholly unseasonable. The sublime stile therefore in general admits the fewest ornaments of this kind.

(Lecture XL, p. 209)

But it is the sublime stile which perfects the orator. This requires the most forceable and emphatical words, the boldest metaphors, and strongest figures. In verbal figures, repetitions, synonyms, gradations, contraries, with others of a like force, and energy, are chiefly [sic] employed here. But figures of sentences are the most considerable, and principally contribute to make up this character.

(Lecture XLVI, p. 304)

To discourse in a lofty and grand way upon a common topic, or in a low and flat manner upon a sublime argument, are both equally injudicious. Cicero refers us to some discourses of his own, as instances of each kind.

(*Ibid.*, p. 310)

In summarizing the extracts from Ward, I can say that his concept of the sublime is quite close to the one that this study attributes to Longinus himself. If Ward deviates from the Greek, it is in the direction of propriety and decorum. It is worth noting, in any event, that as late as 1759 Longinus in a rather pure form is being freshly offered to English readers *via* oratory treatises like this of Ward's, and Lawson's.

John Herries, *Analysis of a course of lectures on the theory and practice of speaking, as they were delivered at Essex House, London*; *the Musick Hall, Dublin*; *the New Assembly Room, Glasgow*; *and the Concert Room, Edinburgh. By John Herries, A.M.* (c. 1760)

This document is a six page outline of the seven lectures in question, and contains no information by which to establish the date that the lectures were first written and delivered. The Folger Library jacket for the pamphlet has the date 'ca. 1760' in brackets after the title. I offer an extract from this outline mainly because of the prolix use of the word sublime therein.

Observations on the sublime. View of Thomson's hymn. Young's elevated thoughts on the immortality of the soul. Cowley's description of heaven. Milton's account of hell. Satan's speech to the sun. Battle of the angels. The

Messiah expelling them from heaven. Shakespeare's sublime thoughts on the dissolution of nature and a future state. Hamlet's meditation on death. It's superiority to that of Cato. Song of Moses. The grand description of a storm from the Psalms and Habbakkuk. The unequalled sublime descriptions of creation from Job, Isaiah, and the Apocrypha. Striking representations of the last judgment, and a future state, from the New Testament. A comparative view of the Bible with other authors.

(Part II, p. 6)

Thomas Sheridan, *A course of lectures on elocution: together with two dissertations on language; and some other tracts relative to those subjects.* (1762)

This work is of interest chiefly for the remarks on Locke in the "Introductory Discourse". Sheridan's main point is that, although Locke contributed much to our knowledge of the processes of mind and language, he did not do anything to further the practical improvement of communicating through language. The author concentrates on speaking over writing and reading, and rhetoric is a side-issue. A perusal of the volume turned up the following usage of the sublime only:

Had there been proper marks for emphasis, such gross errours could not have been committed. And many passages in authours, are on that account, unintelligible to most readers. To give a remarkable instance of this, in the play of Macbeth. There is a passage which as it has been generally spoken on the stage, and read by most people, is downright nonsense; which yet in itself is a very fine one, and conveys an idea truly sublime. I mean an expression of Macbeth's after he has committed the murder, where he says,

> Will all great Neptune's ocean wash this blood
> Clean from my hands? No – – – these my hands will rather,
> The multitudinous sea incarnadine,
> Making the green one, red.

Now the last line pronounced in that manner, calling the sea, the green one, makes flat nonsense of it. But if we read it with proper emphasis and stop, and say, making the green – – – one red. Here is a most sublime idea conveyed, that his hands dipped into the sea, would change the colour of the whole ocean from green to red; making the green – – – one red.

(Lecture IV, pp. 64-65)

In a general way, Sheridan's problem here involves two of the factors that we have found before in the formation and function of the sublime, and those are, of course, the sound and disposition of words. As Sheridan shows by his example, and many of our other authors have indicated by one means or another, a sublime conception can be rendered absurd by faulty disposition and insensitive perception of aural qualities. I see no reason to believe that the disciplines of oratory and rhetoric have exclusive concern with the problem; it is likely to intrude upon any activity that involves expression through the word, and that includes literature.

IV

MILTON

Our Context of John Milton and the sublime does not begin until the end of the first decade of the eighteenth century. It is appropriate that the first extract is in verse.

[Anon.], *Milton's sublimity asserted: in a poem. Occasioned by a late celebrated piece, entituled, Cyder, a Poem; In blank verse, by Philo-Milton.* (1709)

The poem *Cyder* referred to in the title was written by John Phillips (1676-1709) and was widely criticized for its (apparently unintended) bathos, and indecorous use of the Miltonic grand style. *Milton's sublimity asserted* is, therefore, a satiric poem, and consists of about 200 lines. There is a preface of thirteen pages.

> Milton's was warm'd with a Celestial heat,
> Whilst thine is grip'd, and chill'd with Acid Tiff;
> His matchless Genius in transcendent Layes,
> Sung the great Anthem of his Makers Works
> Immense of Eden, and the Innocents,
> Blest Pair! who fell by the forbidden Fruit;
> That Cursed Fatal Fruit, whose damning Juice,
> Is made the fav'rite Subject of thy Song;
> When subtile Thou, by Charm of Milton's Name
> Delightful, play a second Fiends Deceit,
> To Guile the World with Interdicted Verse;
> And whilst in moving Numbers, he excites
> The Vig'rous Soul to the sublimest Thoughts;
> Thou like a bankrupt Wit, with Cheerful Ale,
> And Voice; dull as a Bag pipes Drone, dost Buzz
> Incessant, Thy self pleasing Madrigal;
> Of Shilling, Breeches, and Chimera's Dire.

[Anon.], *Prae-existence. A poem, in imitation of Milton.* (1714)

The poem has 386 lines, composed in the style of *Paradise Lost.*

Preceding it in the volume is a twelve-page "The Publisher's Preface", which outlines the poem. At one point the publisher states that he does not hold with the (anonymous) poet's concept of a pre-existent soul:

> But as the Publisher hereof declares, that this Doctrine of Prae-existence is no Article of his Faith, so he conceives himself not obliged to vindicate the Author's Opinion, or by any Arguments to enforce what he has asserted: And seeing there is no possibility of demonstrating a Point so sublimely Speculative as is that of the Soul's original; he leaves Mankind to the Dictates of their own Judgment, to believe either or neither of the forementioned Hypotheses. (pp. 5-6)

Turning to the poem itself:

> Now had th'Archangel Trumpet, rais'd sublime
> Above the Walls of Heav'n, begun to sound . . .
> (p. 1, lines 1-2)

> But you! commission'd by Commands Divine,
> Have wisely fill'd your Trust, and clos'd 'em all
> Within the fervid Lake, lest any roam
> Into the dark Abiss to shun their Doom,
> And in the Womb immense of Things unborn
> Should seek annihilation; you must rise
> Among the shining Virtues, more sublime;
> On lofty Thrones preferr'd for lofty Deeds.

Both uses of the sublime quoted are in relation to the idea of elevation.

Jonathan Richardson, *Explanatory notes and remarks on Milton's Paradise Lost.* (1734)

Richardson is anything but unknown to eighteenth-century scholars, and, indeed, Monk discusses him at some length in *The Sublime*, but with regard to Richardson's ideas on the sublime in painting. For that reason it seems justified to include the latter's remarks on Milton's sublimity here. The Preface is by Richardson, but he tells us that his son contributed to the text. This fact is of academic interest, however, because all the excerpts below come from the Preface, and are, therefore, presumably the work of the senior Richardson alone.

> He [Milton] Acquir'd Betimes an Uncommon Stock of Learning, and all Those Languages in which the Variety and Sublimity of Humane Knowledge is Treasur'd up for Those who can Unlock the Cabinet, and know how to Judge, and make Use of what they find. (p. xii)

> Now that we have seen This Picture of the Mind of Milton, Drawn by Himself Chiefly . . . and Thus he appears to be Studious, Grave, Chaste, Temperate, to be void of Covetousness, Ambition, or Ostentation; to have a

Warm Zeal for Liberty, Civil and Religious, not for Interest, but as his Duty; to be Irreproachable as to any Wilful and Corrupt Deviations, However he may have been Mistaken; though Otherwise he has not been destitute of a Masculine Judgment. Above all, his Mind Shines with Noble Sentiments of Religion, and Piety: Lastly, it is Truly Poetical. Great, Strong, Elegant, and Sublime; it Raises and Beautifies all its Objects as much as Humanity Can, and Where That Fails, has gone Farther than Any Other Humane Intellect Ever Attain'd to. (p. lxvii)

Well it was for Him that he had So Fine an Amusement, and a Mind Stor'd with Rich Ideas of the Sublimest Kinds: for besides what Affliction he Must have from his Disappointment on the Change of the Times, and from his Own Private Losses, and probably Cares for Subsistence, and for his Family; he was in Perpetual Terror of being Assassinated ... (p. xciv)

A Man always Busied as Milton was, Possess'd of Such Sublime Ideas and Sentiments, and of Such a Consciousness [that his life and occupation were virtuous] – – I enquire not what were the Other Circumstances of his Life, and will admit (as it must happen to the Wisest and Best of Men, and of the most Poetical Genius) Nature Sometimes broke in upon the Strongest Ramparts the Muse, Philosophy, and Religion could Provide; Yet Surely John Milton was in the Main, and upon the foot of the Account, a Happy Man. (p. cv)

For the truth is, though he was in Some respects in a Disadvantageous Situation for Such an Enterprize [the composing of *Paradise Lost*], in Others he had Peculiar Encouragements. That Inexhaustible Fund of Learning in all the Languages in which Science is deposited, particularly what relates to Poetry; a most Intimate Knowledge of All the Poets worthy his Notice, Ancient or Modern; Chiefly the Best, and above All Homer; nor will I forbear to say the Scripture, Infinitely Superior to Homer, as in Other respects, so in its being a Treasure of the Sublimest Poetry. (p. cxii)

... for This Man to be Recompenc'd so Contemptibly for Such a Work! what could be the Meaning of it? Unless Party-Malice, and Folly; or that the Gay Beginning of the Reign of Charles II. diverted the Taste of the Publick from what was of So Sublime a Nature. (p. cxv)

... and 'tis Such a Compliment to the Abilities of Milton, that I confess I cannot come up to; how Poetical soever My Imagination may be thought to be in That Instance; I rather think that we owe some of the most Sublime Beauties of the Poem to That Circumstance [Milton's blindness]; his Mind being not Depress'd with it, but Richly Arm'd against the most Calamitous Dispensations of the Divine Will by an Humble and Devout Resignation ... (p. cxxiii)

Poetry pretends to a Language of its Own. That of the Italian Poetry is so remarkably peculiar that a Man may Well understand a Prose Writer, and not a Poet. Words, Tours of Expression, the Order of them, All has Something not Prosaic. This is Observable particularly in Shakespear. Milton has Apply'd it to that Sublimity of Subject in which he perpetually Engages his Readers, above what Shakespear ever Aim'd at and where This is Peculiarly Necessary. (p. cxliii)

Surely the tenor of this passage is close to that of *On the Sublime*. Richardson even seems to sense poetry in a way which we like to think is more modern.

What Macrobius says of Virgil is Applicable to Milton. "He keeps his Eye Fix'd and Intent upon Homer, and emulates Alike his Greatness and Simplicity; his Readiness of Speech and Silent Majesty." By Silent Majesty, he seems to Mean with Longinus: "His leaving more to the Imagination than is Express'd." (p. cxlv)

if the Sublimity and Peculiarity of the Matter of this Poem, if its Superiority in That Respect has rais'd it above Some of the Rules given by Aristotle, or whatever Other Criticks, and Gather'd From, or Founded on the Iliad, Odyssey, or Aeneid, it has Distinguish'd it to its greater Glory; 'tis not only an Heroic Poem, but the Most So that Ever was Wrote. Milton did not despise Rules, Such as were Built upon Reason, So far as those Establish'd Reach'd; but as his Free and Exalted Genius Aspired Beyond what had Yet been Attempted in the Choice of his Subject, Himself was his Own Rule when in Heights where None had gone before, and Higher than Which None Can Ever go. (p. cxlvii)

But whatever Milton has Woven into his Poem of Others, still his Sublimest Passages are More So than could enter the Heart of Orpheus, Hesiod, Homer, Pindar, Callimachus, etc. Such as the Heathen World were Incapable of by Infinite Degrees, Such as None but the Noblest Genius could attain to, and That Assisted by a Religion Reveal'd by God Himself. We have then in Paradise Lost a Collection, the Quintessence of All that is Excellent in Writing; Frequently Improv'd and Explain'd Better than by the Best of their Profess'd Commentators, but Never Debas'd; and a Sublimity which All other Human Writings put Together have not. to Complete All, He has made use of All These, so as to be subservient to the Great End of Poetry, which is to Please and Inrich the Imagination, and to Mend the Heart, and make the Man Happy. (p.clii)

there is Another Pleasure in Poetry, Oftener Felt perhaps than plac'd to its Account; 'tis This. Much of Art is Essential to This kind of Writing, and to Observe the Address and Capacity of the Poet is vastly Pleasing. 'tis So for Example when we meet with a True Poetical Word, Phrase or Expression, an Apt Simile, a Beautiful Allusion, a Noble Sentiment, a Sublime Image, etc. (p. clvii)

If Ever any Book was Truly Poetical, if Ever Any Abounded with Poetry, 'tis Paradise Lost. What an Expansion of Facts from a Small Seed of History! What Worlds are Invented, What Embellishments of Nature upon what Our Senses Present Us with? Divine things are More Nobly, more Divinely Represented to the Imagination than by Any Other Poem, a More Beautiful Idea is given of Nature than any Poet has Pretended to; Nature is just come out of the Hand of God, in its Virgin Loveliness, Glory, and Purity; and the Human Race is Shown, not as Homer's, More Gigantick, more Robust, more Valiant, but without Comparison more Truly Amiable, more so than by the Pictures and Statues of the Greatest Masters, and all These Sublime Ideas are Convey'd to Us in the most Effectual and Engaging Manner. . . .

in reading the Iliad or Aeneis we Treasure up a Collection of Fine Imaginative Pictures as when we read Paradise Lost; Only that from Thence we have (to speak like a Connoisseur) More Rafaelles, Correggios, Guidos, etc. Milton's Pictures are more Sublimely Great, Divine and Lovely than Homer's, or Virgil's, or those of Any Other Poet, or of All the Poets, Ancient, or Modern. (p. clix)

This commentary is interesting because of the way it incorporates literary criticism with the English connoisseurship in the visual arts that started in the final decades of the seventeenth century.

Without a Solid Establishment of Mind in These Sublime Truths [those of the "Argument" of *Paradise Lost*], All Comprehended in a Just Idea of God, (So far as we are Enabled to Conceive of Him, and He has Sufficiently Reveal'd Himself to Us for that Purpose, More we Need not) whatever Happiness Any One May Seem to Enjoy, 'tis a Cheat, Precarious, and Will Fail, when the Mind is it Self. . . . (p. clx [sic; should be clxi])

O Milton thou hast employ'd all thy Vast Treasure of Wit, Learning and Ability, all the Beauty, Energy, and Propriety of Words our Language was Capable of, all the Sweetness and Harmony of Numbers thy Musical and Judicious Ear furnish'd thee with, All the Fire and Beauty and Sublimity of Imagination Peculiar to thy Self, Added to what could be Supply'd by Those who have most Excell'd in That Angelical Faculty, in whatever Ages or Languages, All the Firmness, Force and Dignity of Mind thy Vertue and Piety Excited in thee, or Rewarded thee with; and together with All These a Genius Perfectly Poetical, if Ever Any Man's was, and That Regulated by a most Solid Judgment. All These thou hast Consecrated to Produce a Poem, more Instrumental than any Other Human Composition, to Calm and Purify the Mind, and through the Delightful Regions of Poetry, to Exalt and Fix it to the Mysteries, Sublimities and Practice of Religion; to a State of Tranquility and Happiness, the Utmost Mortality is Capable of.
(pp. clxii-clxiii)

This kind of Obscurity is so far however from being an Imputation, that it infers One part of the Excellence of the Poem; for it Arises from Causes which help to make it Admirable as it is: Such are the Sublimity of the Matter, and of the Beings which are Introduced, the Variety and Nobleness of the Sciences treated of, or Alluded to, the Perpetual Use made of Ancient Stories and Fables, and of the Writings of the Best Authors in Several Languages, Ancient and Modern, not Commonly Known, or not well Understood; to which must be added a Peculiarity of Language; Words Seldom or Not at all Us'd in English, or not in the Sense Milton Understands them . . . (p. clxvi)

He had from his Youth been Thoroughly Imbu'd with those Noble and Divine Principles of Genuine Christianity, Regeneration, and Union with

God; and Seems to have Persisted in Them to the Last; and indeed the Sublimest Poetry can desire Nothing more for its Purpose; These Include the Idea of God, and his Goodness to Mankind by the Mediation of his Son, the Riches of the Glory of his Inheritance in the Saints. (p. clxxii)

. . . if Moreover I have Help'd to Demolish that too Common Notion that how Excellent and Sublime Soever 'twas in Milton's Mind, and on his Tongue, in Our Hands the Poem is, at least, Imperfect for want of His Eyes to Watch over the Editor and the Printer . . . I shall Rejoice in it More than in Any thing my most Sanguine Expectations have Yet in Store for Me whilst I am Continu'd on the Present Stage of Being. (p. clxxx)

If all of the above passages from Richardson reveal anything, it is that he was not tied down to any one view of the sublime, least of all to a rhetorical view. There is sublime of mind, matter, and the construct of the art work proper.

William Benson, *Letters concerning poetical translations, and Virgil's and Milton's arts of verse, etc.* (1739)

The volume contains 83 pages comprising ten letters. For the most part they are detailed prosodic studies of Milton's art of versification in *Paradise Lost.* Benson believes that rhyme is an essential ingredient of great poetry, but that Milton's achievements in blanks were to be regarded as an exception to the rule. The word 'sublime' occurs as rarely in Benson as it does frequently in Richardson.

I should not part with the Passage in Homer above-mentioned without observing that the Speech of Apollo's Priest is wonderfully Peinturesque, and in Character. We plainly see the Priest holding up his Hands, and pointing with his Crown and Sceptre to Heaven.

> Princes! and Grecian Warriors! may the Gods
> (The Pow'rs that dwell in Heav'ns sublime Abodes)
> (p. 6)

Here are ten dull Words most certainly in one dull Line.

> To take off his great Head, who came with it.

And miserable is the Metre in which they creep on. But hundreds of monosyllable Lines are to be found in Milton that are as sublime, as beautiful, and as harmonious as can possibly be written. Look only into the Morning Hymn in the fifth Book [of "Paradise Lost"]. (p. 12)

Would that Benson had gone on to tell us more about the sublimity of Milton's monosyllabic lines, but the above is the extent of his exposition.

Francis Peck, *New memoirs of the life and poetical works of Mr. John Milton . . .* (1740)

If we compare it [a fine poem] to such a painting we shall find, there faces, here characters; there looks, here speeches; there gesture, here passion; there groupes, here episodes; there coloring, here diction; there every other grace & beauty of the greatest master, here the choicest epithets, the sweetest arrangement, & most charming turn of words; the justest metaphors; the most delightful similes; the boldest figures; the most surprising allusions to the mythology, history, & writings of the antients; & the sublimest flights & descriptions of every thing which is curious in the whole circle of arts & sciences, & in earth & heaven itself, which can be imagined by the wit & art of man; & all this too we may see, as it were, set a moving by the machinery; & yet that in all this infinite variety of design and ornament, there is not one thing too much, or one thing too little. (p. 3)

And again [here Peck quotes from Milton's *Apology for Smectymnuus*, p. 177 in the John Toland edition]. "From the Laureat fraternity of poets riper years & the ceaseless round of study & reading led me to the shady spaces of philosophy, but chiefly to the divine volumes of Plato & his equal Xenophon. Where if I should tell you what I learnt of CHASTITY & LOVE, I meane that which is truly so, whose charming cup is only vertue (the rest are cheated with a thick intoxicating potion, which a certain sorceresse, the abuser of love's name, carries about) & how the first and chieftest office of love begins & ends in the soule, producing those happy twins of her divine generation, KNOWLEDGE & VERTUE; with such abstracted sublimities as these; it might be worth your listning, readers, as I may one day hope to have you in a still time, when there shall be no chiding." (p. 7)

This passage is quoted because of the paucity of Milton's references to the sublime.

And again [here Peck quotes from Dryden's Preface to his *Juvenal*]. "I found in him a true sublimity, lofty thoughts, which were cloathed with admirable Grecisms & antient words, which he had been digging from the mines of Chaucer & Spenser, & which, with all their rusticity, had something of venerable in them."

After him, comes Bp. Atterbury, & in a letter to Mr. Pope, dated at Bromley, 8. Nov. 1717, thus expresses himself. "I return your Milton -- And -- I protest to you, this last perusal of him has given me such new degrees, I will not say of pleasure, but of admiration & astonishment, that I look upon the sublimity of Homer, & the majesty of Virgil, with somewhat less reverence than I us'd to do."[1] (p. 62)

After these appears Monsieur de Voltaire. -- "What Milton so boldly undertook, he perform'd with a superior strength of judgment, & with an imagination productive of beauties not dreamed of before him. The meaness

[1] The accuracy of Peck's quotation is confirmed by George Sherburn, *The Correspondence of Alexander Pope* (Oxford, 1956), whose version of the letter has only minor differences of spelling and punctuation.

(if there be any) of some parts of the subject is lost in the immensity of the poetical invention. There is something about the reach of human force to have attempted the Creation, without bombast . . . The Paradise Lost is the only poem, wherein are to be found, in a perfect degree, that uniformity which satisfies the mind, & that variety, which pleases the imagination; all its episodes being necessary lines, which aim at the centre of a perfect circle. Where is the nation who would not be pleased with the interview of Adam & the angel, with the Mountain of Vision, with the bold strokes which make up the relentless, undaunted, & sly character of Satan? but, above all, with that sublime wisdom, which Milton exerts, whenever he dares to describe God, & to make him speak?" (p. 63)

The quotation from Voltaire comes, of course, from his *Essay on the Epic,* which had wide currency in England shortly after its writing.

On page 64 Peck quotes from Jonathan Richardson, *Explanatory notes* the same passage from page cxliii that I gave above under the head of that work. Likewise, on page 66 Peck quotes from Richardson, page cxlv, and on page 67 from page clii, both given above.

. . . the reverend Mr. John Jortin observes, "that the Paradise Regain'd hath not met with the approbation which it deserves; tho', he thinks, it hath not the harmony of numbers, the sublimity of thought, & the beauties of diction, which are in Paradise Lost; but that it is composed in a lower & less striking style, a style suited to the subject." [from *Remarks on Spenser's Poems*, 1734. p. 171, etc.] (p. 84)

"But how sublime, how rapturous is our author's comparison of Lucifer's diminished spender [sic] & faded beauties to the sun over-clouded or eclips'd?" [Here follows in Peck the appropriate passage -- Book 1, lines 591-600. The quotation is from Ant. Blackwall, *Introduction to the Classic's*, p. 225.][2]

("An Examination of Milton's Stile", p. 124)

No less sublime is that comparison of the rest of his [Satan's] companions, to so many mountain oaks, all new blasted by lightning. [Here Peck illustrates his own comment by citing Book 1, lines 609-615.] (*Ibid.*)

And his imitations of Scripture are as charming.

Under this head I will mention two or three remarkable instances, none which, I think, have been hitherto taken notice of by any writer. . . .

2. There is scarce a more sublime thought in all Milton, than in those three admirable lines which make a part of the description of that grand incident of the Messiah's driving the rebellious angels out of heaven.

> Yet half his strength he put not forth, but check'd
> His thunder in mid-volie; for he meant
> Not to destroy, but root them out of heav'n
>
> P.L. VI. 853[-855]
> (*Ibid.*, p. 131, XLIX)

[2] Editions of this work appeared in 1718, 1719, 1725, 1737, 1746 and even later.

I

Such musick (as 'tis said)
Before was never made,
But when of old the sons of morning sung,
While the Creator great
His constellations set,
And the well-balanc't world on hinges hung,
And cast the dark foundations deep,
And bid the weltr'ing waves their oozy channel keep.
[Milton's] Ode 117

Here our author had many sublime passages of scripture in his thoughts. As, "The morning stars sang together, & all the sons of God shouted for joy." Job xxxviii. 7. God "builded his spheres in the heaven." Amos ix. 6. margin. "He made Arcturus, Orion & Pleiades, & the chambers of the south." Job ix. 9. "the stars of heaven & the constellations thereof." Isaiah xii. 10. "He stretched out the north over the empty space, & hanged the earth upon nothing." Job. xxvi. 7. "I brake up for it my decreed place, & set bars & doors, & said, Hitherto shalt thou come, but no further; & here shall thy proud waves be stayed." Job xxxviii. 10. 11. "Be still, & know that I am God." Ps. xlvi. 10.

("Explanatory & Critical Notes on divers Passages of Milton & Shakespeare: By the Editors", p. 132.)

XXV

At last a soft & solemne breathing sound
Rose like a steame of rich distill'd perfumes
And stole upon the aire, that ev'n Silence
Was tooke e're she was 'ware & wisht she might
Deny her nature, & be never more
Still, to be so displac't. I was all eare,
And took in strains that might create a soule,
Under the ribs of Death! – – – – – –
Comus. 566 [-573]

Pause awhile, good reader, & mark here this wonderful description of a fine song by a fine voice at a distance. It is one of the most sublime passages in all Milton. The last stroke, "I was all eare, etc.," is surprisingly beautiful.

(*Ibid.*, p. 147)

The last two extracts are especially notable. The first for the detailed Biblical allusions given by Peck; the second for being an example of a critic finding a sublimity in Milton that has nothing to do with either elevation or vastness.

[Anon.], *A verbal index to Milton's Paradise Lost.* (1741)

As set up, the following Roman and Arabic numerals refer to book and line in Paradise Lost. It is intriguing that such a verbal index should have entries on the sublime.

Sublime --	II.	528
	III.	72
	IV.	300
	VI.	771
	VII.	421
	VIII.	455
	X.	536
	XI.	236
More Sublime --	X.	1014
Sublim'd --	I.	135
	V.	483

James Paterson, *A complete commentary with etymological, explanatory, critical and classical notes on Milton's Paradise Lost.* (1744)

The word sublime is conspicuous by its absence in the text of this work. However, in a prefatory remark, Paterson says:

> In this I have translated almost every Foreign Word into proper English, . . . and I have omitted none that had the least apparent Difficulty; that this Work might be more serviceable to the meanest Capacities and Strangers; both which lose their Time and Labour in reading this most sublime Poem, without such a Key. (p. v)

William Lauder, *An essay on Milton's use and imitation of the moderns, in his Paradise Lost.* (1750)

Regardless of the honesty or validity of the manner in which Lauder demonstrates the supposed plagiarism by Milton in *Paradise Lost*, this essay has interest for us now in its reflection of what we usually understand as the later eighteenth-century attitude toward originality in poetic genius. It would also seem that Lauder does not understand the function of several devices of the epic form, though this may be only a pose to advance his case. The authors that Lauder says Milton plagiarized the most are Ross, Grotius, Du Bartas, and Masenius.

Significant of Lauder's use of the word 'sublime' is its frequency and impreciseness. There is certainly no progress to be found here toward the esthetic that Monk finds well along in its development by mid-century.

Between the Preface and the text are four letters written to and published by the *Gentleman's Magazine*. The first two of the excerpts to follow are from the second and third of these letters.

Poetry requires the most extensive faculties, an uncommon sublimity of conception, and a very warm imagination, with great regulation of judgment to retrench exuberances; and where this last is absent, the luxuriance of fancy is still preferable to sterility, as far as superfluity to want.

[by G. S. Carlisle]

I have attended to some specimens, that you have lately published, from some modern authors, upon similar subjects with Milton's Paradise Lost; and I must own that they strike me very much. Some of them are truly sublime, and contain nearly the same sentiments with him; and others of them are so exactly the same, that some passages in Milton might pass for a just translation.

[by the Rector of S. Mic. Bassishaw]

Thus Milton: who undoubtedly took these sublime conceptions from the following ones of Masenius, and some other elegant poetical authors, whom I shall have occasion to mention in the progress of this work: For Milton had a large store of materials before him when he first engaged in composing his poem, tho' hitherto he has been thought to have digged them only from the quarries of nature. (p. 26)

Strange perverseness this! two christian poets are both handling the same subject, introducing the same collocutors, an angel and the father of mankind, and both using almost the very same words; (for it is absolutely certain, that Milton had Grotius before him) and yet the vindicator will have it, that his poet, neglecting his christian pattern, alludes to a famous love-story. This is precisely the same way of reasoning, as if any one, after reading Dr. Young's beautiful and sublime description of a horse, paraphrastically translated from the book of Job, should confidently maintain, that the learned doctor had not the sacred book of Job in his eye, but the fourth book of Virgil's Georgics, where the poet treats of bees: there being just as much analogy betwixt Adam and the Angel Raphael, and Dido and Aeneas, as betwixt a horse and bees. Should not a man of common sense be ashamed to fly to such wretched shifts, such unfair altercation, rather than honestly submit to truth? Milton, indeed, has introduced too much of the heathen mythology into his poem, by which he has debased, not a little, the most sublime and sacred of all subjects; according to the opinion of Dr. Bentley, Mr. Addison himself, Rollin, and every other unprejudiced critic: the mixture being not more contrary to the nature of his subject, than to common sense. (p. 60)

The second [of Ramsay's *Sacred Poems*] exhibits a description of man's happiness in a state of innocence, together with a most exalted and sublime encomium on marriage, as the only lawful means appointed by God, for the propagation of the human species, to which Milton often alludes. (p. 77)

As this is the case [the availability of Ramsay's work], I say, I shall content myself with presenting a few passages, only, from it, though Milton has transfused almost the whole substance of it into his poem, but with so much art, that it requires no small degree of attention to trace him out minutely. Ramsay's divine work begins thus, where every line breathes forth a sublime, masterly and truly poetical genius. (p. 78)

I proceed now to another author, the famous Caspar Barlaeus, whom not a few learned men regard, as the best poet of the last century: though, at the same time, I am not ignorant, that others have entertained a quite different opinion of his merit. But be that as it will, he has translated into Latin verse, in a very elegant manner, several pieces of "Jacobus Catsius," an excellent Dutch poet, on matrimonial subjects. Among these, the first in order and dignity, as well as the longest, is one, entitled "Paradisus," or an Epithalamium on the marriage of Adam and Eve: a performance truly sublime! It consists of between eight and nine hundred lines, the substance of which Milton has inserted in various places of his "Paradise Lost." (pp. 111-112)

I now proceed to another author, the celebrated Fredericus Taubmannus, professor of poetry and eloquence in the university of Wittemberg in Germany. This gentleman, in the early part of his life, attempted to write a poem in three books, entitled, "Bellum Anglicum," or the war of the angels. It consists of about nine hundred lines, and appears to be a very masterly performance, for so young an adventurer in poetry. 'Tis pity the author did not finish it, when he arrived at full maturity of judgment and poetical abilities. But such as it is, Milton has served himself most liberally with it, and formed from it the best part of his sixth book, by far the most sublime in his whole poem. (p. 129)

Dr. Zachary Pearce, now bishop of Bangor [and the author of the most popular Latin translation of *On the Sublime* in the eighteenth century], is of opinion, that Milton took the first hint of his design of writing a tragedy, upon the subject of his poem, from an Italian tragedy, called, "Il Paradiso Perso," still extant, and printed many years before he entered upon this work. And, indeed, I have been informed by several persons of unquestionable judgment and veracity, that almost all that is admir'd as lofty and sublime, in Milton's description of the battle of the angels, in his sixth book, is wholly transcribed from this tragedy; where are to be seen the picture of the battle, and the final defeat of Lucifer, with his expulsion out of heaven, as described and delineated in "Paradise Lost." (p. 154)

One comes from these comments of Lauder scarcely able to believe that the man is serious.

John Douglas, *Milton vindicated from the charge of plagiarism, brought against him by Mr. Lauder.* (1751)

Douglas mentions the sublime only once, early in the proceedings of his 77-page defense of Milton, but the entire document is noteworthy because it shows indisputably that as late as 1750 there are men who are independent of the gathering 'pre-romantic' view, and who can, moreover, write as sensible a defense of the Classical and epic esthetic as appeared before or after. The entire piece is an epistle to the Earl of Bath.

Scarce an eminent Writer can be instanced who has not been indebted to the Labors of former Authors; but how absurd would it be to urge this as an

Argument that there is no Merit in their Productions? For as one may be what is called an original Writer, and yet have no Pretensions to Genius, so another may make use of the Labors of others in such a Manner as to satisfy the World of his own Abilities. There may be such a thing as an original Work without Invention, and a Writer may be an Imitator of others without Plagiarism. But as Authority will always weigh more than Assertion, and often more than Argument, I think I cannot take a more effectual Way to confirm and establish what I advance, than to bring up as an Evidence the great Longinus. What then is his Opinion? So far is he from thinking that Imitations of old Authors detract any thing from the Merit and Genius of those who have recourse to them, that, on the contrary, he expressly lays down the Imitation and Emulation of the former great Writers and Poets, as one of the Ways that leads to the Sublime. This he particularly illustrates by the Example of Plato, who, he says, imitated Homer more closely than Herodotus, Stesichorus, and Archilochus had done before, and drew from the copious Stream of that Poet, ten Thousand Rivulets to enrich his own Works. And this, adds he, "is not to be looked upon as a Theft, but (as I find this Passage translated by Mr. Dryden) a beautiful Idea of him who undertakes to imitate, by forming himself on the Work and Invention of another Man." * [footnote reads: Longinus "Peri Hupsous" Ed. Pearce. Page 51. 52. Dryden, whose Translation of the last Sentence of the above Quotation, I have given, from his Preface to *Troilus and Cressida*, seems to have read not *καλωυ ηθων* , but *καλων εγσων*] And if Longinus be so far from looking upon Imitation to be Plagiarism, as to recommend it as one of the Sources of the Sublime, and to praise Plato for his Observation of this Rule, who will venture to assert that Milton's Imitations in his "Paradise Lost" detract any thing from the Merit of the Poem? (pp. 7-9)

John Toland, *The life of John Milton*; *containing, besides the history of his works, several extraordinary characters of men, and books, sects, parties, and opinions*; *with Amyntor*; *or a defense of Milton's life*: *by John Toland. And various notes now added.* (1761)

The date 1761 is that of a later printing of the work; the title page for *Amyntor* says that it was first printed in 1699.[3] Judging from the number of contemporaneous references to it encountered in the holdings of the Folger Library, Toland's *Life* must be one of the most important, if not the most important, works of this genre on Milton stemming from the turn of the century.[4] It is, perhaps, surprising that the sublime is not more ubiquitous in Toland's book.

I send you at length, my best friend [Thomas Raulins of Kilreag, Herefordshire], what you have so often and ernestly sollicited me to write, the life

[3] I have collated this edition with the first edition, of 1699, and found that there are no verbal variations in the passages used.

[4] David Masson does not mention this work, however, in his standard life of Milton.

of John Milton, a man eminent at home and famous abroad for his universal learning, sagacity, and solid judgment: but particularly noted as well for those excellent volumes he wrote on the behalf of civil, religious, and domestic liberty; as for his divine and incomparable poems, which, equalling the most beautiful order and expression of any antient or modern compositions, are infinitely above them all for sublimity and invention. (p. 1)

"These abilities (says he [Milton], speaking of invention and composition) whersoever they be found, are the inspir'd gift of God; rarely bestow'd, but yet to som (tho most abuse them) in every nation, and are of power to breed and cherish in a great people the seeds of virtue and public civility, to allay the perturbations of the mind, and set the affections in a right tune; -- or lastly, whatsoever is in religion holy and sublime, in virtue amiable or grave, whatsoever has passion or admiration in all the changes of that which is call'd fortune from without, or the wily subtilties and refluxes of mans thoughts from within, all these things with a solid and treatable smoothness to paint out and describe." (pp. 23-24)

This passage from the *Reason of Church Government* quoted by Toland is of some interest because of the relative paucity, as noted above, of references by Milton to the sublime.

As to the regularity of the poem [*Paradise Lost*], I never knew it question'd by any but such as would build themselves a reputation on the flaws and mistakes they discover in other mens labours, without producing any thing better or equal of their own. But the unparallel'd sublimity and force of the expression, with the delicacy of his thoughts, and the copiousness of his invention, are unanimously own'd by all ranks of writers. (p. 119)

On page 126 there is a long footnote to the controversy between Lauder and Douglas over Milton's supposed plagiarism.[5]

[Anon.], *A familiar explanation of the poetical works of Milton. To which is prefixed Mr. Addison's criticism on Paradise Lost.* (1762)

A familiar explanation includes a 92-page alphabetically arranged "Explanatory Notes on the Poetical Works of Milton" that has a negative interest for this study. For even though it contains a large number of adjectives and verbs, besides the nouns that one would expect, it does not have a listing for 'sublime', a word one would think more germane to such a listing on Milton than most of the adjectives that are given.

William Massey, *Remarks upon Milton's Paradise Lost.* (1761)

What is the Wrath of Achilles with all its tragical Effects, or the pretended Piety of Aeneas, though set off with all the Beauties of a lively Narration,

[5] Evidently supplied by the editor, since Toland died in 1722 and therefore could not have known Lauder's attack on Milton. The footnote obviously does not appear in the 1699 edition.

in two of the most polished and expressive Languages, compared with the sacred and interesting Truths delivered in our Author's sublime Poem? In which likewise there is agreeably interspersed an useful Variety of moral and religious Observations.

(Advertisement to the Reader, p. 1v)

... Our Author however does not seem here to support the Majesty of his Subject with Sublimity and proper Decorum, in representing the Descent of Raphael in the Shape of this fabulous Bird [the Phoenix].

(from the commentary on Book V, "Verse" 272, p. 128)

... Though Milton is thought to be, and indeed appears, orthodox, in Points of Faith, throughout this whole Poem; yet in these sublime Speeches between the Eternal Father and the Son, it is very difficult to avoid some Terms that seem to favour the Arian Doctrine.

(from the commentary on Book X, "Verse" 56, p. 206)

The desultory nature of Massey's usage of the word 'sublime' is apparent, but whether this stems from the word's prestige status in the 1760's or from his own temperament is hard to determine from such a small sampling.

If I can draw any conclusion from my brief Context of Milton and the sublime, it is that there is no dramatic change or progress in the manner in which the two are used during the first sixty years of the century. I say this, however, with the realization that other primary sources might turn up different results.

V

SHAKESPEARE

Generally speaking, when late seventeenth- and eighteenth-century critics applied the term 'sublime' to the great English writers of the past, they were likely to think foremost of John Milton. In that sense, if not in others, Shakespeare stands in the stern Puritan's shadow during most of our period. That is not to say, on the other hand, that Shakespeare is rarely called sublime; one comes across it now and then. Maybe we should say that there is not the nearly automatic association in the eighteenth-century mind of 'Shakespeare' and 'sublime', as there is of 'Milton' and 'sublime'. The difference in the bulk of this chapter and that of the chapter on Milton attests to the relative number of references in the Folger Library to the sublimity of the two writers respectively.

John Upton, *Critical observations on Shakespeare, By John Upton Prebendary of Rochester.* (1746)

The text proper is divided into three books. The first is general criticism, the second a close textual criticism of the plays, and the third a close textual application of Shakespeare's supposed rules. There is a heavy reliance throughout on the ancient authors, and frequent reference to Milton for principle and illustration. Upton is interesting because he lies somewhere between the strict neo-classical school and what we now call the Romantic approach to the Bard; he retains the foundation of the rules, but makes tolerant exceptions to them in most cases where he believes that such exceptions will advance Shakespeare's case.

Then again those apparitions, being symbolical representations of what shall happen to him, are introduced paltering with him in a double sense, and leading him on, according to the common notions of diabolical oracles, to his confusion. And when the kings appear, we have a piece of machinery, that neither the ancients or modern can exceed. I know nothing any where can parallel it, but that most sublime passage in Virgil, where the great successors of Aeneas pass in review before the hero's eyes. Our poet's closing with a compliment to James the first upon the union, equals Virgil's compliment to Augustus.

(Book I, Section V. pp. 53-54)

Thus every thing in poetry should have manners and passions: and the moral should shine perspicuous in whatever aims at the sublime. And thus he enriches with morals all his sublime passages; as in Prospero's reflections on the transitory state of human grandeur. Isabella's moralizing on men in power abusing their authority. Lear's reflection, when it thunders, on the ingratitude of his daughter. With many more of the like nature. Descriptions without moral or manners, however designed by the poet to raise the passion of wonder and astonishment, are not instances of the "true" sublime. The vast jumps that Juno's steeds take in Homer, is an example of that pompous and astonishing kind of the sublime, which is calculated to raise admiration in vulgar minds; for in poetry the vulgar are to be sometimes considered, as well as philosophers. How careful then should the poet be, to check all childish admiration in himself; tho' he may be allowed, with some reserve, to raise it in his readers?

(*Ibid.*, Section XI, pp. 96-97)

Considering the date he published this work, Upton shows in the above a remarkable dependence on the Longinianism of Longinus himself, and, equally, an apparent disregard of the sublime of the eighteenth-century psychological and natural sublime schools.

And surely that cannot be great, which 'tis great for a man to despise. Hence the eye is to be turned from the distinctions of custom and fashion, to those of nature and truth. The dignity of Socrates and Brutus is to be recognized, before that of Caesar. With what contempt then should that distinction of "high" and "low" life, introduced by our modern comic poets, be treated? For in what other sense can this fantastical distinction be allowed, than as the monkey, that climbs to the top of the tree, is a higher creature, than the generous horse that stands grasing below? So that after all were I to shew the reader instances of the "true" sublime, I should make choice of such as these:

> Aude hospes contemnere opes, et te quoque
> dignum Finge deo.
>
> Virg. Aen. VIII, 369

And in Milton, V, 350.

> Mean while our primitive great sire, to meet
> His godlike guest, walks forth: without more train
> Accompanied than with his own compleat
> Perfections; in himself was all his state;
> More solemn than the tedious pomp that waits
> On princes, when their rich retinue long
> Of horses led, and grooms besmear'd with gold
> Dazzles the crowd, and sets them all agape.

(*Ibid.*, pp. 97-98)

This passage illustrates my point about the way in which Milton tends to shoulder Shakespeare aside even when the latter is supposedly the center of attention.

If on the contrary nature is to be pictured in more colours; if the hero, the friend, the patriot, or prince appears, the thoughts and sentiments alone give an air of majesty to the poetry, without considering even the lofty expressions and sublimity of the diction. What can be more affecting and passionate than king Lear? How does the ghost in Hamlet raise and terrify the imagination of the audience? In a word, the sentiments are so agreeable to the characters, so just and natural, yet so animated and transported, that one would think no other could be possibly used, more proper to the ends he proposes, whether it be to approve or disapprove, to magnify or diminish, to stir or to calm the passions.

(Book I, Section XII, p. 102)

The neo-classical concept of decorum lives on in Upton.

And now I am considering the faulty side of our poet, I cannot pass over his ever and anon confounding the manners of the age which he is describing, with those in which he lived: for if these are at all introduced, it should be done with great art and delicacy; and with such an antique cast, as Virgil has given to his Roman customs and manners. Much less can many of his anacronisms be defended. Other kind of errors (if they may be so called) are properly the errors of great genius's; such are the inaccuracies of language, and a faulty sublime, which is surely preferable to a faultless mediocrity. Shakespeare labouring with a multiplicity of sublime ideas often gives himself not time to be delivered of them by the rules of "flow-endeavouring art"; hence he crowds various figures together, and metaphor upon metaphor; and runs the hazard of far-fetched expressions, whilst intent on nobler ideas he condescends not to grammatical niceties: here the audience are to accompany the poet in his conceptions, and to supply what he has sketched out for them.

(*Ibid.*, Section XV, pp. 136-138)

Once again, Upton seems to be virtually quoting from *On the Sublime.*

When a taste and relish is well modeled and formed, and our general science of what is fair and good improved; 'tis no very difficult matter to apply this knowledge to particulars. But if I have no standard of right and wrong, no criterion of foul and fair; if I cannot give a reason for my liking or disliking, how much more becoming is modesty and silence?

I would beg leave to know, what ideas can he be supposed to have of a real sublime in manners and sentiments, who has never gone further for his instruction, than what a puffy rhetorician, who wrote in a barbarous age, can teach? Or what admirer of monkish sophists and casuists, can ever have any relish at all?

("Book II", "Section 1", p. 150)

It is regrettable that Upton does not name one or two 'puffy rhetoricians', but if he had obliged, I feel confident that Longinus' name would not appear.

> There is one thing, I think, should always be remember'd in settling and adjusting the context of authors; and that is, if they are worthy of criticism, they are worthy of so much regard as to be presumed to be in the right, 'till there are very good grounds to suppose them wrong. A critic should come with abilities to defend, not with arrogance at once to start up a corrector. Is this less finished? Is it not so intended to set off what is principal, and required a higher finishing? Is this less numerous? Perhaps the poet so designed it, to raise the imagination still higher, when we come to sublimer and more sonorous subjects. Does not even variety, which goes so far to constitute what is beautiful, carry with it a supposal of inferiority and subordination? Nay, where no other consideration can be presumed, some allowances surely are to be given to the infirmity of human nature.
>
> (*Ibid.*, pp. 152-153)
>
> And were it not a degree of prophanation, I might here mention the great Designer, who has flung some things into such strong shades, that 'tis no wonder so much gloominess and melancholy is raised in rude and undisciplined minds [a reference to the "Graveyard School?"]: the sublime Maker, who set this universe before us as a book; yet what superficial readers are we in this volume of nature? Here I am certain we must become good men, before we become good critics, and the first step to wisdom is humility.
>
> (*Ibid.*, p. 153)

Considering these passages from Upton all in all, I believe that they rank with a select few in this Context as an example of rather pure eighteenth-century Longinianism. Upton does not acknowledge Longinus as his critical master, but that really is not important. It is instructive to find how sensible is the majority of these extracts as a general guide for us modern critics. This becomes only more evident when Upton is compared with some of his more fashionable contemporaries, whose ideas on the sublime are likely to strike us now as somewhat quaint and unsoundly based.

Thomas Edwards, *The canons of criticism, and glossary, being a supplement to Mr. Warburton's edition of Shakespeare. Fourth edition.* (1750)

This is a judicious and devastating criticism of Warburton's criticism of Shakespeare. Edwards does not use the word 'sublime', but does give a noteworthy quotation from Warburton:

> It will be proper, in order to shew his wit, especially if the critic be a married man, to take every opportunity of sneering at the fair sex.
>
> Example 1, Vol. VI. p. 468. Coriolanus.

"My gracious 'silence', hail."

"The expression is extremely sublime; and the sense of it conveys the finest praise, that can be given to a good woman." Warb.

Edwards' procedure in *The Canons* is to present (generally) a group of quotations from Warburton, and then to comment on the entire group. This accounts for the fact that he does not comment directly on the above quotation; it gets lost, apparently, in the group of quotations of which it is a part, and gets no individual attention from Edwards.

John Roberts, *An answer to Mr. Pope's preface to Shakespeare. In a letter to a Friend.* (1729)

Roberts' work is offered here as a sort of after-thought. There is no mention of the word 'sublime' in its 46 pages, but there is a dependence throughout on the idea of great beauties overcoming minor blemishes in the productions of geniuses like Shakespeare. The burden of Roberts' *Answer* to Pope's preface is that Ben Jonson was wrong in saying that he wished Shakespeare had blotted a thousand lines, and Pope is equally wrong in blaming the Elizabethan players for the corruptions in the Quartos, which were due, he says, to the errors of diverse mechanics.

As Rosenberg points out in his dissertation, eighteenth-century literary commentaries that sound as though they were inspired by Longinus, frequently stem from another source entirely, but I offer the above echo of one of Longinus' most prominent concepts for what it is worth.

VI

PERIODICALS

There is little question that in a Context of this sort, there must be some account of the commentary to be found in the popular media of the period, that is to say the magazines and newspapers that devote at least part of their columns to literary and esthetic matters. In the process of selecting passages from these periodicals it becomes apparent immediately that there is inherently both an advantage and disadvantage. The advantage is, of course, that the very nature of the genre lends itself to the establishing of a context of popular usage of a word like 'sublime', certainly more popular than the usage to be found in the formal productions of leading critics. The disadvantage, on the other hand, bears on methodology; because of the enormous bulk of periodical matter available, any choice of periodical, and, especially, passages therein is bound to be somewhat arbitrary. The searcher may discover an interesting item only to miss an exciting one. Nevertheless, assurance can be given that all of the excerpts that follow enjoyed a certain amount of currency in the society of this period.

The Free Thinker.

The *Free Thinker* was published on Mondays and Fridays, March 24, 1718-1721. The editor was Ambrose Philips. As a general rule the essays contributed to it are on non-literary subjects.

In Consequence of what was said, on Monday last, I come now to consider how far Learning disqualifies Men for Business.

It is generally thought, the student is so deeply immerst in Contemplation on the Philosophy and Transactions of Former Ages, that he can give no Attention to the Affairs of the Present; or, that he is so intent upon General and Sublime Truths, that his Observation stoops not to the minute and trifling Occurrences of Life: And that, notwithstanding the comprehensive Rules of Wisdom he may have formed in Theory, he has not the Skill and Dexterity to apply those Maxims to the particular Circumstances of Action, in which he may be engaged.

(No. LXXXIX; Monday, January 26, 1718)

Note the aura, to be found in passages in other chapters of the Context, surrounding the usage of the sublime in the above; whatever else it may connote, the sublime here surely refers to the impractical aspect of human life, that which is not measured by the requirements of utility.

The same General Remarks [regarding the technique of the pulpit for clerics] will hold equally True with Regard to Sentiments. One may excell in the Sublimity of his Thoughts; Another in familiar and happy Illustrations of Notions not clearly apprehended by the Vulgar . . .

(No. XCIII; Monday, February 9, 1718)

Another Discouragement several Branches of Knowledge labour under is, a Fashionable Contempt fixed upon them by our gay Readers of Men. The Unlearned for the most Part look on all Sciences conversant about abstracted Subjects, or Speculations remote from Common Life, to be Matters of meer Curiosity, or vain, unprofitable Enquiries; which indeed in an Instance or Two may be True; Then, they are apt to consider all Rudimental Knowledge, as Mean, Trifling, and Useless. Whereas to One, who understands those sublime Truths, and comprehends at a View the long Chain of Reasoning by which some Abstruse Propositions are made Evident, it is a Matter of Admiration, that the Capacity of Humane Nature should be able to extend itself to such Lengths of Progressive Deductions. Neither ought any Rudiments to be dispised, or accounted mean and trifling, or useless, without the Assistance of which we can never climb up to the superior Heights of Knowledge.

(No. CXI; Monday, April 13, 1719)

It is apparent that in the preceding excerpt the word 'sublime' combines the ideas of the esoteric and the lofty.

How different is the Mode of Conversation, I have hitherto described [of the best of the Ancients] from that, which at present obtains amongst Us! Our Countrymen seem to have forgot, of late more than ever, that Reason and Speech are the Endowments, by which Mankind is distinguished from the Brute Creation, and fitted for all the Offices and the Pleasures of a social Life. How rare a Piece of good Fortune is it to fall into Company, where either the Understanding may be enlightened by any useful Observations, or even the Imagination entertained, either by the Facetiousness of Wit, or just and sublime Representations of Nature.

(No. CCLII; Friday, August 19, 1720)

Once again there is unmistakably an element of the supra-common and non-practical associated with the sublime.

The St. James's Journal; with Memoirs of Literature, and the Freshest Advices Foreign and Domestick.

This periodical was published weekly, during the period May 3, 1722 –May 18, 1723.[1]

To the Author of the St. James's Journal.

Sir,

The following Dissertation is prefixed to a little Book, entitled, "Epigrammatum Delectus". What you have here, is but a Summary of the Discourse itself, unelegantly, indeed, expressed, wanting both Style and Diction; my Design being to keep as close as possible to the Author's Meaning, and to enclose as much of his Materials in as little compass as conveniently I could. It does not appear who was the Author of it, but if one might guess from some Passages I could mention in his Dissertation, I shou'd judge him to be a Frenchman. If this little Labour of mine shou'd chance to find its way into your Paper, I may perhaps be encourag'd to be your future Correspondent. In the mean time, I am, Sir,

Your most Humble Servant, and Admirer,
Marcus.

(*Memoirs of Literature,* p. 141)

I give this correspondence between contributor and editor by way of introducing the passages that follow. Note the indication of the sort of French-English collaboration that is so prominent in my chapter on oratory and rhetoric.

In the next Section he [the author of the dissertation in question] comes to speak of Words, and in what manner they are to be accommodated to the Expression of Nature; which he considers in a twofold View, either in regard to the things themselves of which we speak, or the Persons spoken to, or that read them.

The first consists in suiting Words to Things; i.e. in describing Things grand and sublime, such Words are to be us'd as raise the Idea equal to the Subject treated of; and things humble and submissive, in Language as low and abject. Every Oration requires a Simplicity but such a Simplicity, as, when Occasion offers, will admit of the Sublime, or be precipitated into the Pathetick; but in such a manner as not to exceed or come short of the Expression of Nature. An Oration does not always put on Figure and Ornament, nor does it always refuse them; but they are us'd to the best advantage, when thereby the Similitude of Words and Things is render'd more perfect.

(*Ibid.*, p. 142)

The Form of it [the Epigram] some wou'd have depend altogether upon the last Clause or Sentence, and deny that to be an Epigram that does not conclude with a Turn of Wit. This he [the author of the dissertation] will not allow always to hold true, and gives us one, every Line of which is full of the Sublime, and ends with the same Majesty of Thought and Expression

[1] None of the standard studies of the English eighteenth-century periodical, by Walter Graham; R. S. Crane and F. B. Kaye; George Marr; and K. Weed and R. P. Bond, gives the editor. Neither does the *Union List of Serials.*

as it begins. Others run on in a certain Simplicity, and please with the Humour of their Style.

He comes in the last place to the Matter of Epigrams, and their various Kinds. The Matter or Subjects of an Epigram comprehends every Thing, and may admit of many Divisions. The chief are these, viz. The Sublime, Grand, and Majestick, whose Argument is Noble, pursu'd in Language as Bold, and concluding with a Sentence equally Magnificent. In which Martial, Grotius, and Barclay are peculiarly happy.

(*Ibid.*, p. 143)

The divisions by classifications are quite orthodox here, but the remarks concerning the epigram are interesting, and not commonly encountered.

In its number LIV for Saturday, May 4, 1723, *The St. James's Journal* presents *in toto* the first two of John Dennis' *Letters on Milton and Wycherly* (1721). Both are on the subject of *Paradise Lost* and have numerous references to the sublime.[2]

The Plain Dealer: being select essays on several curious subjects, relating to friendship, love, and gallantry, marriage, morality, mercantile affairs, painting, history, poetry, and other branches of polite literature. Publish'd originally in the year 1724. And now first collected into two volumes. (1730)

The Plain Dealer was published March 23, 1724–May 7, 1725, and was edited by a number of men, among them Aaron Hill and William Bond.[3] As its title promises, this periodical discourses on assorted subjects. The incidence of the word 'sublime' is not infrequent, and reflects a certain variety of usage.

So weak is the Frailty of Human Nature, that we can never be too secure, tho' arm'd with the sublimest Vertue, against the repeated Attacks of so many Passions, as constantly besiege us . . .

(No. III; Monday, March 30, 1724)

But, though this venerable, undress'd Nature, is seldom to be met with now; and has, indeed, been lost among us, for above a Century, it was so frequent Two or Three hundred Years ago, that their lowest Class of Poets, and the Composers of our good Old Ballads, have left us some of the noblest Examples of the Sublime, in its most striking Energy.

(No. 36; Friday, July 24, 1724)

In the above the sublime is associated with simplicity and the lack of sophistication, the opposite, it would seem, from a rhetorical concept of the sublime.

[2] They are quoted in Chapter IX below, on Dennis, pp. 182-185.

[3] Information supplied by Ronald S. Crane and F. B. Kaye, *A Census of British Newspapers and Periodicals 1620-1800* (Chapel Hill, 1927), p. 89.

"Modern Writers," said our Critick [unidentified], the other Evening, "have gone into a different Turn of Thinking: They extol, to the Skies, the indifferent Actions, and palliate the Blemishes, of Titled People, who disgrace the Figure of Life they appear in; but meanly, decline the right Use of Art upon Subjects, where they might point out the Greatness in obscure Men, who were never little in any Thing but the Accident of their Birth, and who living and dying, did an Honour to Human Nature. Such Pen-men may be called, "The Rabble of the Wits," who are dazzled by the false Glare of the Great, but can look at solid, Virtue, without the least Emotion, or Sign, of being able to see it. The Stiles of these petty Panegyrists, are, like their Subjects, glittering, but not solid; swelling, but rather empty than great; they seem never to have heard of that beautiful Simplicity, which arises out of Nature, and forms the Sublime, so much admired by the Readers, and so masterly executed by the Writers of Antiquity."

(No. 50; Friday, September 11, 1724)

Interestingly, the above extract both looks backward to Pliny and anticipates Wordsworth, the latter somewhat in the manner of Le Clerc and Fenelon.[4]

Wit and Beauty, are the Arms they [female lovers] conquer by; It is with Jealousy, therefore, that they behold them in any Hands but their own. The Praise of one Lady, is considered by another, as a Reproach: And her Soul must be sublimely Great, who, not only observes with Pleasure, the Fame and Influence, of a powerful Rival; but contributes her own Endeavours, to the Supports, and Increase of them!

(No. 53; Monday, September 21, 1724)

The early eighteenth century is obviously capable of using the word 'sublime' in a loose, non-literary sense when discussing the fairer sex!

I shall consecrate Three future Papers, to the Great, and different Excellences of Three English ladies, who are all now living; And whose Writings shall be tryed, in a most impartial Comparison, with the finest, and most celebrated Remnants of Female Genius, which have been preserv'd and wonder'd at, through a Length of applauding Ages. -- And, I doubt not, but I shall make it demonstrable, in those Three Papers; that the English Ladies have excell'd the Antients, in the Depth, the Tenderness, and the Sublimity of their Compositions.

(*Ibid.*)

Another indeterminable usage.

Here [regarding the panegyricks of Blackmore], the admirable Critick [Dennis], his old Friend, had, Himself, set an Example; such, as can never be too much applauded. -- The noblest, the most extensive, the most astonishing Ideas, which can expand the Human Soul, had inrich'd his powerful

[4] See Chapter III, p. 95.

Conception. And one wou'd have hop'd, that Mr. Dennis had made it impossible for any future Writer to treat this Subject, in a mean and groveling Manner; after he had oblig'd the World, so nobly, in his Paraphrase on Te Deum, with Verse, and Sentiments, sublimely suited to the Vastness of the Occasion.

(No. 54; Friday, September 25, 1724)

Because of the victory that history is thought to have given Pope in the dispute between him and Dennis, it is refreshing to see in this number, on the rightful place of critics in the production of great literature, a supporter of the beleaguered Dennis. I surmise that the latter and the writer of this passage see eye-to-eye on the subject of the sublime.

I have lately received a Letter containing some Remarks on the Battle of the Angels, as 'tis describ'd by Milton in the VIth Book of his "Paradise Lost," and I thought I could not find a more proper Occasion of publishing that Letter, than just after the Feast of St. Michael, on the 29th of the last Month, which was set apart by the Church to celebrate the Victory which that Arch-Angel got over Lucifer, and his rebellious Crew. I make no Doubt, but it will appear, that Milton, by the Account which he has given of that Victory, has gained a very glorious one himself, and has carried away the Praise of Sublimity from all Poets, both Antient and Modern.

(No. 57; Monday, October 5, 1724)

"Thus with this very pretty trifling Remark [on Milton's battle of the angels], does Mr. Addison stop short, within the very Touch of one of the vastest, and the sublimest Beauties, that ever was inspired by the God of Verse, or by Milton's Godlike Genius; when the very next Lines, the very next Words, strike and astonish us with such wonderful Ideas, as are able to lift up the Reader's Imagination to a Thousand Times a greater Height, than either the Shout of Armies, the Rattling of brazen Chariots, the Hurling of Rocks and Mountains, the Earthquake, the Fire, or the Thunder. But that these Beauties may be seen in all their Lustre, and in all their Glory, give me leave to set the whole Passage before you.

Th' Arch-Angel's Trumpet through the Vast of Heav'n
Resounded, and the faithful Armies rung
Hosanna to the Highest: nor stood at gaze
The adverse Legions, nor less hideous join'd
The horrid Shock [. . .]
What Wonder! when
Millions of fierce encountring Angels fought
On either Side, the least of whom could wield
These Elements, and arm him with the Force
Of all the Regions?"[5]

(No. 57; Monday, October 5, 1724)

[5] The entire passage is placed within quotation marks because it is supposedly a letter received by the editor of *The Plain Dealer*.

"But let us proceed to the Combat of the Two Arch-Angels, and we shall see something more, in a Passage that is wonderfully sublime, and worthy the Mouth of the Angel who relates it.

> They ended Parle, and both addrest for Fight
> Unspeakable [. . .]
> from each Hand, with Speed, retir'd
> Where erst was thickest Fight, th'Angelic Throng,
> And left large Field, unsafe within the Wind
> Of such Commotion."

(*Ibid.*)

"The Conflict of Two Worlds crushing and confounding each other, appear'd but trivial and light to him [Milton], to express his Idea of the Combat of the Two Arch-Angels; And therefore he says, that he's oblig'd 'to set forth Great Things by Small.'

"What immediately follows, accounts for all this, and is transcendentally Sublime.

> Together both, *with next-to-Almighty-Arm*,
> Uplifted, imminent, one Stroke they aim'd,
> That might determine, and not need repeat,
> As not of Power at once.

"That Expression, *With next-to-Almighty Arm*, includes more than the Thoughts of the greatest Reader can ever comprehend; which recalls to the best of my Remembrance, that noble, that wonderful Image, which the Poet gives of Satan, in the Second Book of this exalted Poem.

> The Stygian Council thus dissolv'd, and forth
> In order came the grand infernal Peers,
> Midst came their mighty Paramount, and seem'd
> Alone th'Antagonist of Heav'n.

"I defy any one to name any Thing so sublime in Homer, as the latter End of this Passage above."

(*Ibid.*)

"I have been so long conversant with you, and have so just a Knowledge of you, that I make no Doubt but that you are charm'd with these sovereign and immortal Beauties of Milton. But if any one into whose Hands this Letter may happen to fall, should think, that these vast Conceptions of so great a Genius, are rather extravagant and temerarious, than noble and sublime; I desire, that he would consider the Gradation of animal Beings which we find here below; what a prodigious, what an indefinite Distance is there, between a Mite and a Man?"

(*Ibid.*)

The above is a nice illustration of the interplay of two leading concepts of the period, the sublime and the great chain of being.

He [the author of *The Plain Dealer*, as compared with Addison in his *Spectator*] is as refined, polite, easy and genteel a Writer, as graceful and familiar, as sublime and as facetious, as sharp and as sprightly, as smooth and as strong, as pathetic and concise at Times, and yet, at Times, as copious too and as fluent, as learned and sententious, in fine as full of all Kinds of Seasonings and Ornaments, according as the Subject and the Circumstances of Persons, Places, Times, and Things treated of, occasionally, require.

(Dedication, pp. v-vi)[6]

An interesting set of opposite, or at least contrasting, terms. Here the word 'sublime' would appear to denote something like high seriousness.

To carry on the Resemblance a little further between these two masterly Authors in this Way ... It is peculiar to them two, to give a Signification to Trifles, to make common Things appear the most uncommon, by their surprizing and uncommon Turns; by the finest Ridicule they teach Men how to avoid it, and turn our very Follies into Wit; and in Subjects that are sublime, they raise Men's Minds with Ease to Heights, to which they must judge that of themselves they could never de capable to reach, even tho' they put themselves to the greatest Exertion and Difficulty.

(*Ibid.*, p. vi)

It is Nobly and Generously observed by an Excellent Poet of the present Age, that, To do one good Action, is preferable to the writing, however sublimely, the most Glorious Deeds of others. But methinks, on the other hand, it gives an unspeakable Pleasure to deliver in writing, what may give occasion to good Actions.

(No. 62; Friday, October 23, 1724)

Among the Beauties of Magnanimity, there is none, of a nobler Quality, than the Power of forgiving Injuries. -- It throws a Majesty over the Mind, and illustrates the Person, with an Air of Sweetness, and Serenity. -- We ought the more to admire it, since, where-ever it is found, It is in Company with the Sublimest Virtues: There not being Room for it, in a narrow, vulgar, Soul; because, overfill'd with Little Sentiments, such as have their Rise, and Revolution, within the Circle of Self-Interest.

(No. 72; Friday, November 27, 1724)

The above passage is an application, apparently, to human beings in general, of the Longinian idea that a leading source of the sublime is the nobility of the artist.

There is a single, heroick, Word, in the History of the Life of Adrian, which I could never read, without Emotions of the highest Admiration; and, which carries in it the Instruction, and Sublimity, of many Volumes! -- After That Great-Spirited Prince became possessed of the Empire, He met a Person, in the publick Way, who had been his most implacable, and bitter, Enemy. -- The Wretch, whose Heart was as contracted, as His Malice had been extensive, began to tremble, with Expectation of some severe, and sudden, Punishment, -- such as, He knew, He would, Himself, have inflicted on Adrian, had the Emperor's Power been His. But Adrian, with the

[6] This and the remaining excerpts from *The Plain Dealer* are from volume two.

serenest Gravity, only whisper'd, as He pass'd him, EVASISTI -- "You have Escap'd me."

All, that Largeness of Soul could inspire, or Eloquence adorn, and utter, seems to have been express'd, in this ESCAP'D ME!

(*Ibid.*)

But, it is not only the Manner in which Psalms are commonly sung, that I consider as an Indecency: The Psalms Themselves, as we have them in the old English Version, are a Disgrace to our Learning, Language, and our Religion! -- Who, that forms his Notion of David's Genius, from his Poetry, as This Translation gives it us, could possibly *believe* Him the Sublimest, of All Human Writers?

(No. 74; Friday, December 4, 1724)

He [the young patentee of the "New Theatre"] try'd every Reasonable Art of Pleasing, without Success! -- He reviv'd the best Old Plays, and brought on several New Ones! but had, often the Mortification to oppose his own Industry, and the sublimest Scenes of Shakespear, to the cold Encouragement of Empty Boxes!

(No. 82; Friday, January 1, 1725)

"Moses was a great Lawgiver, and David was a Warriour: But Solomon, whom God was pleased to honour, with still sublimer Marks of his Favour, and to whom He gave the wisest, and most Understanding Heart . . ."

(No. 85; Monday, January 11, 1725)

"But, not to digress farther, There are infinitely Sublimer Sentiments in the Sacred Writings [than in the writers of Classical Antiquity], and the lives of their Authors shone, illustrious Examples of their Doctrine!

(No. 87; Monday, January 18, 1725)

The Hebrew Prophets abound, Everywhere with Idea's, so sublimely Enthusiastick, that they transport and carry away the Reader, with a Power that is resistless; and worthy of the GOD, who is honour'd by them! -- Among These, the Description of That Desolation from the East, which was prophesied against the Jews, by Habakkuk (as we see it, in his first Chapter) has something in it, so strongly painted, and so terrible! that it strikes us, (thro' the most un-ornamented Simplicity,) with a Force, that was never excell'd, by all the Elaborate Productions of Poetry!

(*Ibid.*)

The sentiments of the author of *The Plain Dealer* above are a rejoinder to the letter quoted just previously, and are evidently inspired by the conviction that the lack of popularity of this kind of sublime Scriptural writing is due to the English translations available to the reading public.

The above passages on the sublime in Scripture parallel what we find in the more famous writers of the period. Although its frame of reference ranges across a number of other meanings, the sublime usually seems to pertain to the subject matter of the Bible first, and the mode of its expression second, but a close second.

The Sea is the most Vast, of all the visible Objects of Nature: And, when the Wind adds Disturbance and Motion, to its Immensity, There is nothing, that seems so Dreadfully proportion'd to the Greatness of its Almighty Creator! -- Yet, as the Art of the Painter gives us a sensible Delight, from the Representation of Prospects, of Creatures, or of Actions, which, in their Natures, are Productive of Horror; so, we are never more pleas'd, by any Descriptions, in Poetry, than by Those, which set before us the strongest, and liveliest Pictures, of Shipwrecks and Storms at Sea: Whether it is, that the Soul exults, and prides its self, in a Consciousness of its own Capacity, to move and conceive so greatly? -- Or, That we derive a sharper Taste, and Enjoyment, of our own Safety, from a Comparison, with those represented Dangers?

(No. 88; Friday, January 22, 1725)

The author is undoubtedly indebted to some extent to Addison's earlier discussions of 'Greatness' in *The Pleasures of the Imagination*, but his emphasis on the distinction in the viewer's mind between the terror of the scene and his own personal safety appears to anticipate by some thirty years the same concept in Burke's *Original Enquiry*.

"I have seen with a great deal of Pleasure some Excellent Specimens of the ancient Hebrew Poetry distinguish'd in your Paper, with the Applause which is so justly due to them: For every Body, who weighs these Things with Judgment, must agree with a late Writer, That 'there is nothing, so soft, so tender, and pathetick; and, at the same Time, nothing so grand, so majestick, so terrible, and so harmonious, as the Poetick Part of the Bible.'

I send you one of their Lyrick Odes (which is the Song of Moses, on the Overthrow of the Egyptians, in the Red Sea) and I believe it will be readily allow'd, That there is more of the Sublime in this Hebrew Ode, than can be found among the Writings of any Greek, or Roman Poet."

(No. 95; Monday, February 15, 1725)

"Homer's famous Catalogue, of Grecian Ships, and their Commanders, would, then, I am apt to believe, cease to pass for one of his Sublimest, and most Poetical Beauties. [That is, if the moderns were not afraid to censure the errors of the most popular among the ancient writers.] Its Geographical Exactness would no longer be pleased as a Ballance, against the Dryness, and the Tediousness, of its Historical Enumeration: Since it is no Part of a Poet's Business, to teach the Situation, Bounds, and Quality, of Countries. Little, occasional Descriptions of that kind, 'tis true, may sometimes, be necessary; and, being artfully introduced, and handled, might not only diversify a Poem; but also render it delightful: Without which last Quality, the whole Labour is lost. And nothing, certainly, can delight, that is tiresom, and heavy."

(No. 109; Monday, April 5, 1725)

The above letter to *The Plain Dealer* is one of the few negative criticisms of the great Greek poet that occur in the Context, but it serves to remind us that the dispute over the relative merits of the ancients and moderns was conducted in divers circles in our period.

The Grub-street Journal, 1730-1737.

The Grub-street Journal was published January 8, 1730–December 29, 1737, and was edited by Alexander Russel and John Martyn.[7] During the winter of 1733-1734 the *Bee* sponsored a contest in ode-writing in honor of the recently deceased Dr. Tindall. The first prize of a golden medal went to two odes, one of which was *Carmina sunt dicenda: neget quis carmina Gallo? The Grub-street Journal* reprinted the poem, alternately by Latin and English stanzas, and offered commentary after each pair of stanzas.

Torquens honores Tindalius poli
Vulgo videtur Stella nimis vaga;
Quin semper, aspectu Sophorum
Spaera gravi manet axe constans.

Whirling the pole's bright honours Tindall seems
To vulgar eyes a star that's too erratic;
But still in sight of Sophs the sphere
On pond'rous axle constant keeps.

Tho' several of our members endeavored to find out the meaning of "Torquens honores Tindalius poli," they could make no discovery of any meaning at all; and therefore it was concluded to be a beautiful expression in "The unintelligible Sublime", a sort of stile in which only those of our fraternity who have very "great talents" are able to write.

Orbem administro lumine Gratiae
Virtutis ornant; lene fluens modus
Tranquillat hinc mores & illinc
In Patriam pius aestus ardet:

Virtue's fair Graces with attendant light
The orb adorn; a mean here gently flowing
His manners calms, and tow'rds his countrey
His pious ardour there burns strong.

This stanza is almost as unintelligible as the former, tho' not so sublime: we shall pass them both over, not pretending to criticize what we do not understand.

(Thursday, October 9, 1735)

There is no need to comment at length on the satirical use of the sublime in the above extract. This procedure was quite common in the first half of the eighteenth century, having received a certain amount of

[7] Supplied by Crane and Kaye, *op. cit.*, p. 44.

impetus from such wits as Swift and Pope. We have seen that from the time of Longinus right up through the era covered by our Context, there was a general recognition of the danger that the sublime could fall into the inanities of bathos and unintelligibility unless the reins of artistic control were kept taut.

The London Magazine.

This periodical was published monthly, 1732-1779, averaged about 50 pages in length, and was divided into two distinct parts.[8] The first and longer of these is the *London Magazine*, the second the *Gentleman's Monthly Intelligencer*. The former is mostly a digest of essays that had appeared earlier in other periodicals, the latter a compendium of notices and advertisements.

The oldest Writings in the World are those of Moses; and next to them the Books of Homer. The first of these are, without Comparison, the noblest Treasure of Antiquity Time has left us, and contain the best Account of the Creation, and of the first Ages that can any where be met with; they are written in a Way so plain and simple, but with so much Force and Fire, that, even in the Translation, they retain a Grandeur and Sublimity which pierce the very Soul; as any Body may be convinc'd, who will but take the Pains to read attentively the History of Joseph, which, without any Ornament of Language, will affect the Mind more sensibly, and has, perhaps, more of the true Pathetick than any Piece that ever yet was written.

Nothing but the sacred Writings can exceed the Grandeur and Magnificence of these Descriptions [six from *The Iliad*], which express the Majesty and Omnipotence of the Supreme Being in a Manner as sublime as the Faculties of Man seem capable of conceiving, without Heaven's more immediate Assistance.

(January 1733, 30-31; abstracted from the *Universal Spectator* for January 27, 1733; No. 225, "Observations on Homer".)

Bayle died at the Age of fifty five, and many Years of his Life had been spent in the Professor's Chair; Yet his Works fill seven or eight great Folio's, and are all excellent in their Way; many of them upon Subjects the most sublime and important, Religion, Government, Philosophy, History, Criticism, and curious Disquisitions; many serious, many gay, often mixed, all handled with infinite Delicacy and Justness, and with immense Thought, Knowledge and Profoundness.

(March 1733, 150, "A Character and Recommendation of Monsieur Bayle's Dictionary")

I have lately had the Pleasure (says Walsingham) of seeing the Statue of our great and brave King William the Third at Mr. Rysbrack's. This Statue was voted by the Corporation of Bristol, and will stand in perpetual Memory

[8] Crane and Kaye give as editors 'J. Wilford, etc.' (*op. cit.*, p. 56).

of that zealous Affection, which the Citizens of Bristol worthily cherished for the Restorer of the British Constitution.

This Statue is worthy of publick Attention, not only as it regards the Memory of King William, but as it is a Work of Genius, and will, in that Respect, do Honour to this Nation. The ingenious Statuary [maker of statues] seems to have exerted the utmost Powers of his Invention, and to have laboured with the truest Judgment, as if, conscious of the vast Debt due to the fame of the Hero, he thought it incumbent on him to discharge it by the greatest Profusion of his Art.

Indeed, no Hand can give the Expression of a Hero to any Figure, unless he is blest with Genius to conceive the Reality of Heroism. There must be the true Sublime in the Artist's imagination, otherwise he will never reach or describe the Sublime of such an elevated Character.

(August 1733; from the *Free Briton* of August 16, 1733, no. 195, "Of Statuaries")

The most notable aspect of this passage is probably the emphasis, as late as 1733, on the sublime in the artist, as distinguished from the object or the audience.

A Collection of political and humorous letters, poems, and articles of news, publish'd in an evening paper, intitled, the national journal, or, country gazette. (1748)

The National Journal was published from March 22, 1746 to June 12, 1746.[9] Collected, the papers comprise a volume of about 100 pages, but this considerable bulk yields only the following passage alluding to the sublime:

Sir,

No Doubt if you have read an Imitation of Horace by Dr. Free, you will not think me guilty of Flattery, if I beg to return my publick Acknowledgments to him by your Paper, in some Observations upon his most excellent Ode.

I am, Sir, Yours,
Hertfordiensis.

The Guardian.

An Imitation of the 5th Ode of the 4th Book of Horace. . . .

II.

(2) You broke the Clouds that gather'd o'er our Heads;
You like the Spring make ev'ry Object gay:
Your Presence universal Gladness spreads,
And mends the Sunshine of the Summer's Day.

[9] *The Union List of Serials* (p. 75) gives June 28 as the terminal date as opposed to the earlier date given in the Folger Library catalogue. I could not obtain the name of the editor.

Observations.

(2) It is well known that firing Cannon will clear the Air, by dispelling the Clouds, thus the Doctor [Free] introduces at once an Allusion Military, Philosophical, and Political.

(3) I have heard a proposed Alteration.

And makes us wish to see a Summer's Day.

A Wish not at all improbable for the Soldiers to make in so cold a Climate as Scotland, and in so rigorous a Season. Another Critick proposed to read,

And Winter's Ice, converts to Flow'rs of May.

But I prefer the original Text, since of all Employments a "Mender of Sunshine" is surely the most Noble, the most Sublime, and the most Poetical.

(No. 28, Saturday, May 24, 1746, pp. 89-91, "A Criticism upon a Poem in Praise of the Duke")

Because of the fact that this comes from a collection of humorous letters, I number it among the non-serious commentaries on the sublime. Of itself it has little interest aside from its very occurrence.

The Adventurer.

The Adventurer was published November 7, 1752–March 9, 1754. Dr. J. Hawkesworth was the principal editor,[10] with Samuel Johnson also serving as an editor.

To the Adventurer

Sir,

As the business of Pantomimes is become a very serious concern, and the curiosity of mankind is perpetually thirsting after novelties, I have been at great pains to contrive an entertainment, in which every thing shall be united that is either the delight or astonishment of the present age; I have not only ransacked the fairs of Bartholomew and Southwark, but pickt up every uncommon animal, every amazing prodigy of nature, and every surprising performer, that has lately appeared within the bills of mortality. As soon as I am provided with a theatre spacious enough for my purpose, I intend to exhibit a most sublime Pantomime in the modern taste; but far more ostentatious in its feats of activity, its scenes, decorations, machinery, and monsters. A sketch of my design I shall lay before you; and you may possibly think it not inconsistent with the character of Adventurer to recommend it to public notice.

(No. III, Tuesday, November 14, 1752, pp. 13-14)

Numbers LI (Tuesday, May 1, 1753) and LVII (Tuesday, May 22, 1753) are devoted in their entirety to translations of sections from *On the Sublime*. No. LI begins:

[10] Supplied by Crane and Kaye, *op. cit.*, p. 14.

Sir,

In the library of the Benedictine Monks at Lyons, has lately been discovered a most curious manuscript of the celebrated Longinus. As I know you will eagerly embrace every opportunity of contributing to promote, or rather revive, a reverence and love for the Sacred Writings, I send you the following extract translated from this extraordinary work.

From the above we can see that as late as the 1750's Longinus was used as a gloss to demonstrate the sublimities of the Bible.

Let the Iliad be ever ranked at the head of human compositions for its spirit and sublimity; but let not the milder, and, perhaps, more insinuating and attractive beauties of the Odyssey be despised and overlooked.

(No. LXXV, Tuesday, July 24, 1753, p. 26)[11]

Thus the sublimities of Homer still have their advocates in mid-century.

However indelicate I may be esteemed, I freely confess I had rather sit in the grotto of Calypso, than in the most pompous saloon of Louis XV. The tea and the card tables can be introduced with propriety and success only in the mock-heroic, as they have been very happily in the Rape of the Lock; but the present modes of life must be forgotten when we attempt any thing in the serious or sublime poetry: for heroism disdains the luxurious refinements, the false delicacy and state of modern ages. The primeval, I was about to say, patriarchal simplicity of manners displayed in the Odyssey, is a perpetual source of true poetry, is inexpressibly pleasing to all who are uncorrupted and "unhackneyed in the ways of men," and may therefore prove equally instructive and captivating to younger readers.

(No. LXXX, Saturday, August 11, 1753, p. 58)

The Romantic view of Antiquity is easily seen in the two preceding passages. Like the Neo-classic, this view finds the age of Homer a repository of sublime subject matter, but for different reasons.

... the Natural is as strong an evidence of true genius, as the Sublime. It is in such images the Odyssey abounds; the superior utility of which, as they "come home to our business and bosoms," need not be pointed out. Let Longinus admire the majesty of Neptune whirling his chariot over the deep, surrounded by sea monsters, that gambolled before their king: the death of the dog Argus, creeping to his masters feet, whom he alone knew in his disguise, and expiring with joy for his return, is so inexpressibly pathetic, that it equals if not exceeds any of the magnificent and bolder

[11] George S. Marr, *The Periodical Essayists of the Eighteenth Century* (New York, 1924) attributes numbers 75, 80, and 101 to Joseph Warton (pp. 139-140). Walter Graham, *English Literary Periodicals* (New York, 1930) also credits to Warton nos. 49, 51, 57, 63, 71, 75, 76, 80, 83, 87, 89, 93, 97, 101, 109, 113, 116, 122, 127, 129, 133, 139 (p. 126).

images, which that excellent critic hath produced in his treatise on the sublime.

(*Ibid.*, p. 59)

Once again I invite comparison of this sublime of the homely with the passages in the chapter on oratory and rhetoric cited above in this chapter.

Against his battle of the Angels I have the same objections as against his garden of Eden [Milton's]. He has endeavoured to elevate his combatants, by giving them the enormous stature of giants in romances, books of which he was known to be fond; and the prowess and behavior of Michael as much resemble the feats of Ariosto's Knights, as his two-handed sword does the weapons of chivalry. I think the sublimity of his genius much more visible, in the first appearance of the fallen Angels; the debates of the infernal peers; the passage of Satan through the dominions of Chaos, and his adventures with Sin and Death; the mission of Raphael to Adam; the conversations between Adam and his wife; the creation; the account which Adam gives of his first sensations, and of the approach of Eve from the hand of her CREATOR: the whole behavior of Adam and Eve after the first transgression; and the prospect of the various states of the world, and history of man, exhibited in vision to Adam.

(No. CI, Tuesday, October 23, 1753, pp. 183-184)

The appreciation of the writer for the sublime possibilities of Satan certainly foreshadows the Romantic interpretation of the *Paradise Lost* that made a hero of the great rebel.

If an apology should be deemed necessary for the freedom here used with our inimitable bard [Milton], let me conclude in the words of Longinus: "Whoever was carefully to collect the blemishes of Homer, Demosthenes, Plato, and of other celebrated writers of the same rank, would find they bore not the least proportion to the sublimities and excellencies with which their works abound."

(*Ibid.*, p. 186)

[In discussing Addison's assertion that the ancients excelled the moderns in arts and sciences that depend more on genius than experience, the author of *The Adventurer* says:] That Tasso, Ariosto and Camoens, the three most celebrated of modern Epic Poets, are infinitely excelled in propriety of design of sentiment and style by Homer and Virgil, it would be serious trifling to attempt to prove: but Milton, perhaps, will not so easily resign his claim to equality, if not to superiority. Let it, however, be remembered, that if Milton be enabled to dispute the prize with the great champions of antiquity, it is intirely owing to the sublime conceptions he has copied from The Book of GOD. These, therefore, must be taken away, before we begin to make a just estimate of his genius: and from what remains, it cannot, I presume, be said, with candor and impartiality, that he has excelled

Homer, in the sublimity and variety of his thoughts, or the strength and majesty of his diction.

(No. CXXVII, Tuesday, January 22, 1754, p. 338)

Basically this argument begs the question of Milton's genius, since most great writers take the best of the literary past and shape it to their own ends. In addition, there seems to be some ambiguity here concerning the sublime conceptions in the Bible, and the sublime diction of Scripture. Does the author mean to say that Milton borrowed both, or just the former? This is the only commentary along these lines in the Context.

But no modern Orator can dare to enter the lists with Demosthenes and Tully. We have discourses, indeed, that may be admired for their perspicuity, purity, and elegance; but can produce none that abound in a sublime which whirls away the auditor like a mighty torrent, and pierces the inmost recesses of his heart like a flash of lightning; which irresistibly and instantaneously convinces, without leaving him leisure to weigh the motives of conviction.

(*Ibid.*, p. 340)

The above is another example of the eighteenth-century tendency I have noted elsewhere to find sublimity in both literature and rhetoric, and to minimize the differences between the two forms of expression.

If it be now asked, to what can we ascribe this superiority of the moderns in all the species of Ridicule; I answer, to the improved state of conversation. The great geniuses of Greece and Rome were formed during the times of a republican government: and though it be certain, as Longinus asserts, that Democracies are the nurses of true sublimity; yet monarchies and courts are more productive of politeness. The arts of civility, and the decencies of conversation, as they unite men more closely and bring them more frequently together, multiply opportunities of observing those incongruities and absurdities of behavior, on which Ridicule is founded. The ancients had more Liberty and Seriousness; the moderns have more Luxury and Laughter.

(No. CXXXIII, Tuesday, February 12, 1754, p. 378)

This statement is as reactionarily Augustan and neo-classical in spirit as several of this chapter's earlier passages are pre-romantic. Note how the author over-estimates the importance of Longinus' remarks on the interrelationship of the artist and the state of his nation.[12]

The Gray's Inn Journal. By Charles Ranger, Esq: London.

[12] See Chapter I, pp. 24-25.

The Gray's Inn Journal was published weekly during the period October 21, 1752–October 12, 1754. The editor was one Arthur Murphy, who also achieved a modest reputation as barrister and playwright.[13] The numbers of this journal treat of various subjects, but none as often as literary matters.

Milton also, who has every softer Delicacy in minute Descriptions, as well as every lofty Image in the sublime, has inserted many beautiful Colourings of this Species in his "Paradise Lost," and his "grinn'd horrible a ghastly Smile," is an admirable Instance.

(No. 4, Saturday, October 20, 1753, p. 22)

With Regard to Dramatic Poetry, our Advantage over every Nation in the Known World is, I think, very apparent. The best Critics have laid it down as a Rule that a Performance is to be judged by its Number of striking Beauties, and not by some Inaccuracies, and the Instances of occasional Conformity to the vicious Taste of the Times. . . . I remember a Passage in Voltaire's Writings, where he is at infinite Pains to bring together a String of Quotations from the best French Tragedies, to evince their great Talents at Strokes of the sublime . . .

Our Poets are sufficiently possessed of the Spirit of Tragedy, but they are not attentive to the minute Rules of correct Taste and the Trouble of blotting. It may be added that they have more real Fire, sublimer Sentiments, and Characters better marked than any Nation whatever, and in Painting and Music, we can boast so many Masters in both as might have prevented the French Author [Voltaire] from charging us with a want of Genius.

(No. 20, Saturday, February 9, 1754, p. 118)

A possible measure of the depth of Longinus' influence on English literary criticism during the span of the Context is to be found in the statement "The best critics . . . of the times". The author attributes the principle to critics in the plural sense, and his tone is that of a reference to recognized authority. Keeping Rosenberg's caveat in mind,[14] I feel that it is this kind of literary commentary that best reflects the cultural penetration of a document like *On the Sublime*.

Were I to declare in which of the three Powers of Genius, already mentioned ["Its Aim is, says he (Horace), to afford at once Utility and Delight, to offer what may be agreeable to the Fancy, and also what may conduce to the Advantages of human Life"], I think Homer, Virgil and Milton to be most eminently shining; I should ascribe to Homer the strongest and most vigorous Efforts of Imagination, and an amazing Faculty of alarming

[13] Supplied by George S. Marr, *op. cit.*, p. 157.

[14] That a dictum that sounds like Longinus may have been inspired by an entirely different source. See my Preface, p. 11.

us with noble and amazing Descriptions of all the magnificent Objects in Nature. As to our own Milton I should be inclined to declare him a Rival of the Greek Poet for a comprehensive Sublimity of Conception, and Virgil's Excellence I should place in beautiful Touches of poetic Eloquence.

(No. 47, Saturday, August 17, 1754, p. 279)

Another very common Method of Burlesque is by making frequent Application of grand and sublime Passages in our best Poets, to Things unworthy and mean. Boileau, is in my Opinion, the happiest of all modern Poets in this Particular. As Passages of this Nature are frequently mistaken for an Intent to burlesque the Author, from the Images borrowed, it may not be improper in this place to observe, Parody does not always carry with it any Sneer at the Author parodied.

(No. 50, Saturday, September 6, 1754, pp. 297-298)

In light of the place that Boileau holds as the single most important neo-classical popularizer of Longinus, the above comment showing another side to the French critic's command of the sublime is interesting.

Benjamin Martin, *The General Magazine of Arts and Sciences, Philosophical, Philological, Mathematical, and Mechanical --- 6 Vol.* (1755)

In general this magazine has no interest for a study in esthetics, which makes the use of the word 'sublime' in the introduction to the work somewhat more interesting, culturally speaking, than it would ordinarily be.

The fourth great Part [of the magazine] will consist of a continued Series of mathematical and mechanical Institutes or Principles of geometrical Science, beginning with those that are the most simple and easy, and proceeding to the more compounded and sublime . . .

(An Account of the Plan and Design of this Magazine, p. viii)

No one would accuse the author in this case of using the sublime in any of the esthetic senses that we have seen in this chapter!

There is in this relatively modest sampling a variety of usages of the sublime that is quite astonishing. Nearly every quotation offers a different aspect of the term. By way of summary, this prolix usage is outlined as follows:

1. Utility versus non-utility *vis-à-vis* the sublime
2. The false sublime; sublime used satirically
3. French-English collaboration on literary commentary pertaining to the sublime
4. The periodical as an organ for the serious critic on the sublime, like Dennis

5. The sublime as simplicity
6. The sword 'sublime' used in a non-literary sense
7. The sublime related to intellectual history
8. Sublimity and scripture
9. Sublimity and the natural sublime
10. Longinus criticized negatively
11. The sublime as residing in the artist
12. Sublimity in Homer
13. Sublimity in Milton's Satan

There is no telling what conclusions could be developed concerning the context of the eighteenth-century sublime, if a full-length study of the era's periodicals were to be undertaken; the present chapter at least serves notice of the complexity of the situation.

VII

HOLY SCRIPTURES

It is well known that a number of writers on the eighteenth-century sublime, either under the influence of Longinus or independently, found in the Holy Scriptures the preeminent source for the sublime. A search of the Folger Library's holdings pertinent to this general area, however, turned up a disappointingly small number of passages suitable for our study. As a result the entries in this chapter are only five, and all of them date from the years before the turn of the eighteenth century. I present them, nevertheless, with the hope that they will contribute just a bit to the picture of the eighteenth-century sublime.

Robert Boyle, *Some considerations touching the style of the Holy Scriptures. Extracted from several parts of a Discourse (concerning divers Particulars belonging to the Bible) Written divers Years since to a Friend.* (1663)

Boyle is a relativist as to what comprises rhetorical eloquence in the style of a given time and place (pp. 158-170), his discussion of the matter being one of the most judicious seventeenth-century English denials of the 'Rules' that one is likely to find.

What Boyle says in his allusions to the sublime takes on added interest because of the early date of this document; he states in "To the Reader" that he wrote the treatise ten years previous to the date of publication, so I date it with some assurance from *circa* 1653.

And if such Dilucidation [critical commentary and annotation on Roman literature] be necessary to make us value writings that treat of familiar and secular affairs, and were written in an European Language, & in Times and Countries much nearer ours, how much do you think we must lose of the Elegancy of the Book of Job, the Psalms of David, the Song of Salomon, and other Sacred composures, which not only treat oftentimes of sublime and supernatural Mysteries, but were written in very remote Regions so many Ages ago, amidst Circumstances to most of which we cannot but be strangers? And thus much for my first general Consideration. (pp. 15-16)

And shall we then wonder that those Texts of Scripture, that treat of the Nature and Decrees of God, and of such sublime Mysteries as the Trinity, the Incarnation, the Influence of the Spirit upon the Soul of man, and such other abstruse things, which it cannot be Reasonably expected that humane words should keep from being hard to be comprehended by humane understandings, should be Obscure to us, especially if we suffer our not understanding their full meaning at first to deter us from endeavouring to find it out by further study? (p. 39)

Nay, there is no other Book whatsoever that Teaches us any thing at all, concerning divers of these sublime Subjects, that may be safely Rely'd on, save in what it is beholden to the Scripture for. (p. 104)

Thus when God himself is pleas'd to reveal what is Vice or Virtue, Sublime or Despicable, Truth or Falshood, Happiness or Misery, I have an otherguess Acquiescence in his Decisions, than in the same met with in an human Author, who having necessarily Frailties and Passions, is both obnoxious to Mistake, and capable to Deceive. (p. 125)

Nay, many of the very Flowers of Rhetorick growing there [the instructional passages in the Bible], have (like the Marygold that in hot Countries points at the Sunn) a Virtue of hinting the usefullest and the sublimest Truths: the Bible being in this like the Tree of Life, (flourishing in the New Jerusalem) which not only afforded seasonable fruit, but of which the very "Leaves were for the healing of the Nations." (p. 131)

Some famous Writers have Challeng'd Demosthenes and Cicero, to compare with the Prophet Esay [sic]; in whom they have not only Admir'd that Lofty Strain which Artists have term'd the Sublime Character, but even that Harmonious Disposition and Sound of Words, (I mean in their Original) which the French prettily call, "La cadence des Periodes." (pp. 173-174)

"'Tis pleasant to Observe in how many of such Copies of Verses [profane, sensual, etc.], the Themes appear to have been made to the Conceits, not the Conceits for the Themes; how often the Words are not so Properly the Cloaths of the Matter, as the Matter the Stuffing of the Words; how frequently Sublime Non-sense passes for Sublime Wit; and (though according to my Notion of it, that is indeed True Wit, which 'tis more easie to Understand, than 'tis not to Admire it,) how commonly Confus'd Notions, and Abortive or Unlick'd Conceptions are in Exotick Language, or Ambiguous Expressions, expos'd to the Uncertain Adoption of the Courteous Reader."[1] (p. 184)

An interesting association here of Boyle's familiar drive for clarity of expression, in line with the policy of the Royal Society's emphasis in the 1660's, with the sublime. This kind of sublime of simplicity is, of course, not exactly what Longinus delineated, though who is to say

[1] This and the following passage occur in a lengthy section running from page 177 to 220, which the author calls a long digression against profaneness. The entire 44-page passage is set off in quotation marks, but Boyle does not use it as the opinion of another persona in the manner, say, of a satirist like Swift.

that the results of the pursuit of such sublimity by the two lines of thinking would be very different after all?

"Certainly, Transcendent Wits, when once they Addict themselves to Theological Composures, Improve and Grace most excellently Themes so capable of Being so Improv'd. They need small Time to Signalize their Pens; for Possessing already in a Sublime Degree all the Requisites and Appropriates of Rare Writers, they need but Apply that Choice Knowledg and Charming Eloquence to Divine Subjects, to handle them to Admiration . . ." (p. 224)

It is interesting to note that, although Boyle ostensibly devotes this work to considerations of style, he makes at least six allusions to the sublime in a broader, or even contrasting, sense.

Benjamin Keach, *Troposchematologia: Tropes and Figures; or, a treatise of the metaphors, allegories, and express similitudes, etc. contained in the Bible of the Old and New Testament . . .* (1682)

This is an enormous volume of well over 1,000 pages, which makes it rather formidable to peruse for allusions to the sublime. A search of the "Epistle to the Reader" developed the following extracts, but similar efforts in other parts of the work were not so successful.

And if we improve not all these Mercies [the advantages aiding to the knowledge of Scripture that Keach sees as existing in his England as never before] to the acquisition of this divine and sublime Knowledg, how inexcusable shall we be, and how just in God, should he in one day deprive us of all?

(the Epistle.)

And tho the Stile of the Holy Scripture is not varnish'd with that Delicacy of superficial Ornament, that jingling Cadence of Sounds, and Fancy-pleasing Trifles, as the pompous Oratory of Greece and Rome is beautified with; yet it has Qualities far more excellent: 'Tis grave and masculine; it hath a magnificent, commanding Elegance, peculiar to it self, suitable to the lofty Things it treats of, which no other Writing can imitate, reaching the inner Rooms of the Soul, and stirring up Affections, in so spiritual and sublime a kind, as the artificial Bravery of Cicero, or Quintilian's Elocution could never do.

(*Ibid.*)

Surely no more explicit opposition of rhetoric and the sublime is to be found in our period than the one in the above passage.

And tho there is a great difference between Metaphorical or Allegorical, and Typical Scriptures [that is, type, or factual; historical]; yet we thought an Essay to open the most eminent Types found in the Old-Testament, would well suit with this sublime Subject . . .

(From remarks on the general purpose of the work.)

Simon Patrick, *A paraphrase upon the books of Eccleasiastes and the Song of Solomon. With arguments to each chapter, and annotations thereupon. By Symon Patrick D.D. Dean of Peterburgh, and one of His Majesties chaplains in ordinary.* (1685)

Some shall service I hope I have performed in the Explication of these two holy Books. [Ecclesiastes & Song of Solomon]. In the first of which (according to the ancient Opinion) the foundation is laid for a due progress unto the other: the Mind not being fitted for such sublime thoughts, as lye hid under the Figures, in the Book of Canticles, till it hath learnt by the Ecclesiastes, the vanity of all earthly Enjoyments; and, by looking down upon them with contempt, be disposed to value heavenly Blessings. To this purpose Origen discourses in his Preface to the Song of Songs.

(The Epistle Dedicatory.)

Patrick opposes 'sublime thoughts' and 'figures'.

Simon Patrick, *The Song of Solomon paraphrased. With annotations.* (1685)

Nor doth it seem hard, either to find out what that spiritual matter is, of which the Wise man here treats (especially, since all Christian Writers have from the beginning applied this Song to Christ and his Church) or to give an account of the rise and Original of such sublime contemplations: which I take to be this. [Here follows Biblical history.]

(Preface, p. ii)

Thomas Beverley, *An exposition of the divinely prophetick song of songs which is Solomons. Beginning with the reign of David and Solomon, ending in the glorious kingdom of our Lord Jesus Christ. Adjusted to the expositor's Line of time, and Illustrating it. And composed into verse.* (1687)

The only mention of the sublime in the entire volume occurs on the first page of the Preface. There are, however, numerous places in the annotations that the sublime would have been appropriate for mentioning, in connection with both Biblical subject matter and the requirements of rhetoric.

It is enough known, that the Jews prohibit any to read it [Song of Songs], till the Sacerdotal or Thirtieth Year of Age; Now though this may favor of an over Fear, which in Religious Matters dwells at the next door to Superstition; Yet still it shews of how sublime a Majesty and Estimation this Song appear'd to them.

John Edwards, *A discourse concerning the authority, stile, and perfection of the books of the old and new testament.* (1693)

The text of Edwards' work runs 430 pages; the excerpts from it below make no claim to completeness of its references to the sublime.

The Internal Testimonies or Arguments to evince the Authority of the Holy Scriptures, viz. 1. The Matter of them, that is, the Sublime Verities, the Holy Rules, the Accomplish'd Prophecies contain'd in them . . .

(From the heading of the first chapter, p. 1)

A God is plainly discovered in them [Scriptures], for the most improved Creatures could never have reach'd to this pitch. Any serious and thinking Man cannot but discern the peculiar Turn and singular Contrivance of these Mysterious Doctrines, which argue them to be Divine. We may therefore believe the Writings of the Prophets and Apostles to be the Word of God, because of the wonderful Height and Sublimity of those Truths which are contained in them. (p. 5)

And here [the Gospel] also you will find an excellent and admirable Composition of Simplicity and Majesty together. Though the Strain be High and Lofty, yet you may observe that at the same time it is Humble and Condescending. To which purpose a Learned Father saith well, "The Language of Divine Wisdom in the Scripture is Low, but the Sense is Sublime and Heavenly; whereas on the contrary, the Phrase of Heathen Writers is Splendid, but the things couched in them are Poor and Mean." The Scripture-Writers make it not their work to set off and commend their Writings, by being Elaborate and Exact. (pp. 29-30)

The tenor of this passage is close to that of Longinus himself, although the 'Learned Father' quoted therein is obviously not the Greek critic.[2]

In support of his statement that the styles of the various contributions to the Scriptures (apparently he means here both Testaments) show an extraordinary uniformity, Edwards quotes the following passage from *Judg Hale of the Knowledg of God, and of our Selves*:

Excellently to this purpose a very Wise and Judicious Man thus speaks: "When several Men in several Ages, not brought up under the same Education, write, it is not possible to find Unity in their Tenents or Positions, because their Spirits, Judgments and Fancies are different; but where so many several Authors, speaking and writing at several times, agree not only in Matters Dogmatical, of sublime and difficult Natures, but also in Predictions of future and contingent Events, whereof it is impossible for humane Understanding to make a Discovery, without a superior Discovery made to

[2] At the bottom of p. 29 there is a footnote giving the source of the quotation along with its equivalent in Greek. It reads: Lib. 1 [the Greek passage] Isid. Pelus. Ep. 1. 5. This probably means the first Epistle of the first Book of Isidore of Pelusium. The translation in the *Discourse* is probably by Edwards.

it, I must needs conclude one and the same Divine Spirit declared the same Truths to these several Men." (p. 39)

In concluding this chapter on the Bible and the sublime, I am tempted to the observation that the contents partly make up for their brevity by their wide-ranging usage of the word 'sublime'.

VIII

LETTERS

This chapter offers a very restricted sampling, but the four entries seemed of sufficient worth to justify inclusion in the Context.

Claudius Mauger, *French and English letters, upon all subjects, mean and sublime . . . Printed by Tho. Royscroft and sold by Samuel Lawndes, Second edition.* (1676)

This book of some 300 pages has the French on the left page and the English on the right. Mauger is evidently a Frenchman, and the English versions of the letters tend toward a literal translation of the French. Curiously enough, in view of the name of the volume, the word 'sublime' occurs practically not at all in the text. Importantly, the word 'sublime' in the title of the English version is a translation of the French title's 'grands', thus showing that only two years after Boileau's translation of Longinus the word 'sublime' in a non-rhetorical sense was current in secondary works in both France and England.

You never testifie any thing to me but admiration for Master – – – – – as if his learning composed all his good fortune, and as if it were enough to be knowing to be perfectly happy. Although I revere his person, and honour his knowledge, yet I am obliged to confess ingeniously [sic], that science is not able to render a man content in the Earth, for everyone knows that grief is affixed to it, that great Scholars are hidden Martyrs, who give themselves much trouble, to arrive to the end of their intentions. . . . One may say, they renounce the sweetness of life, when they seek learning with so much eagerness, that they are blind enough to prefer labour before pleasure; and that they are resolved to die, while their blood boyles still in the veins, and the vigour of their body priviledges them from all the attaques of death. Extol to me as much as you please that sublime [in this case, Mauger's original is "sublime."] man, as you call him, you will never perswade me to be his follower; though with you I admire him, yet I have no mind to imitate him. I love my liberty too well, to lose it for so difficult an acquisition.

(Letter XLVI, to Doctor Hemery, London, August 25, 1675; pp. 163-7)

You know that I have no other pensil than a barren Pen, nor colours but imperfect words, and as one cannot make a Picture without shadows, what shall I do in this case to find any, seeing there is nothing in her but what is resplendent? Therefore not disobey you [sic], content your self with the idea which I give you of her, by telling you that she is a good soul much fearing God, and to do her right, she is a true rendezvous of all vertues, she has a sublime [Mauger's original: 'elévé'] wit, an admirable judgment, a happy memory, a strong reasoning, a charming discourse, she speaks all languages, sings beyond expression, touches the Lute to astonishment, dances perfectly, she is beautiful as an Angel . . .

(Letter LXVI, to my Lord the Earl of – – – – –, London, Sept. 16, 1675; p. 233)

Your sublime [Mauger's original: 'elévé'] wit surprises your admirers, they are taken with your great judgment, your fine memory makes you be considered of every one, and the modesty which is so natural to you, joined to your humility so laudable, extols you in all places.

(Letter LXX, to Madam Clemence Hovell, [no place or date given]; p. 247)

. . . But it is to be feared lest Nature should be jealous of your work, for you make Forrests, Eminences, Valleys, and Rivers, besides so many fine views with which you adorn them, that it seems that you have a desire to surmount her. However, permit me to tell you, that she has much advantage over you, since all her care is but to repair the ruines which accidents do to her, and that yours is but to make some to enrich your pictures with the remainders of old Palaces and Castles. But what I do admire in your Art, is that your Pencil is so elevated [Mauger's original: 'elévé' which is above translated 'sublime'] that it reaches even to the Stars, and that it represents to us Aurora so naturally, that though one be in the heart of Winter, one would think that he were in the Spring. . . .

(Letter LXXIV, to my Brother-in-law, Master G. Keyser, Picture-drawer, London, July 10, 1675; pp. 295 & 261)

Gilbert Burnet, *Some letters. Containing, an account of what seemed most remarkable in Switzerland, Italy, etc.* (Rotterdam, 1686)

These letters are devoted mainly to politics, economics, commerce, religion, husbandry, architecture, and historical anecdotes. There are barely a dozen passages of natural description, and these are short. None contains the word 'sublime'. I found only one mentioning of sublime, and that in a context especially close to the heart of a divine like Burnet.

He [a cleric named Tronchin] is a man of Extraordinary vertue and of a readiness to oblige and serve all persons, that has scarce any measures. His Sermons have a sublimity in them that strikes the hearer as well as it edifies him. His thoughts are noble, and his Eloquence is Masculine and exact, and has all the Majesty of the chair in it tempered with all the softness of persuasion, so that he not only convinces his hearers, but subdues them and triumphs over them.

(Fifth of the volume's five letters, p. 260)

Actually, this usage is one of the more rhetoric-orientcd in the Context.

Letters of the Critical Club, containing Miscellaneous Observations upon Men, Manners, and Writings. Begun in the Month of January, 1738 and published Monthly at Edinburgh. Volume I. From the Month of January, to the Month of June, inclusive. . . . (Edinburgh, 1738)

Letter XII, Monday, February 27, 1738, by 'Will Portly' (pp. 81-88), is a piece on the picturesque and terrible. It denies that the pleasure from beholding terror in art stems from the sense of safety of the beholder, and attributes the pleasure, rather, to the art of the artist. Hence, this letter debates in terms that Burke was to use twenty years later in his *Enquiry*, but takes the opposite position. I mention this letter because it is obliquely related to the problem of the sublime, and because it has unusual interest *per se*.

Letter XXVIII, Wednesday, May 17, 1738, by 'Ned Rhymer' (pp. 229-236) is significant in a negative way. It is concerned with the beauties of nature, and the immensity of the universe, and hence contains many passages where the use of the word 'sublime' would have been appropriate. The word never occurs, however.

Or, if your Patience cannot endure much reading, and you incline more for Chit-Chat, go into the Booksellers Shops and publick Libraries, and you'll find there, in every Corner, Clubs of Philosophers, talking very sagely about her [Selima, who in this context obviously stands for virtue]; sometimes taking her to pieces, and examining her with the outmost Nicety; sometimes patching her up in such an odd Dress, as she looks scarce like herself; but, for the most Part, all (except your alamode Folks) talk well of her; and tho' she meets with bad Treatment, when present, yet, when absent, she is seldom or never abus'd or scandalized. These Philosophers are easily known, both by their Looks and Dress; they resemble, in both, pretty much the Sublimity of a Garret, and in outward Appearance are not very unlike Virtue in Rags.

(From Letter XXXIII, Saturday, June 10, 1738, by 'Dick Crotchet"; pp. 279-80)

The comment I made above really applies to the letters as a whole in this sizable volume (304 pages). There are numerous passages where one might reasonably expect to find the word 'sublime' used, but a close reading of the first half of the collection, and a glance at the second turned up only the negative usage of Letter XXXIII.

William Melmoth, *Letters on several subjects. By the late Sir Thomas Fitzosborne, Bart.*[1] *Published from the Copies found among his Papers.* (1748)

The subjects of the letters are literary and non-literary.

To say of this noble work [Pope's *Iliad*], that it is the best which ever appeared of the kind, would be speaking in much lower terms than it deserves; the world perhaps scarce ever before saw a truly poetical translation: for, as Denham observes,

> Such is our pride, our folly, or our fate,
> That few, but those who cannot write, translate.

But Mr. Pope seems in most places to have been inspired with the same sublime spirit that animates his original; as he often takes fire from a single hint in his author, and blazes out even with a stronger and brighter flame of poetry.

(Letter XI, pp. 41-2)

I fear the enthusiastic admirers of Homer would look upon me with much indignation, were they to hear me speak of any thing in modern language as equal to the strength and majesty of that great father of poetry. But as the following passage has been quoted by a celebrated author of antiquity [Longinus], as an instance of the true Sublime, I will leave it to you to determine whether the translation has not at least as just a claim to that character as the original. [Here follow five lines of Homer's Greek, and then six lines of Pope, beginning "As torrents roll, encreas'd by num'rous rills."]

(*Ibid.*, p. 45)

It must be confessed however, these admirers of the false sublime in friendship, talk upon this subject with so much caution and in such general terms, that one is inclined to think they themselves a little suspected the validity of those very principles they would inculcate. [The idea suggested by certain writers of Antiquity that justice itself ought to yield in some cases to the desires of supreme friendship.]

(Letter XV, p. 69)

This is quite obviously an unusual non-literary use of the sublime.

One cannot indeed but regret that he [Dr. Tillotson], who abounds with such noble and generous sentiments, should want the art of setting them off

[1] The card catalogue of the Folger Shakespeare Library identifies Sir Thomas Fitzosborne as a pseudonym for William Melmoth.

with all the advantage they deserve; that the Sublime in morals should not be attended with a suitable elevation of language.

(Letter XXIV, p. 110)

Apparently Melmoth sees the sublime as comprising both matter and manner. In this he is close to the spirit of *On the Sublime.*

IX

JOHN DENNIS ON THE SUBLIME

The allusions of John Dennis to the sublime form this chapter, included in the Context because of the fact that Dennis is of foremost importance in the history of the eighteenth-century sublime, and yet has not been the subject of a full-length study in this connection.[1] Not that I pretend to such a study here, but rather intend to present all together in one place the corpus of Dennis' usages of the word 'sublime'.

My source throughout for the quotations from Dennis is E. N. Hooker, ed., *The Critical Works of John Dennis* (Baltimore, 1939). In his introduction, Hooker informs us of Monk's implication that Dennis practically ignored the category of the beautiful, and in fact failed to recognize that it was a category in the first place. It would seem that Dennis' crime of negligence stemmed from his penchant for rating the passions according to their intensity instead of by their quality as both Monk and Hooker apparently feel he ought to have done. Hooker does defend Dennis to the extent that he says he tried to define the unique quality, contributed by reflection, that differentiates the enthusiastic from the ordinary esthetic responses, and thus, by implication, acknowledged the two separate categories of the sublime and the beautiful.

Hooker goes on to say that Dennis in a letter of 1717 attached names to the categories, to wit, the 'pulchrum' for the experience in which enthusiastic passion (or passion in which reflection has an active role) is involved, and the 'dulce' for the experience in which ordinary, non-reflective passion holds sway. As far as Hooker is concerned, the identical categories existed in Dennis' critical thought as in Addison's except that it was reserved for the latter critic to score the *coup* of naming them the sublime and the beautiful.[2]

[1] In Chapter I, I said that Monk barely acknowledges that Dennis is an important figure in the history of the sublime, and that grudgingly (p. 25), while Hamilton is more appreciative and fair, but just as brief (pp. 40-41).

[2] All of Hooker's remarks that I have summarized to this point occur on p. xcv of his Introduction in Vol. II.

It is to the extent that Dennis does not categorize the sources and responses accruing to the sublime, however, that he assumes added interest for this Context, since it is virtually meaningless to describe all of the attributes of the sublime on the one hand, and those of the beautiful on the other. And that applies, say, to either the poem or the reader of the poem. It would seem that all we can say, and it is not far from Dennis, is that the sublime can be defined only in the most general terms as regards the subject of the art work's content and the intensity of the person's response thereto. We have seen that Longinus stopped short of trying to determine the ineffable, and Dennis evidently followed his example in part.

But only in part, for Dennis has much more to say about the passions than does *On the Sublime*. (It will be remembered that the essay on the passions which Longinus is supposed to have appended to his treatise has never been recovered.) Dennis believes that the chief characteristic of poetry is passion, and that all genius is passion, both for the reason that they move. And since the desideratum of poetry is the greatest amount of passion possible, poetry must be built of the greatest possible thoughts and images. And these, in turn, come from religious subjects, which Dennis considers to be from their very nature the most profound. To us, of course, all of this seems somewhat *a priori* and circular, but is self-evident to Dennis.

Another assumption made by Dennis without too much effort at demonstration is that English is more elevated and harmonious by nature than French. Whether or not he is right in this, the important point is that he is aware of the aural element in evaluating poetry.

Having established, hopefully, the fundamentals of Dennis' view of the sublime, I turn to the large number of examples of his usage, remembering that part of the purpose of the Context is the creation of a compendium where the student can find most of Dennis' pronouncements on our subject. I observe the same chronology, which is not strict, as Hooker.

I am not so miserably mistaken, as to think rhiming essential to our English Poetry. I am far better acquainted with Milton, than that comes to. Who without the assistance of Rhime, is one of the most sublime of our English Poets. Nay, there is something so transcendentally sublime in his first, second, and sixth Books, that were the language as pure as the Images are vast and daring, I do not believe it could be equall'd, no, not in all Antiquity.

(Preface to *The Passion of Byblis*, p. 3)

It is at once apparent that Dennis does not try to avoid the issue, so much debated in his time, of the place of rhyme in poetry. This is the first of several passages we will see that discuss the interrelationship of rhyme and the sublime in poetry, and because of the definition that Dennis gives the latter these passages inevitably must consider both poetry and reader.

Never man thought more clearly, more truly, more justly than he [Roscommon] did; never man express'd himself more fitly and more becomingly. In every thing that he writ, his Language was as perfect as his Conceptions were often sublime. On every thing that came from him, he has stamped the Character not only of an exalted Wit,[3] but of a Man of a high Condition, and of a courtly Mind.

(*Ibid.*, p. 4)

In his remarks on Lord Roscommon, Dennis is thinking particularly of the former's translation of Horace's *Art of Poetry*. Notice that it is Roscommon's conceptions that are sublime, while 'perfect' is the word used to describe his language.

For the Pindaric way, if you'l give credit to a great Master, is dangerous both to Writer and Reader. The first must have some qualities at the time of writing, which are rarely to be found together, as Precipitation and Address, Boldness and Decency, Sublimeness and Clearness, Fury and Sense ...

(Preface to *Miscellanies in Verse and Prose*, p. 6)

In this definition by opposites, not uncommon in our period, we gather that Dennis appreciates the sublime's potential for creating an effect through obscurity. This was to become an important aspect of the natural sublime.

A Man may in many places of Mr. Waller's Works, see not only Wit, Spirit, good Sence, but a happy and delicate turn of Thought, with clearness, boldness, justness, sublimeness, and gallantry.

(*The Impartial Critick: Or Some Observations upon a Late Book, Entituled, A Short View of Tragedy, Written by Mr. Rymer*, 1693, p. 13)

The best thing in the World is as liable to be ridicul'd as the silliest. Has not Scarron impudently diverted all Europe at the Expence of Virgil, the best of Poets, and the justest of Writers? upon which an ingenious French-man has made this Observation, That as all Human Grandeur is but Folly, so Sublimeness and the Ridiculum are very nearly related.

(*Ibid.*, "First Dialogue", p. 16)

[3] In his Preface to *Miscellanies in Verse and Prose* (1693) Dennis defines wit as a 'just mixture of Reason and Extravagance'.

In addition to referring to what is presumably the source of the expression 'from the sublime to the ridiculous', Dennis shows here that he is well aware of the ubiquitous peril, in the attempt to achieve the sublime, of producing instead some such unwanted effect as bathos, bombast, or fustian.

Freeman. ... And Terrour and Compassion may be ixcited without a Chorus, perhaps better than with it.

Beaumont. Pray, why so?

Freeman. Because the Chorus in some measure must calm an Audience which the Episode disturb'd by its Sublimity, and by its Pathetick ...

(*Ibid.*, "Fourth Dialogue", p. 33)

The Ode (says Rapin) ought to have as much greatness, elevation and violence, as the Eglogue is oblig'd to have modesty, restraint and simplicity. It is not only great by the sublimeness of its Spirit, but by the greatness of its Subjects.

(Preface to *The Court of Death*, p. 42)

Dennis echoes Longinus in his emphasis on the spirit underlying an impassioned poem.

But 'tis now time to consider how far he [Pindar] may be imitated in our Language and Climate. An English Writer may endeavor to imitate him in several of his greatest qualities, by the Genius of our Nation, which is bold and sublime, as Mr. Waller has observ'd. But then he ought to be discreet in his boldness; for our Language is not capable of some of the most violent figures of Pindar; and in aiming at two of his principal qualities, which are his Sublimity and his Magnificence, he ought carefully to avoid two things, and those are Fustian and Superfluity of Epithetes ... it may serve for an eternal rule, that there can be no Fustian, for a man of Sense must have a very fantastick opinion of himself, if he thinks that the false Sublime can warm him.

(*Ibid.*, p. 43)

The third [error of Cowley in imitating Pindar's odes] is the Neglect of his Style, which seems in several places not to have Pomp and Majesty enough to answer the sublimeness of Pindar's Genius.

(*Ibid.*, p. 44)

For tho' true Sublimity, like Grace, may exalt Nature, it can never invert it.

(*Ibid.*, p. 91)

The terrible and tender are every where in the *Aeneis*; but the last of them is never to be seen in *Prince Arthur*, and the first but very rarely, though it is exceeding proper for epick Poetry, as being in its own Nature sublime, and grave, and majestick.

(*Ibid.*, p. 127)

So that the Stage is not only absolutely necessary for the instructing and humanizing those who are not Christians, but (the best of all human Things) to prepare them for the sublimer Doctrines of the Church.

(*The Usefulness of the Stage*, 1698, p. 185)

Thus Dennis introduces the sublime into his defense of the stage against the attack of the Puritan forces that began in earnest after the Restoration. This is the utilitarian side, if you will, of Dennis on the sublime.

I resolv'd therefore, to do my Endeavor to treat this Subject, with something at least, of that at once Sublime and Pathetick Air, which reigns in the renown'd Sophocles. I resolv'd to use some Effort to make the Greatness of the Sentiments, and of the Images, answer to the Height of the Subject; and the Dignity of the Expression, to the Greatness of the Sentiments. I design'd in this Poem, to make Terror the prevailing Passion, which is likewise the predominant Passion in that admirable Grecian.

(Preface to *Rinaldo and Armida*, 1699, p. 195)

It can be seen that Dennis does not find terror and the sublime incompatible as Longinus does.

So that from what we have said, we may venture to lay down this Definition of Poetical Genius: Poetical Genius, in a Poem, is the true Expression of Ordinary or Enthusiastick Passions proceeding from Ideas to which it naturally belongs; and Poetical Genius, in a Poet, is the Power of expressing such Passion worthily: And the Sublime is a great Thought, express'd with the Enthusiasm that belongs to it, which the Reader will find agreeable to the Doctrine of Cecilius. Longinus, I must confess, has not told us what the Sublime is, because Cecilius, it seems, had done that before him. Tho' methinks, it was a very great Fault, in so great a Man as Longinus, to write a Book which could not be understood, but by another Man's Writings; especially when he saw that those Writings were so very defective, that they were not likely to last. But tho' Longinus does not directly tell us what the Sublime is, yet in the first Six or Seven Chapters of his Book, he takes a great deal of Pains to set before us the Effects which it produces in the Minds of Men; as for Example, That it causes in them Admiration and Surprize; a noble Pride, and a noble Vigour, an invincible Force, transporting the Soul from its ordinary Situation, and a Transport, and a Fulness of Joy mingled with Astonishment. These are the Effects that Longinus tells us, the Sublime produces in the Minds of Men. Now I have endeavor'd to shew, what it is in Poetry that works these Effects. So that, take the Cause and the Effects together, and you have the Sublime.

(*The Advancement and Reformation of Modern Poetry*, 1701, p. 222)

As Dennis says, you have the sublime, but not exactly the sublime of Longinus, because *On the Sublime* has more to say on the cause of the sublime than Dennis is either able to, or chooses to, see. We have discovered as much in Chapter I.

> For their [the ancient poets'] Invocations, Apostrophes, and the like, which were all of them either a sort of Prayers, or Divine Attestations, they are most of them very Sublime, and attended with a strong Enthusiasm.
>
> (*Ibid.*, p. 231)

Another example of the way in which Dennis links religion and the sublime.

> For the Apostrophe, we have given Examples of it already, and therefore we shall only say here, that Longinus mentions it as one of the Figures that contribute the most to the sublime.
>
> (*Ibid.*, p. 232)

The above declaration is pretty surely conclusive evidence of one of two possible situations. Either Dennis in this passage, as opposed to the one from page 222 of *The Advancement* above, sees certain causes of the sublime in Longinus, or, more probably, he means literally that such devices as Figures merely contribute to the sublime, but are definitely not to be considered a cause.

> In short, any Thing that immediately concerns Revelation, has so great an Influence upon Poetry, that it is able to change even the Nature of Writing, and exalt that very sort of Poetry, which by its Character is Low and Humble; as for Example, The Eclogue. The Fourth Eclogue of Virgil, will be easily granted by all to be very Sublime. But what is it that makes it so? Why, there is at once in that Eclogue, an Invocation, and an Apostrophe, and a Revelation of sundry Miracles to come.
>
> (*Ibid.*, p. 233)

Obviously, Dennis argues quite dogmatically about the sublime when Revelation is involved, since he proceeds on the assumption that the sublimity of the latter is self-evident. Thus any poetic genre is potentially sublime if it alludes to Revelation. This is the Longinian indifference to genre with a difference!

> But it is not only in his Invocation, that Lucretius is pleas'd to have Recourse to Religion: For after that in the Two First Books, he has been taking a great deal of pains to destroy the Belief of Gods and Providence, that in his Third he may be very Poetical, and very Sublime, he is forc'd to erect a new Divinity in the Room of those whom he has been just subverting, and that is Nature; tho' by what he makes her say, in that noble Prosopopoeia, we might very well mistake her for Providence.
>
> (*Ibid.*, p. 250)

Indeed, sometimes he [Lucretius] was so, for I do not remember, that I affirmed, that there can be no Poetry without Religion, but only, that Religion gives Occasion for the best, the greatest, and the most exalted, and it makes for my purpose sufficiently, that Lucretius is most Poetical and Sublime, where he is Religious.

(*Ibid.*)

I point out for the last time what will indeed occur again and again in Dennis' criticism, the assumed principle of the sublime in religion and the circular reasoning therefrom.

So that in Places where there is no mention of Religion, Lucretius in some measure, derives from that his Impetuous Golden Torrent of Verse, his Vehemence and his Sublimity.

(*Ibid.*, p. 251)

We could well wish that Dennis had seen fit to expand a bit on the above, where there is 'no mention of Religion'!

But in a sublime and accomplish'd Poem, the Reason, and the Passions, and Senses are pleas'd at the same Time superlatively.

(*Ibid.*, p. 263)

On the contrary, no Man [Milton] knew them [Aristotle's rules] better, or esteemed them more, because no Man had an Understanding that was more able to comprehend the necessity of them; and therefore when he mention'd them in a little Treatise which he wrote to Mr. Hartlib, he calls the Art which treats of them, a sublime Art.

(*The Grounds of Criticism in Poetry*, 1704, p. 333)

The main value of the above passage is that it adds to my slender listing of references to the sublime by Milton.

And by laying down either the general Rules of it [Poetry], or by tracing out that sublime Art . . .

(*Ibid.*, p. 335)

And such are the Thoughts concerning God, which are spread thro that Divine Dialogue between God and Adam, in the Eighth Book of the same Poem [*Paradise Lost*]: I believe the Reader will pardon the length if I repeat it, which I am very much inclin'd to do, not only because I challenge the most zealous Admirers of Antiquity to produce any thing like it, from among all the Dialogues in Homer and Virgil, that are between either a God or a Man, or between one God and another; but because the Reader who sees the Inequalities in it, will easily see that it derives its Greatness and its Sublimity from the becoming Thoughts which it has of the Deity.

(*Ibid.*, p. 342)

The Reader may easily see, that here [Adam's description to Raphael of God in *Paradise Lost* VIII] is all that is great and sublime in Reason, express'd with the Spirit of that just Admiration, with which such worthy Thoughts of the Deity must naturally fill the Soul.

(*Ibid.*, p. 344)

And therefore whenever in Poetry there is a great Spirit which is derived from Ideas, whose Objects are unworthy to move the Soul of a great and wise Man, then that Spirit is either false, or at least has nothing sublimely admirable in it.

(*Ibid.*, p. 345)

And this puts me in mind of an extraordinary Argument of Monsieur Paschal, proving the Divinity of our Saviour by the Simplicity of his Stile; for, says he, our Saviour speaks of the sublimest Subjects, even the Glories of the Kingdom of Heaven, without being moved at all, which shows that he was really God . . .

(*Ibid.*, p. 353)

And now I mention Longinus, this is the properest place to shew, by his Authority, that Religious Ideas are the most proper to give Greatness and Sublimity to a Discourse. And this I shall shew, First, by his Examples; and, Secondly, by his Precepts.

(*Ibid.*, p. 357)

I now come to the Precepts of Longinus, and pretend to shew from them, that the greatest Sublimity is to be deriv'd from Religious Ideas.

(*Ibid.*, p. 358)

Despite his repeated assertions that he takes his ideas of the sublime in religion from Longinus, a familiarity with both critics reveals the fact that Dennis leans more to the religious side, Longinus more to the esthetic, as I have defined it in Chapter I.

. . . tho Longinus did by long Study and Habitude know the Sublime when he saw it, as well as any Man, yet he had not so clear a Knowledge of the nature of it, as to explain it clearly to others. For if he had done that, as the Objector says, he would have defin'd it; but he has been so far from defining it, that in one place he has given an account of it that is contrary to the true nature of it. For he tells us in that Chapter which treats of the Fountains of Sublimity, that Loftiness is often without any Passion at all; which is contrary to the true nature of it. The Sublime is indeed often without common Passion, as ordinary Passion is often without that. But then it is never without Enthusiastick Passion: For the Sublime is nothing else but a great Thought, or great Thoughts moving the Soul from its ordinary Situation by the Enthusiasm which naturally attends them. Now Longinus, by affirming that the Sublime may be without not only that, but ordinary Passion, says a thing that is not only contrary to the true nature of it, but contradictory to himself. For he tells us in the beginning of the Treatise, that the Sublime does not so properly persuade us, as it ravishes and transports us, and produces in us a certain Admiration, mingled with Astonishment and with Surprize, which is quite another thing than the barely pleasing, or the barely persuading; that it gives a noble Vigour to a Discourse, an invincible Force, which commits a pleasing Rape upon the very soul of the Reader; that whenever it breaks out where it ought to do, like the Artillery of Jove, it thunders, blazes, and strikes at once, and shews all the united Force of a Writer. Now I leave the Reader to judge, whether Longinus has not been saying here all along that Sublimity is never without Passion.

That the foremention'd Definition is just and good, I have reason to believe, because it takes in all the Sources of Sublimity which Longinus has establish'd. . . .

Thus the Definition which we have laid down being, according to Longinus's own Doctrine, the true Definition of the Sublime, and shewing clearly the thing which he has not done, nor given any Definition at all of it; it seems plain to me, that he had no clear and distinct Idea of it; and consequently Religion might be the thing from which 'tis chiefly to be deriv'd, and he but obscurely know it: but that Religion is that thing from which the Sublime is chiefly to be deriv'd, let us shew by the Marks which he has given of the latter; which will further strengthen our Definition. 1. Says he, that which is truly Sublime has this peculiar to it, that it exalts the Soul, and makes it conceive a greater Idea of it self, filling it with Joy, and with a certain noble Pride, as if it self had produc'd what it but barely reads.

(*Ibid.*, pp. 359-360)

What Dennis apparently does not understand is Longinus' perception that certain kinds of emotional turmoil, or passion, are irrelevant to the sublime in the arts. Also, because Longinus does not cite religion as the paramount source of the sublime, Dennis alleges that he has no clear idea of it, which is not very sound reasoning. Dennis is more astute on the question of terror than he is on the place of religion in the sublime:

But to return to Terror, we may plainly see by the foregoing Precepts and Examples of Longinus, that this Enthusiastick Terror contributes extremely to the Sublime; and, secondly, that it is most produced by Religious Ideas.

First, Ideas producing Terror, contribute extremely to the Sublime. All the Examples that Longinus brings of the Loftiness of the Thought, consist of terrible Ideas. And they are principally such Ideas that work the Effects, which he takes notice of in the beginning of his Treatise, viz. that ravish and transport the Reader, and produce a certain Admiration, mingled with Astonishment and with Surprize. For the Ideas which produce Terror, are necessarily accompany'd with Admiration, because ev'ry thing that is terrible, is great to him to whom it is terrible; and with Surprize, without which Terror cannot subsist; and with Astonishment, because every thing which is very terrible, is wonderful and astonishing: And as Terror is perhaps the violentest of all the Passions, it consequently makes an Impression which we cannot resist, and which is hardly to be defaced: and no Passion is attended with greater Joy than Enthusiastick Terror, which proceeds from our reflecting that we are out of danger at the very time that we see it before us.

And as Terror is one of the violentest of all Passions, if it is very great, and the hardest to be resisted, nothing gives more Force, nor more Vehemence to a Discourse.

But, secondly, it is plain from the same Longinus, that this Enthusiastick Terror is chiefly to be deriv'd from Religious Ideas. For all the Examples which he has brought of the Sublime, in his Chapter of the Sublimity of the Thoughts, consists of most terrible and most religious Ideas; and at the same time every Man's Reason will inform him, that every thing that is terrible in Religion, is the most terrible thing in the World. . . .

Now of all these Ideas none are so terrible as those which shew the Wrath and Vengeance of an angry God; for nothing is so wonderful in its Effects: and consequently the Images or Ideas of those Effects must carry a great deal of Terror with them, which we may see was Longinus's Opinion, by the Examples which he brings in his Chapter of the Sublimity of the Thoughts. . . .

But further, nothing is so terrible as the Wrath of infinite Power [God], because nothing is so unavoidable as the Vengeance design'd by it. . . .

And therefore Reason, which serves to dissipate our Terrors in some other Dangers, serves but to augment them when we are threatned by infinite Power; and that Fortitude, which may be heroick at other times, is down-right Madness then. . . .

'Tis very plain that it is the Apprehension of Danger which causes that Emotion in us which we call Terror, and it signifies nothing at all to the purpose whether the Danger is real or imaginary . . . For the warmer the Imagination is, the less able we are to reflect, and consequently the things are the more present to us of which we draw the Images; and therefore when the Imagination is so inflam'd, as to render the Soul utterly incapable of reflecting, there is no difference between the Images and the Things themselves . . .

(*Ibid.*, pp. 361-363)

The argument in the penultimate paragraph by which Dennis disposes of reason when the sublimity of God is involved is quite ingenious, and, within the confines of his theory, quite logical. A most interesting divergence in the theories of the sublime of Dennis and his successor, Burke, is seen where Dennis declares that it does not matter whether the danger is real or imaginary. Burke, of course, stipulates that the spectator must distinguish the degree of danger to his person in order to have the ability to obtain delight from the sublime of terror in the cases where he is not physically threatened.[4] All of this is very awkward for the clear formulation of Burke's esthetic. Dennis' theory is less encumbered with objects of the natural world, and his view of the imagination as fusing things and their images strikes us as somewhat

[4] *Philosophical Enquiry*, IV. pp. 6, 7.

more satisfactory than Burke's intellectually self-conscious process of ascertaining the relative safety of the spectator.

A possible discrepancy in Dennis' theory of the sublime appears in the last paragraph above, in which he states that "the warmer the imagination is, the less able we are to reflect", which leads in turn to the desired fusing of object and image I mentioned above. Yet, we remember that another vital ingredient in the theory is the 'enthusiastic passion', which is characterized by the fact that it is reflective. So we are left with the question of 'to reflect, or not to reflect'.

But not only the Tragedies in Blank Verse are the best, but the very best of our Epick Poems is writ in the same Verse. And that is the Paradise lost [sic] of Milton. And though this may in some Measure be attributed to the admirable and extraordinary Choice of the Subject, yet I am satisfied that something of its Excellence is owing to the Blank Verse. For Mr. Dryden has handled the very same Subject in Rime, but has faln so infinitely short of the Sublimity, the Majesty, the Vehemence, and the other great Qualities of Milton, that they are never to be nam'd together.

(Preface to *Britannia Triumphans*, 1704, p. 377)

It belongs to Poetry only, to teach publick Virtue and publick Spirit, and a noble Contempt of Death, with an Expression and with an Air becoming its Godlike Notions ... That great Minds bravely condemn Death to further that Felicity; that Fate is unavoidable to Mankind, and that thirty, forty, fifty Years is so very much nothing in the view of a comprehensive Soul, that a Hero must esteem it wiser as well as nobler, rather than languishingly to expect Death, to go out and meet him, for the publick Good, and so to make a sublime Virtue ev'n of the last necessity ...

(*An Essay on the Opera's* ..., 1706, p. 388)

In the above passage the sublime is extended to include the action that inspires poetry, but which is not necessarily dependent on the poetry for its existence.

For why should not a modern Critick imitate the great Qualities of Longinus; and when he treats of a Subject which is sublime, treat of it sublimely? Now he who writes any thing with Sublimity, let it be Prose or Verse, let it be Criticism or Poetry, writes sometimes with Fury, as Longinus hath shewn both by his Doctrine and his Example in the first Chapter of his Treatise.

(*Reflections Critical and Satyrical, upon a Late Rhapsody, Call'd, An Essay upon Criticism*, 1711, p. 409)

...from whose noblest Poem you [George Granville] formerly gave us a Tragedy, in which, in Imitation of Homer, you are daring yet just, fiery yet regular, sublime yet natural and perspicuous, chast yet alluring, and easie yet strong and powerful.

(Dedication to George Granville, Secretary at War in *An Essay on the Genius and Writings of Shakespear*, p. 2)[5]

The fifth Quality of the poetic Diction is that it be harmonious, that it may maintain that great and majestic Air, with which Poetry is wont to adorn it self, and may express all the Force and the utmost Dignity of the great Things which it utters. It ought to reject all Terms but those that are proper to fill the Mouth and content the Ear, that it may attain to that Sublime and that Wonderful, which it always and every where aims at.

(*Of Simplicity in Poetical Compositions, in Remarks on the 70th Spectator*, 1711, 1721, p. 37)

Some modern critics would find that the above passage concerns itself with rhetoric, but as I have said so often there seems no reason to exclude such matters as the aural properties of poetry from the domain of poetry proper.

But these are Figures [in the Psalm of Sternhold] which are another Person's, which the Transverser repeats like a Parrot, without understanding them, and without being mov'd by them, and which consequently have neither Passion nor Sublimity to sustain them. For 'tis a just Observation which is made by Longinus, that as the Figures support the pathetick and the sublime, they are wonderfully supported by each of them. Let us now see how the Force of Milton's Genius hides and conceals the Assistance of Art, while these lofty Figures, at the very time that they raise and transport his exalted Soul, are lost in his Enthusiasm and his Sublimity, as the glittering of numberless Stars is swallow'd and lost in the blaze of Day, and that golden Deluge of Light which on every side overwhelms them.

(*Ibid.*, p. 39)

This is one of the most interesting excerpts we have from Dennis. For once he does not argue at cross purposes with the Greek critic. Perhaps it requires the example of a Milton to act as catalytic agent in Dennis' reaction to the function of figures in the sublime. There seems to be real integration here of spirit and expression. In addition I am tempted to make an observation that is not strictly germane to my purpose in this Context: The final sentence of the passage above is strikingly similar to those parts of Ruskin's prose that blaze with color and visual imagery as they take flight. When we recall that Elizabeth Nitchie found a sober Longinian strain in Pater's writing (Chapter I, p. 33), the idea quite logically occurs to us that this kind of writing by the prose stylists of the nineteenth century may be indebted, at least in part, to a combination of the eighteenth-century sublime of Dennis and the disciples of the natural sublime.

[5] This and the following passages occur in Hooker, Vol. II.

England has certainly produced great Men in every part of Learning. But that Branch of it, which did most Honour to Greece and to Ancient Rome, has likewise done most to England. We have a Poet, who in Sublimity has excell'd both Ancients and Moderns.

(*Remarks upon Mr. Pope's Translation of Homer, Observations*, 1717, p. 120)

The sublime poet referred to is Milton, Pope having already incurred the prolonged enmity of Dennis.

In the Reign of King Charles II, Milton, who was an Honour to Great Britain, and an Ornament to Humankind, continued long neglected and obscure. How few of those to whom he wrote, had Eyes for his matchless Beauties! How many of them were more blind than he! Upon the other Side of Parnassus, the admirable Pleasantry of Butler found still worse Quarter than the Force, and Elevation, and Sublimity of Milton.

(*Ibid.*, p. 121)

... the Reader ... would believe that ... he [Pope] had the Force and Sublimity, and Elevation of Milton ...

(*Ibid.*, p. 122)

And yet I have all along known, that nothing in the greater Poetry can grow immediately popular without a Cabal or Party. I have a long time been convinced, that the more sublimely any thing is writ in Poetry, and the nearer it comes to Perfection, the longer it will be before it grows popular, without such a Cabal; because the more sublimely it is writ, and the nearer it comes to Perfection, the more it is rais'd above the Apprehensions of the Vulgar.

(Letter to Sir Richard Steele of September 4, 1719, p. 174)

The history of the public's reaction to great works of art, music, and literature down to our own time leads us to agree with Dennis. But the vital question is why this should be so. The conventional answer that it requires the vulgar a longer time to become 'educated' in a particular artistic tendency or technique begs the question all over again, because the exact nature of the educational process is too little understood. It is at this point that the ideas in Chapter I can make a useful contribution to the solution of the general problem, and especially of the particular phenomenon noted by Dennis, for the very opposite to the cabal-led popular acceptance of sublime literature, which Dennis obviously disdains, is the understanding of the sublime reached almost at once by the individual with the kind of nervous organization that instinctively comprehends. The popularity induced by a cabal is based on an appeal to fashion and non-artistic verbal explanations, while an individual's appropriate response involves a rapport that is quite independent of fashion and exegesis.

Because you have been told, that the French Genius has neither the Force nor Sublimity of the English; therefore you conclude, that the Rules are in fault. Whereas I have clearly shewn you, that nothing perfectly beautiful can be produc'd in the Drama, without the Help of the Rules.

(*The Characters and Conduct of Sir John Edgar, Call'd by Himself sole Monarch of the Stage in Drury-Lane; And His Three Deputy-Governors. In Two Letters to Sir John Edgar. Letter II*, 1720, p. 196)

Indeed there is evidence throughout the Context that where the sublime is concerned many English writers agree with Longinus and Dennis that a judicious use of the rules is required.

Would he [Dryden] prefer Nat Lee to Etherege, as he does Juvenal to Horace, because the Thoughts of Lee are more elevated than those of Etherege, his Expressions more noble and more sonorous, his Verse more numerous, and his Words more sublime and lofty?

(*To Matthew Prior, Esq. Upon the Roman Satirists*, 1721, p. 219)

I believe, Sir, that I have told you more than once, that I, who have all my Life-time had the highest Esteem for the great Genius's of the Ancients, and especially for Homer and Virgil, and who admire them now more than ever, have yet for these last Thirty Years admir'd Milton above them all for one thing, and that is for having carried away the Prize of Sublimity from both Ancients and Moderns . . . In the "Remarks on Prince Arthur", I cited at large the sublime Description of Satan in the first Book of that Poem . . .

(*Letters on Milton and Wycherly*. Letter I, "Observations on the Paradise Lost of Milton. To Dr. S", 1721, p. 221)

. . . but I should not be in the least concern'd at the treating me so unfairly and ungenerously, if they had done Justice to Milton, thro' the Course of their Criticisms, of which they have grossly fail'd in the following Respects.
I. They have not allow'd that Milton in the Sublimity of his Thoughts surpass'd both Ancients and Moderns.
II. In their Observations which they have made on the "Paradise Lost," they have insisted too much upon things in which Milton has Equals, instead of dwelling intirely on that Sublimity which is his distinguishing and Characteristick Quality, and which sets him above Mankind.
III. In citing Passages from him which are truly sublime, they have often fail'd of setting his Sublimity in a true Light, and of shewing it to all its Advantage.
IV. In those Passages whose Sublimity they have set in a true Light, they

have not observ'd, to the Honour of Milton, and our Country, that the Thoughts and Images are Original, and the genuine Offspring of Milton's transcendent Genius.

V. They have not shewn how Milton's Sublimity is distinguish'd from that of all other Poets in this Respect, that where he has excell'd all other Poets in what he has exprest, he has left ten times more to be understood than what he has exprest, which is the surest and noblest Mark, and the most transporting Effect of Sublimity.

(*Ibid.*, p. 222)

Items II, IV, and V are particularly astute on the part of Dennis, because of his recognition of Milton's originality and daring. Dennis' achievement is the more notable in light of the fact that most of his contemporaries' critiques of Milton are comprised of little else than explications of the allusions, similes, and the like in *Paradise Lost*. Dennis' remark on the sublimity of what Milton leaves unexpressed appears to be indebted to *On the Sublime* IX, 2, the famous reference to the silence of Ajax in Homer's *Odyssey*, XI, l. 543.

I affirmed in my last [letter] that the Persons who had writ Comments upon the "Paradise Lost" of Milton, had not done Justice to the great Author in several Respects which are there particulariz'd. And, first and principally in this, that they have not acknowledg'd that he has born away the Prize of Sublimity from both Ancients and Moderns.

(*Ibid.*, Letter II, 172½, p. 222)

Evidently Milton's having won the universal prize for sublimity is uppermost in Dennis' mind!

... Mr. Addison, who expresly here either equals or prefers Homer for the Greatness of his Sentiments before Milton, contradicts himself at least no less than twice in the Course of his Observations: for says he, in the 74th Page of the foresaid Edition, "There is an indisputable and unquestion'd Magnificence in every part of 'Paradise Lost', and indeed a much greater than could have been form'd upon any Pagan System." Now if there is a greater Magnificence in every Part of Milton's Poem, there is by Consequence a greater Sublimity than there is in the "Iliads", which was form'd upon a Pagan System. ...

Now, Sir, if Milton's Subject is the most Sublime that could enter into the Thoughts of a Poet, and his Genius is every way equal to his Subject; it follows that Milton is more exalted than any Poet who has not a Subject so elevated, and consequently than Homer, or any other Poet ancient or modern.

(*Ibid.*, p. 223)

Dennis' quibble with Addison really centers on the meaning of the term 'greatness of sentiments', and illustrates a point that has some importance in the history of the sublime. We have discovered that for Dennis the ultimate source of the sublime lies in the divine precepts of the Christian religion. Taken by and of itself, this idea is not very close to an esthetic, as we now understand the latter. Nevertheless we grant Dennis that there is greatness of sentiment in the Christian precepts. Addison, on the other hand, distinguishes greatness of sentiments and sublimity in Milton, and thus shows himself, to that extent, nearer a purely esthetic concept of the sublime.

Thus with this very pretty trifling Remark does Mr. Addison stop short, within the very touch of one of the vastest and the sublimest Beauties that ever was inspir'd by the God of Verse, or by Milton's Godlike Genius . . .

(*Ibid.*, p. 224)

The above passage refers to some lines from the war in Heaven in *Paradise Lost.*

But let us proceed to the Combat of the two Arch-Angels, and we shall see something more in a Passage that is wonderfully sublime, and worthy the Mouth of the Angel who relates it.

(*Ibid.*, p. 226)

The Conflict of two Worlds crushing and confounding each other, appear'd but trivial and light to him, to express his Idea of the Combat of the two Arch-Angels; and therefore he says, that he's oblig'd "to set forth Great things by Small."

What immediately follows accounts for all this, and is transcendently Sublime. . . .

I defy any one to name any thing so sublime in Homer, as the latter End of this Passage above. [The description of Satan in Book II.]

I am sensible, that this Letter runs into too great a Length, and 'tis high time to conclude it. I have endeavour'd to prove in it, that there is a Sublimity in Milton's Battle of Angels, infinitely superior to that which is in the Battle of Homer's Gods and Heroes in the twentieth "Iliad": And as I have set sublime Beauties before you, of which neither Mr. Addison, nor my Lord Roscommon, have taken the least Notice, so in my next I shall make an Objection which has not been yet made. If I have any where pass'd the Bounds of the Epistolary or the Didactic Stile, you will have the Goodness to consider, that it was next to impossible to resist the violent Emotions which the Greatness of the Subject rais'd in me.

(*Ibid.*, p. 227)

As in my last I endeavour'd to shew Beauties in Milton, which no one had taken Notice of before me, and greater Beauties than any which I believe had been taken Notice of: I shall in this lay before you an Objection, which no one that I know of has made against those very Machines of Milton, from the Force and Power of which those sublime Beauties were drawn.

(*Ibid.*, Letter III, p. 228)

But with all the Veneration that I have for this great Poet, I cannot help thinking, that when in the first and second Books of his Poem, which yet are transcendently Sublime, he describes the fall'n Angels in Shapes that come near to humane . . . methinks his Paintings, as to that Point, are not so easily to be justified.

(*Ibid.*, Postscript, p. 229)

The above passage hints at the kind of infringement on his concept of the sublime that Dennis' religious conservatism produces.

Now in this passage of Milton [*Treatise of the Education of Youth*] there are Two or three Remarkable things. First He tells you that the Art of Poetry, as tis Deliver'd by Aristotle and Horace is a sublime art, whereas Mr. W [elsted] has told us just now that tis nothing but a sett of very obvious thoughts and observations. Now which shall we believe of the Two, the writer of Madrigals and Bawdy Tales, or the Immortal Authour of the sublimest Poem that ever was writ in the world?

(*The Causes of the Decay and Defects of Dramatick Poetry, and of the Degeneracy of the Publick Tast,* 1725? p. 286)

In light of the fact that Welsted is capable very often of being judicious in his literary criticism, his differing view of the two Ancients is one measurement of the change in taste from Milton's time to his own, about a half century later.

I shall now come to the Practice of the antient Poets, and the Method which they made use of in introducing their Machines, in order to render their Poems more instructive and delightful. . . .

They shew'd a just Subordination among them, and a just Proportion between their Functions. While one was employ'd about the greatest and the sublimest Things, another was not busied about the most trifling and most contemptible.

(*Remarks on Mr. Pope's Rape of the Lock, in Several Letters to a Friend.* Letter IV, 1714, p. 336)

Pray which of the aerial Kind [Pope's Sylphs in *The Rape*] have these sublime Employments? . . .

There is a Difference almost infinite between these vile Functions and the former sublime ones, and therefore they can never belong to Beings of the same Species.

(*Ibid.*, p. 338)

If this Prefacer [Pope] had not been superlatively ignorant, he would have known, that the most judicious and methodical Genius's have been the greatest and the most fruitful ones; the most admirable, and the most sublime. The Epick Poems of Homer and Virgil are infallible Proofs of this.

(*Remarks Upon Several Passages in the Preliminaries to the Dunciad . . . And upon Several Passages in*

Pope's Preface to His Translation of Homer's Iliad, 1729, p. 363)

We do not discern any dramatic change in Dennis' view of the sublime in the chronological unfolding of his commentary in this chapter.

After that, I determined to shew that all Conversation is not familiar; that it may be Ceremonious, that it may be Grave, nay, that it may be Sublime, or that Tragedy must be allow'd to be out of Nature: That if the Sublime were easy and unconstrain'd, it might be as consistent with the Epistolary Style, as it was with the Didactique, that Voiture had admirably joyn'd it with one of them, and Longinus with both. After this, I resolv'd to have said something of those who had most succeeded in Letters amongst the Ancients and Moderns, and to have treated of their Excellencies and their Defects . . . That the Elevation of Balzac was frequently forced and his Sublime affected . . . that I had always taken to suit my Style to my Subject, whether it was Familiar or Sublime, or Didactique.

(*Letters Upon Several Occasions*, 1696. The Advertisement, To the Reader, p. 382)

Thus have I endeavour'd to give the reason, why a Fool succeeds better in Business than a Man of Wit, who has a Multitude of thoughts, and which fly at the Noblest Objects; and who finds that there is something so pleasing, and so noble, in thinking rightly, and more especially in the sublime Speculations of exalted Reason, that he finds it intollerably irksome to descend to Action, and abhors the very thought of being diligent in things, for which he has an extream Contempt.

(Letter to Wycherley of October 30, 1695, p. 383)

We found in Le Clerc and Fenelon (Chapter III) and *The Free-Thinker* (Chapter VI), to mention the most prominent, that the sublime is discussed in relation to what I call utility, or the practical considerations of life, but none of these three sources is quite as explicit as Dennis in the extract above. And yet it is a curious fact that Dennis reserves for the sublime the most important of assignments for the best conduct of human life, that is, inspiration for investigating and embracing the highest spiritual precepts. Without a certain degree of attainment in the moral arena, man's successes in the purely mundane practicalities avail him nothing, so maybe we should conclude that Dennis' view of the sublime in the above passage is practical in the highest sense after all.

I appeal to the reasonable and impartial Reader, if this must not be the Sense of all knowing French and Italians who have seen these Translations. Let the reasonable and impartial Reader judge then, if a just Criticism upon "Cato" was not absolutely necessary, both for the Advantage of Dramatick Poetry, to which the undeserv'd Success of this Tragedy has done infinite Harm, and for the Vindication of the National Honour; let the Reader judge, if it was not necessary, that a Man who owns that he admires the noble Genius of Shakespear, admires the unparallell'd Sublimity of the "Paradise Lost" of Milton, that he is infinitely pleas'd with the Master-Pieces of Ben Johnson, and exceedingly delighted with several of our other Comick Poets, should give his Reasons to all the World why he has no Esteem for "Cato"?

(Preface to the *Original Letters*, 1721, p. 414)

As Longinus in treating Sublimity is himself often sublime, so Alexander P– has writ of the Profund with the utmost Profundity, and is himself a perpetual Example of that Absurdity and that Stupidity for which he gives vain and impertinent Rules.

(Letter to the *Daily Journal*, May 11, 1728, p. 416)

After examining the allusions to and discussions of the sublime contained in this chapter, I conclude that Dennis' contribution to and understanding of the sublime esthetic is somewhat greater than Monk, for one, is willing to grant when he states, "Dennis is no psychologist, and certainly he is no aesthetician, but surely ... we have a crude attempt at both psychology and aesthetic"[6] and "he has seized on one or two statements [of Longinus] and has expanded them, building a theory on them, and forcing Longinus to conform to his views."[7] Certainly Dennis is no pure Longinian, but then it is doubtful that one can be found in the eighteenth century. Least of all Edmund Burke! But by turning Monk's appraisal around and looking at it in a positive way, the modern student can begin to see the importance of Dennis' remarks on the sublime in the history of that term's development during the eighteenth century. It has already been demonstrated (Chapter I) that according to Monk's definition of esthetic any critical orientation not directly related to the natural and Burkeian sublime cannot rate as esthetic, but even Monk has to admit that Dennis makes a 'crude attempt at both psychology and aesthetic'. Surely there is no doubt that Dennis is attentive to the reaction of mind and soul, which really means the entire personality, to the effect of literature. Whereas Monk would qualify Dennis' right to the title of esthetician on the grounds, presumably, that he fails to take sufficient cognizance of extra-literary elements, the quotations in the Context suggest that he is more deservedly censured on a different score, which is overemphasis on the role of religion, particularly Christianity.

There is, furthermore, an identity of interest that ties Dennis to Longinus, and that is, of course, the preeminence each assigns to the

[6] *The Sublime*, pp. 52-53.
[7] *The Sublime*, p. 53.

passions, the latter being broadly, if vaguely, defined as the agency that, once roused by the stimulus of sublime art, is capable of producing transport in the reader or listener. It could be argued that in failing to speculate further on the precise nature of the passions and on the forces in nature that stimulate them, Dennis is rather prudent than crude or inadequate.

X

DICTIONARIES

Our discussion of the word 'sublime' could hardly make the smallest claim to comprehensiveness without the inclusion of a representative cross-section of the word's definition in a goodly number of the dictionaries appearing between 1650 and 1760. An examination of the fifty-old lexicons held by the Folger Library revealed that slightly over half of them defined the word 'sublime', and these follow in chronological order. In the case of dictionaries, however, it may be just as significant to know which and how many of them omit the sublime; accordingly, these are listed separately in Appendix 2.

In the extracts that follow, I make every effort to render them exactly as they appear in their sources.

John Florio, *Queen Anna's New World of Words, or Dictionarie of the Italian and English tongues.* (1611)

This is the first of two dictionaries preceding 1650 that are included in order to lend additional perspective to our survey. It is an Italian to English dictionary only.

Sublíme, sublime, high and aloft, extolled, above us lofty. Also the upper post of a doore. Also the mantle of a chimny.
Sublimità, sublimity, highnesse, the top or tip of any thing, height, loftiness.

Ambrosii Calepini, *Dictionarium* . . . (Lugduni, 1634)

Written mostly in Latin, the definitions are frequently many lines long. The definition of 'Sublimis' requires 27 lines, including several references to ancient authors, but not to Longinus. Its copiousness is in contrast to the very brief definitions of the sublime in most of the later English dictionaries.

Edward Phillips, *The new world of English words: or, A general dictionary.* (1658)

Sulimation [sic], (Lat) a raising, or carrying up on high: on high: also a Chemical Operation, wherein dry exhalations ascending upward, stick to the sides of the Alembick.
Sublimity, (Lat.) heighth.

Gio. Torriano, *Vocabolario Italiano & Inglese, A Dictionary Italian and English. Formerly Compiled by John Florio, and since his last Edition, Anno 1611. augmented by himself in His life time, with many thousand Words, and Thuscan Phrases. Now Most diligently Revised, Corrected, and Compared, with La Crusca, and other approved Dictionaries extant since his Death; and enriched with very considerable Additions. Whereunto is added A Dictionary English and Italian, with several Proverbs and Instructions for the speedy attaining to the Italian Tongue. Never before Published.* (1659)

Sublíme, sublime, high above others, by Met. the mantle of a chimney or a door.
Sublimità, Sublimézza, sublimity, height or top of any thing
(From the Italian – English section.)

Sublime, sublime.
Sublimitie, sublimità.
(From the English – Italian section.)

As we shall see in many subsequent cases, brevity is apparently the essence of wit in the defining of the word 'sublime'.

John Florio, *Vocabolario Italiano & Inglese, A dictionary Italian & English. Formerly Compiled by John Florio, and since his last Edition, Anno 1611, augmented by himself in His life time, with many thousand Words, and Thuscan Phrases. Now Most diligently Revised, Corrected and Compared, with La Crusca, and other approved Dictionaries extant since his Death; and enriched with very considerable Additions.* (1659)

Sublimáre, to sublimate, to extoll, to advance on high.
Sublíme, sublime, high above others, by Met. the mantle of a chimney or a door.
Sublimità, Sublimézza, sublimity, height or top of any thing.
(From the Italian – English section.)

Sublime, sublime
Sublimitie, sublimità
(From the English – Italian Section.)

James Howell, *Lexicon tetraglotton, an English-French-Italian-Spanish dictionary . . .* (1660)

Sublime; Sublime, transendent; Sublime, transendente; Sublime, transcendiente.

Henry Hexham, *A copious English and Netherduytch dictionarie, composed out of our best English authours.* (Rotterdam, 1660)

Sublimity – Hooghte ofte hoogheyt

Francis Gouldman, *A copious dictionary in three parts. Second edition.* (Cambridge, 1669)

Sublimity, Sublimitas, fastigium
("Part I. English before Latin.")

Fastigium [Many definitions given. Among them is:], Mart. The top, head, or height of a thing: also the bottom or depth of a pit or like thing.
("Part II. Latin before English.")

This is our first incidence of the sublime of depth, an idea that develops during the eighteenth century, and attains its fullest statement in the *Enquiry* of Burke.

Sublìmè, . . . Up aloft, on high.
(*Ibid.*)

John Bullokar, *An English expositour, or Compleat dictionary: teaching the Interpretation of the hardest words, and most useful terms of Art used in our Language.* (Cambridge, 1671)

Sublime. High, lofty, honourable.

The last section of this dictionary is "A brief Nomenclator, Containing a Summary of the most memorable Things, and famous Persons, whether Inventours and Improvers of rare Arts and Ingenuities, or others". The name of Longinus does NOT appear therein.

Randle Cotgrave, *A French and English dictionary* . . . (1673)

Eleveur: m. A raiser, or lifter up.
Sublime: com. Sublime, high, lofty, haughty, honourable, stately.
(From the French – English section)

In this section Cotgrave lists seven other variations of the word 'sublime', and defines them similarly to the above.

Sublime. Sublime, sublin, sublim [plus five variations]
(From the English – French section.)

Elisha Coles, *An English dictionary.* (1676, 1701)

Coles was a schoolmaster and teacher of the English tongue to foreigners. In light of the fact that his dictionary promises the reader etymological derivations, it is disappointing to discover the brevity of the definitions below:

Sublime, lofty.
Sublimity, height.

Thomas Blount, *Glossographia: or a dictionary, interpreting the hard words . . . now used in our refined English tongue . . . Fifth edition.* (1681)

Sublimity (sublimitas) height, highness.
(p. 617)

Abel Boyer, *The Royal Dictionary, In Two Parts. First, French and English. Secondly, English and French.* (1699)

S'élever dans son Stile, to raise one's Stile. [one of five definitions under 's'élever']
(From the French to English section.)

Elevation, (noblesse, sublimité du Stile) loftiness, sublimity of Stile, nobleness of Expression. [one of seven definitions under "Elevation."]
(*Ibid.*)

Sublime, Adj. (Haut, grand, relevé) sublime, lofty, high, great.
(*Ibid.*)

Le sublime, S.M. [Substantif du Genre Masculin] (le style sublime) the sublime, the lofty Style.
(*Ibid.*)

Sublime, Adj. (or lofty) Sublime, relevé, grand, haut, extraordinaire.
A sublime Genius, Un genie sublime, grand, extraordinaire.
A sublime Style, Stile sublime, le sublime.
[plus four variations similarly defined]
(From the English to French section.)

There is considerable emphasis on the sublime style in Boyer's dictionary, more than in the majority of the dictionaries quoted here.

John Kersey, *A new English dictionary.* (1702)

In his preface Kersey makes the following statement, which serves, of course, to qualify his definition of 'sublime'.

For that purpose, we have taken care to make a Collection of all the most proper and significant English Words, that are now commonly us'd either

in Speech, or in the familiar way of Writing Letters, etc; omitting at the same time, such as are obsolete, barbarous, foreign or peculiar to the several Counties of England; as also many difficult, abstruse and uncouth Terms of Art, as altogether unnecessary, nay even prejudicial to the endeavours of young Beginners, and unlearned Persons, and whereof seldom any use does occur . . .
Sublime, or lofty.
A Sublimeness, sublimity, or loftiness of style.

Edward Cocker, *Cocker's English dictionary*. (1704)

There is a 'Historico-Poetical Dictionary' following the main text. Like most other contemporaneous examples of this sub-genre, it concentrates on persons and places, instead of abstract terms, poetic technique, and the like. Quite naturally, then, the sublime does not appear in Cocker's poetical dictionary. For that matter, he gives short shrift to the sublime in the main dictionary:

Sublime, great, high, honourable, lofty
Sublimity, Grandeur, Advancement, Nobleness.

Note that Cocker, like several other lexicographers, includes the ideas of honor and nobility in his definition.

John Stevens, *A new Spanish and English dictionary*. (1706)

Sublíme, lofty, high, Lat. Sublimis.
(From the Spanish – English section.)

Sublime, Alto, Levantádo.
Sublimely, Altaménte.
Sublimity, Altúra.
(From the English – Spanish section.)

A.D., *Glossographis Anglicana nova: or, a Dictionary, interpreting such Hard Words of whatever Language, as are at present used in the English Tongue, with their Etymologies, Definitions, etc*. (1707)

Sublime, (Lat.) high, lofty, great.

The only significant thing about this definition is that it is skimpy in comparison with a good many others to be found in this dictionary of words that do not seem particularly interesting to us today.

William Sewell, *A large dictionary, English and Dutch, in two parts*. (Amsterdam, 1708)

SUBLIME, Hoog, verheeven, hoogzweevend, hoogwigtig.

Sublimity, Verheevenheyd, hoogzweevendheyd, hoogwigtigheyd.
(From the English – Dutch section, p. 547)

HOOG, high, tall.
Hoogwichtig, Very weighty, sublime.
Hoogzweevend, High-soaring, towring aloft, sublime.
(From the Dutch – English section, pp. 183-184)

John Harris, *Lexicon technicum: or an universal English dictionary of arts and sciences: explaining not only the terms of art, but the arts themselves. Two volumes. Second edition.* (1708)

The second volume is actually a supplemental volume printed two years later than the first, and includes material barely mentioned in the first, or omitted entirely. Neither volume includes the sublime, but I place this entry here rather than in the Appendix because of the passage below, which evidently reflects a strong current of the times, and is indicative of the procedure followed by most of the dictionaries in this Context.

> In Logick, Metaphysicks, Ethicks, Grammar, Rhetorick, etc. I have been *designedly short* [my emphasis]; giving usually the bare Meanings only of the Words and Terms of Art, with one or two Instances to explain them, and illustrate them.
> (Preface, p. 6)

Ferdinando Altieri, *Dizionario italiano ed inglese.* (1726)

Sublime, adj. [high, lofty] sublime, alto, eccelso.
A sublime genius, un ingegno sublime.
A sublime style, uno stilo sublime.
(Sublimeness, s.
(Sublimity, ì [height, loftiness] sublimità, altezza, eccelenza, grandezza, s.f.
(From the English – Italian section.)

Sublíme, adj. m. f. [alto, eccelso] sublime, lofty, high, great.
(From the Italian – English section.)[1]

B. N. Defoe, *A compleat English dictionary.* (Westminster, 1735)

Sublime, high, lofty, great
Sublimity, Height, Loftiness

[1] All of the brackets in this entry's definitions appear in the original, as will be the case throughout the chapter. Brackets in the other than definition passages will, of course, be mine.

Nathaniel Bailey, *An universal etymological English dictionary. Thirteenth edition.* (1749)

SUBLIME [sublimis, L.] high, Lofty, great; as a sublime Style, Notion, etc.

Samuel Johnson, *A Dictionary of the English Language.* (1755)

Johnson defines 'sublime' in the adjectival form by giving five definitions of a very few words each, followed in each case by an example from the poetry of Milton, Dryden, Prior, or Wotton in which the word 'sublime' appears. The substantive is defined as 'the grand or lofty style'. Johnson then adds, "'The sublime' is a Gallicism, but now naturalized." As a poetic example of the substantive he gives:

> Longinus strengthens all his laws,
> And is himself the great sublime he draws.

which is, of course, the famous eulogy of the Greek critic from Pope's *Essay on Criticism.*

Johnson next provides a prose illustration by Addison, still for the substantive:

> The sublime rises from the nobleness of thoughts, the magnificence of the words, or the harmonious and lively turn of the phrase; the per-sublime arises from all three together.

Johnson defines "To Sublíme. v.a. [sublimer, Fr. from the adjective.]" by giving three variations of the general meaning "to raise on high", and illustrates each of them by poetic excerpts from Donne, Denham, Milton, and Pope, and by prose passages from Glanville and Dryden's *Dufresnoy.*

One of the three meanings that Johnson gives of 'sublimity' is worth quoting.

> 3. Loftiness of style or sentiment.
> Milton's distinguishing excellence lies in the sublimity of his thoughts, in the greatness of which he triumphs over all the poets, modern and ancient, Homer only excepted. Addison.

From his assorted definitions, we gather that Johnson takes a rather broad view of the sublime. One thing is certain; he does not emphasize the rhetorical, pictorial, 'natural', or psychological alone. If any one aspect of the sublime seems to predominate in Johnson's dictionary definitions it is greatness of thought. In any event, Johnson is more interested in the problem of defining the sublime than most of the lexicographers represented in the present chapter.

[Diderot], *Encyclopedie*. (Paris, 1755)

Although it is entirely in French, Diderot's massive work finds its place here in order that I might mention the fact that it contains a four-and-one-half page discussion of the word 'sublime' (Volume 15, [1765], pp. 566-570). Longinus is treated at some length therein. This is by far the longest definition of the word 'sublime' in all the dictionaries held by the Folger Library.

Giuseppi Baretti, *A dictionary of the English and Italian languages.* Two volumes. (1760)

Baretti refers to the *Dizionario italiano ed inglese* of Altieri (see above) in his Preface in Volume I, and that none too kindly. Yet it is obvious that he has virtually lifted Altieri's definitions *in toto*, there being only the most trivial of variations between the two sets of definitions, as regards punctuation, the use of the article, accent marks, and the like.

Samuel Derrick, *A poetical dictionary*. (1761)

This is a miscellany, divided in the customary fashion by subject. The sublime is not the subject of a section, but the word occurs several times in the Preface:

> As there is no modern language more happily adapted to express the various and delightful stiles of poetry than the English, it being not only strong, copious, and energetic, but comprehensive and melodious; fit for the most sublime, sufficiently soft for the tenderest and most simple subjects; so no nation can boast greater poetical ornaments. (pp. vii-viii)

> France and Italy have long since pleaded their title to literary fame, by publications of this nature [Derrick's own volume]; as we yield not to them in genius, why should we decline exhibiting an equal claim? Something of this kind has been attempted by Byshe [sic], in his art of poetry; and one or two others have trod in his steps, and copied his imperfections. Their choice of authors has been very injudicious; and two parts out of three of their works are filled with quotations from Pope's Homer, Dryden's Virgil, and other translations of the classics. Here we are indeed struck with contrivance, conduct, fancy, sentiment, and character; but these are not the perfections of Dryden and Pope: it is Homer and Virgil we compliment in our admiration; the only merits of our great countrymen that occur, are classical knowledge, and talents for smooth versification. It is in their original works, their imitations of nature, and not of men, that we must look for that excellence in our most celebrated writers, which reflects honour upon the nation, and helps to exemplify its literary character. We must seek it in the rapid boldness of Shakespear; the astonishing sublimity of Milton; the unbounded genius of Dryden, and others of our great poets, whose names and some of

> whose beauties will be found in the ensuing performance; and while they shew the strength of Britain-born talents, they will convince the reader that we can justly boast as bold imagery, as daring metaphors, as warm fancy, as glowing imagination, as spirited language, and a strain of poetry as sublime and enthusiastic, as any nation under heaven. (pp. ix-x)

This passage is notable for a middle-of-the-road critical position, neither strongly neo-classical nor pro-original genius, and for a generalized use of the word 'sublime' that is no different than many instances we encounter sixty years earlier. Apparently the 'development' of the sublime fell upon some deaf ears and sightless eyes during the first half of the eighteenth century. And as far as that is concerned, a perusal of the contents of this chapter is not calculated to excite the cultural historian who everywhere seeks the evidence of vibrant evolution in the realms of art and ideas. If we know of men who theorized over the sublime during the eighteenth century, and there were many, we also see here a few who were content to remain, at least in connection with the sublime, esthetic reactionaries.

XI

MISCELLANEOUS

The Folger Library holds several documents containing references to the sublime that do not fit conveniently under the somewhat specialized headings that comprise the other chapters of this Context. In view of the unusual interest of several of these 'misfits', however, I deemed it appropriate to include all of them in a chapter entitled "Miscellaneous". As might be expected, there is no attempt made herein to interrelate the extracts, even to the slight degree of the other chapters. I let each quotation merely speak for itself as an independent entity.

Sir Balthazar Gerbier, *A brief discourse concerning the three chief principles of magnificent building.* (1664)

Curiously enough, all of the references to the sublime in this volume occur in certain of the thirty-eight letters that make up the bulk of the prefatory matter. The text itself, furthermore, has little value for inquiry in esthetics.

Your Aspect My Lord, speaks indeed that which no memory can fall short of; And your Heroick minde affecting that which is the Purest, speaks Buckingham in perfection; your Grace can by a sublime quality separate Spiritual from Terrestrial, and without venturing a stock to fetch Aurum Horisontalis from the East Indies, or with me to the West, the most concocted and most pure from el Dorado, which if it had a speaking quality, your Grace would hear its Hessian Alembick sing the Gold its joy, for having approved it self the more pure by its often passing through a Furnace . . .

(To the Duke of Buckingham His Grace)

It may be, that at the first sight of an Epistle, with Your Lordships name, will be expected a Treatise concerning the most sublime parts of the Metaphisicks . . .

(To the Right Honourable the Earle of Leicester)

Possibly there are not wanting such who accustomed themselves to carp at all things not directly of their humour, that will (upon sight of the Title of this ensuing discourse) think it strange, that I should in an Epistle to you, treat on the case of the perishing Buildings of mortals, though you already have been entertained with observations made on the bills of mortality; as also the Vegitation of Plants, when as indeed your Apollo's Oracle-like Arcenal, may challenge the most sublime proffers of men of parts; And that if I would follow the practise of men, who tell strange things, (having been in parts remote from this Region) I should not begin with Clay, Sand and Chalk, whereof Bricks and Lime are made, and is daily digged here at home.

(To the Right Honourable Lord Brunckhord, Viscount Lyons in Ireland, President of the Royal Society of Phylosophers Meeting at Gresham Colledg, and the rest of that Honourable Society.)

Criticks knowing also that (among such Eminent Phylosophers who like stars in the Firmament, do with the approbation of the great Apollo of this Monarchy, and his sacred influence, dive in matters most sublime) would fit more seasonably from me an account of a day of rejoycing . . .

(*Ibid.*)

The Nation in reference to a lively Image of the Supream sacred, by an assembly of Representatives, takes notice of your Lordships great Genius in representing Solomons Temple -- like Foundations of a State, to free it from the fate of the Hebrews, Assyrians, Persians, Lacedemonians, Medes, Greeks, Affricans, Romans, and even the Gots, who were sent packing by the Mores, whereof but too many (as black in mind) are left; and therefore though a poor small thing which treats but of Surveyors, Clarks of Works, Master Workmen, Materials, and their Prizes, be not of a sublime, nor of State matter; yet since from the least that lives, to the greatest Building is a main necessary, either for one conveniency or other; (My Lord) this apparent Demonstration of Zeal, and Respect is humbly offered by . . .

(Entire letter To the Right Honourable Anthony Lord Ashley, Chancellor of the Exchequer, and one of his Majesties most Honourable Privy Council.)

Balthasar Gracian y Morales, *The critick. Written originally in Spanish: by Lorenzo Gracian . . . Translated into English by Paul Rycaut . . . London: by T. N. for Henry Brome, 1681.*

This is a treatise on morals (in the broadest sense of the word) and the anatomy of the world, cast in the form of a Spanish romance form popular at the time. The moral content is conveyed through the discourses of Critilo, an older man shipwrecked on the island of St. Helena, and a youth, Andrenio, who believes himself born and reared of an indigenous wild creature, and who has not had the benefit of human company or language until the fortuitous arrival of Critilo.

Your Query [concerning the existence of purpose or chance in the creation of the universe], said Critilo, is not from the purpose, for you must know that the Divine Wisdom directing, and disposing of them [the stars of the firmament] in this manner, had more Sublime Reason, than is easily conceivable, placing their Harmony, and Rule not so much in their situation, as the conveniency of their Motion, and Temperature: for there is not a star in heaven, which hath not his different nature, and influence . . .

("The Second Chrisis", p. 20)

That [the color green that Andrenio noticed was not to be seen in the heavens], said Critilo, partakes too much of an Earthly quality, greeness being a Symptome, or Badge of Hope, is more agreeable to the future Wishes, and growing expectation of the Earth, than to that sublimer Region, which is swallowed up wholly in a happy Possession.

(*Ibid.*, p. 21)

The Sun, said Critilo, at the second view doth not amaze, nor at the third strike admiration. My curiosity began by this time to abate, as my stomach became more sharp; so after I had repeated some applauses, and praises in his honour, I descended lower by the direction of his light (which I perceived was a Creature, and an Instrument to serve my use) for the strengthening of the Mind is subject to the necessities of the Body, and sublime contemplations cannot be continued but by new supplies made to the decays of nature.

(*Ibid.*, p. 23)

The Variety of Nature is one part of its comely adornment, and affords us matter to busie our Heads in Contemplation, and our Tongues in Praises: our Souls are naturally propense to observe the effects of Nature: The wisest man called it the worst employment, and indeed so it is, when our considerations arrest themselves in satisfaction of our own Vanity, not proceeding to such sublime Raptures as may serve to raise in us the returns Gratitude and Glory to the supream Creator.

("The Third Chrisis", p. 25)

Hear me, said Adrenio, this last truth the greatest, and most sublime of any, that I have yet declared. I confess, that though I have admired four strange Prodigies in this Universe, viz. The multitude and variety of Creatures, the harmony and agreement in Contraries, their beauty and ornament mixed with profit, and convenience, and their mutations with Permanency. Yet above all, I remained confused in the knowledge of the Creator, who is so manifest in his Creatures, and yet hid in himself . . .

(*Ibid.*, p. 38)

I [Critilo] studied the noble Arts, and sublime Sciences, devoting my self with great affection to Moral Philosophy, which is the Food of the Judgment, the Centre of Reason, and the Life of Discretion.

(*Ibid.*, p. 58)

If this [the precepts of Galateus] doth not content you, said the Bookseller, because he treats of material Ceremonies, his Doctrine being only of outward carriage: Here is then, and it may be better to your liking, the judicious and grave Instruction of Juan de Vega, which he gave his Son when he sent him to the Court: This sublime Doctrine is not delivered with the affected gravity of a Portagues, but is as much as the Count of Portalegre could say when he sent his Son upon the like occasion. This Work, replied the Courtier, is too sublime, and too high for me, and fit for those only who move in the supream Sphere of the Commonwealth . . .

("The Eleventh Chrisis," p. 205)

Let us now reflect, said Critilo, on the Journy which we have made. Do not you observe those green and trampled paths, which we have left behind us, how mean, how vile do all those matters seem, which we have already passed? How childish and vain appears every thing in respect of that great Province into which we are now entred? How empty and void do past matters appear? How little do they show from our sublime place of residence?

("The Conclusion", p. 256)

The passages above do not necessarily represent all those in the work mentioning the sublime, but the uniformity of usage here is notable. The sublime is invariably used to express elevation or height, and in a generally non-literary context.

Dominique Bouhours, *The art of criticism: or, the method of making a right judgment upon subjects of wit and learning. Translated from the best edition of the French, of the famous Father Bohours, by a Person of Quality. In four dialogues.* (1705)

The following extracts are to be found in the first fifth or so of the 296-page text.

The fabulous System Salves all the Falshood which these sort of Thoughts have in themselves; and it is allow'd, nay, it is even glorious for a Poet to lye in so ingenious a manner. But then setting the Fiction aside, Truth ought to be found in Poetry as well as in Prose. Hereby I do not pretend to take away the marvellous from Poetry, which distinguishes it from the noblest and the sublimest Prose: I mean only that Poets ought never to destroy the Essences of things, when they would raise and adorn them.

(Dialogue I, p. 9)

I confess also that in a work which is profane and perfectly Poetical, it is allowable with Virgil* [footnote refers to his *Aeneid 4*] to bury the Manes, and yet one has a Right to make the Souls of the dead wander about the Places where they are interred; but I question whether in a Christian Discourse all of a Piece, that has nothing Poetical in it but the Numbers, such as Malherbs is, one may speak in the Language of the sublimest Poetry. Ronsard's Poem upon the Miseries of the Times, allows of Ideas and Expressions, which a Spiritual Stanza upon the Vanity of worldly greatness would not away with.

(*Ibid.*, p. 25)

A contrast to the prevalent association in the early eighteenth century of the sublime and Christian subject matter.

When they were in the Study, Eudoxus took up some Sheets [extracts he had made from his library collection of the works of the ancients], and read what follows.

"All kinds of writings please us only because of the Secret corruption of our Heart: if in a Discourse that is well written we love the Sublime of the Thoughts, the free and noble Air of some Authors: it is because of our vanity, and because we love to be great, and independent."

You have set this down, says Philanthus, for a false Thought? yes, replies Eudoxus: for what can be falser than to attribute that to the Corruption of the Heart, which is the effect of an exquisite discretion, and the Mark of a True Tast? Discourses that are well Writ please men of Sense, because it is a regular thing for them to be pleased with what is finely said, and the Mind is contented for the most part with any thing that is perfect in its own way. Vanity has no more part in the Pleasure which the reading of Virgil and Tully gives, than it has in that which is taken in seeing excellent Pictures, or in hearing excellent Musick. The humblest Man in the World is touched with these Beauties as much as any Body else, provided that he understands them, and is able to relish them. When I read the Holy Scriptures, whose simplicity has so much Sublime, think you that it is the Love of my own Loftiness, or the Corruption of my Heart which makes me relish what I read? Is it not rather that simple and majestical Character of the Word of God which makes the Impression on me? And may not much the same thing be said of the Language of the great Masters in Poetry and Eloquence? What a Fancy it is, to imagine that we love the nobleness and the easiness of their Stile, from a Spirit of haughtiness and independency!

(*Ibid*., pp. 31-32)

Bouhours lays much less stress on psychology and the ego in the sublime, and criticism generally, than his contemporary John Dennis. Bouhours' realization of the democratic, or classless, appeal of the sublime is a concept encountered above in several passages in the Context, perhaps most notably in Chapter III, p. 101.[1]

For my part, replies Philanthus, I chiefly love Thoughts which have softness in them, and which represent only great things to the Mind. Your Tast is not very bad in that, says Eudoxus, the Sublime, (11) [footnote refers to: Non ad persuasionem, sed ad stuporem rapiunt grandia. Long de sublimi. Sect. 1.] the Grandeur in a Thought is that properly which carries all before it, and which ravishes, provided the Thought agrees to the Subject: for this is a general Rule, that one ought to think according to the matter he treats of, (*) [footnote refers to: A Sermone tenui sublime discordat, fitq; corruptum, quia in plano tumet. Quintil, Lib. 8. cap. 3.] and nothing is more foolish than to have sublime Thoughts on a Subject which requires only mean ones: and it would almost be better to have none but

[1] For a brillant book-length discussion of the relationship between class and the art of fiction see Erich Auerbach, *Mimesis: the Representation of Reality in Western Literature* (Princeton, 1953).

mean Thoughts upon an Argument which might require sublime ones: so that Timaeus whom Longinus speaks of, that commended Alexander for Conquering all Asia, in fewer Years than Isocrates composed his Panegyrick upon the Athenians, troubles me less than Balzac who says thus to la Motte Aigron; "Let me dye if the least part of the work which you show'd me, be not worth more than all that ever the Hollanders did; provided you except the Victories of the Prince of Orange."

The Truth is, Longinus condemns this Comparison of the King of Macedon with a Sophist, and of the Conquest of Asia with a simple Discourse, as low and childish: But yet there is more proportion between an illustrious Conqueror, and a Famous Orator; between an effect of Heroick Vertue, and a Masterpiece of Eloquence; than there is between a small part of a little Work, and all that a powerful and happy People have done . . . [Philanthus disagrees]

(Dialogue II, pp. 54-55)

Methinks, reply'd Philanthus, that well chosen Comparisons, taken from the great Subjects of Nature, always produce very noble Thoughts. Yes, reply'd Eudoxus, and (*) [footnote refers to: Longinus. Sect. 10.] Longinus who gives rules of the sublime not only in Words, but in Thoughts, thinks very nobly himself; when he compares Demosthenes to a Tempest and Thunder that ravages and carries all away; Cicero to an everlasting Fire, and who according to the proportion it goes on gets new Strength. The Comparisons of art, persued he, excell sometimes those we borrow from Nature . . .

(*Ibid.*, p. 82)

But concerning the Divine Word, remember, I beseech you, that the Holy Scripture is a Foundation of noble Thoughts, great and sublime, such as these: "I am he that is. The Lord shall Reign in all Eternity and beyond. That there be light, and there was light." The last so plain in appearance and looking only upon the Terms, gives a Magnificent Idea of the Power of God; and Longinus for all he was a Pagan, proposes it for a Model of sublimity in the Thought: For an elevated Thought may agree very well with the plain words; (*) [footnote refers to a thirty-word quotation from Longinus *On the Sublime*, Sect. 2.] it happens even that the plainess of the Expression makes us often more sensible of the Greatness of things; and that is true according to the Sentiment of Longinus, that sometimes we admire the Thought of a generous and magnanimous Man, tho' he says nothing: We admire him, I say, through his silence, which shews the nobleness of his Soul, and we have an Example of it in the Odysses. Here Ulysses makes his submissions to Ajax, to which Ajax does not so much as Answer; and that very Silence has something greater than all what he cou'd have said.

(*Ibid.*, p. 86)

Here Bouhours presents the orthodox view of the sublime and Holy Scripture. It is important to note that throughout his remarks, Bouhours emphasizes the sublimity of thought rather than the sublimity of words or tropes.

William Mears, *A catalogue of modern books in divinity, history, law, Philosophy, mathematicks, poetry, etc.* (1722)

This is a sixteen-page catalogue. On page 11 occurs the following interesting discrepancy *vis-à-vis* the correct name of the book in question:

XIX The Art of English Poetry, containing, 1. Rules for making Verses. 2. A Collection of the most Natural, Agreeable and Sublime Thoughts, Viz.

Some party, we will probably never know who or for what reason, has substituted the word 'Sublime' in the place of the word 'Noble' of the author's (Edward Bysshe) own title. The conclusion to be drawn therefrom is that the two words were interchangable in the minds of at least some people of the time.[2]

In a miscellany of a dozen poems, including well known ones by writers like Denham, Roscommon, Dryden, Mulgrave, Congreve, Addison, and Sprat, printed and sold by H. Hills in Black-fryars, near the Water-side, London, in 1708 and 1709 appears the following passage from an advertisement placed in the miscellany just before Dryden's *Absalom and Achitophel*:

A Catalogue of Poems, Printed and Sold by H. Hills, in Black-Fryars, near the Water-side . . .
The Flight of the Pretender, with Advice to the Poets. A Poem, in the Arthurical, -Jobical, -Elizabethecal Style and Phrase of the sublime Poet Maurus.

[2] See also Chapter II, p. 52, above.

XII

CONCLUSIONS

As stated in the Preface and Chapter I, the purpose of my study was twofold. The first objective was to summarize several of the leading critical works on the Longinian and the eighteenth-century sublime to appear since the beginning of the present century, and to indicate ways in which they perhaps leave something to be desired. As the basic text on the subject, Samuel Monk's *The Sublime* received the bulk of my attention as far as negative criticism is concerned. I tried, on the other hand, to demonstrate how certain more recent studies, notably those of Menuez and Olson, help to balance assessments of Longinus that, like Monk's, weigh too heavily the element of rhetoric in the make-up of the eighteenth-century sublime. And as an introduction to the discussion of the modern critics and to aid in interrelating them with my own ideas I employed several esthetic concepts of Susanne Langer.

My second objective was the compilation of a Context, which, it is hoped, brings together in one place a number of eighteenth-century usages of the word 'sublime' that have not hitherto appeared in a formal study of the term. In addition to helping the student to evaluate the nature and influence of the idea of the sublime in the eighteenth century, these passages suggest a half dozen fundamental questions about the sublime touched on in the Context commentary. I intend to try here to come to some conclusions on these questions, which are: Are there early eighteenth-century responses to the Longinian sublime that are neither anticipations of the psychological and natural sublime nor *jejune* reiterations of a rhetorical sublime? Is there evidence that the role of the artist continues to be emphasized despite the cant opinion that the eighteenth century switched its attention to the psychological state of the audience? Are there writers who call Longinus an extra-rhetorical critic? Is there an application of the sublime to nature before Boileau's translation of *On the Sublime* in 1674? Is there a narrowing interpretation of 'hupsous' during the century? What evidence is there for the supposed shift of interest from artist to subject matter?

The first question above is undeniably the most important for this study. Indeed, it was Monk's insistence on limiting the eighteenth-century sublime to the two alternatives of rhetoric and psychology that first led me to investigate the validity of such a rigid formulation of the problem, for it seemed unlikely that in a period when so many contrasting tendencies were striving for ascendency that the sublime could be so neatly and narrowly compartmented. My initial step was to deny that esthetic is limited to man's emotional response to external nature and literature treating of the awesome phenomena of nature. Having, I hope, proven this point, with the aid of recent criticism, I presented throughout the Context a large number of allusions to the sublime that clearly do not lend themselves to the Monk dichotomy. They are too numerous for mention here, but are easily found, particularly in Chapter III, on oratory and rhetoric.

Before turning to the other questions at hand, I should point out that a corollary to my thesis that Monk and others are wrong in saying that the sublime from Longinus to Boileau is exclusively rhetorical, and from Boileau to Burke gradually more psychological, is that there is no reason to dismiss eighteenth-century references to the sublime that depend on the ancients in some important way. That is not to say, of course, that there are no documents to support Monk's view and that all eighteenth-century writings linking the sublime with Homer, Virgil, and Demosthenes are interesting and independent of rhetorical considerations. But the fact is, as established by the Context, that there are many passages in which invoking antiquity leads to unpredictable results, several of the latter bearing on the remaining central questions raised by this study.

There is abundant evidence in the Context that, whatever success in the period is enjoyed by the adherents of the schools of the natural sublime and psychology, the artist continues during the first half of the century to be the focus of much attention in matters relating to the sublime. Weekes' satiric poem *On the abuse of poetry* (1754) alludes throughout to the sublime in terms of the poet. (Ch. II, p. 63). In his *Dissertation* (1763), John Brown calls Ossian a 'sublime and original Bard' (Ch. II, p. 67). In both general principles and specific application John Lawson, in his *Lectures concerning oratory* (1759), stresses that sublimity springs from the nobility of the writer (Ch. III, p. 106 f). John Ward's *A System of oratory* (1759) discusses the sublime in terms of the speaker primarily (Ch. III, p. 113 f.). As might be expected, the chapter on Milton offers a general emphasis on the role of the artist, in this case the Puritan poet himself. I cite as examples Jonathan Richardson's apostrophe to Milton in *Explanatory notes* (1734; my Ch. IV, p. 122); G. S. Carlisle's letter on the requirements for a poet in the *Essay* (1750) of William Lauder (p. 128); and in his *The life of John Milton* (1699) John Toland's descriptions of the attributes and abilities of Milton (p. 131). John Upton's *Critical observations on Shakespeare* (1746) offers a caveat to the poet who would attain to the sublime (Ch. V, p. 134). In an essay abstracted by *The London Magazine* from the *Free Briton* (1733) there is noteworthy emphasis on the sublime in the artist as distinguished from the object or the audience (Ch. VI, p. 150). The same thing, with the element of pleasure from terror in art superadded, is the subject of one of the letters (1738) of the Critical Club (Ch. VIII, p. 166). William Melmoth, in *Letters on several subjects* (1748) writes of Pope's being inspired with the same sublime spirit that invests the *Iliad* (*Ibid.*, p. 167). Finally, in his great dictionary of 1755 Samuel Johnson gives the sublimity of Milton's thoughts as part of the definition of the sublime (Ch. X, p. 195). The above is by no means an exhaustive listing of the passages in the Context that illustrate the importance which the critics of the eighteenth century apparently continued to assign to the artist's capacity for the sublime in his own mind and soul.

In recapitulating allusions in the Context to the matter of critics' regarding Longinus as an extra-rhetorical theorist of the sublime, I must admit that the validity of any conclusions drawn therefrom is seriously qualified by the virtual impossibility of determining when a given writer has obtained intimacy with Longinus through the good offices of Boileau. Although this problem is a factor of some importance for the Context as a whole, it is obviously especially germane to the task of interpreting the extent to which the eighteenth century recognized the non-rhetorical possibilities of *On the Sublime*. Nevertheless, allowing for the Bolevian influence, the Context contains enough passages on the non-rhetorical sublime of Longinus to support the view that it did not require a psychological esthetic to free the sublime from a rhetorical orientation in the eighteenth century. Henry Pemberton, *Observations on poetry* (1738), says, "Yet Longinus has judiciously distinguished between the design of poetic and oratorial imagery" (Ch. II, p. 59). In a work concerned with aspects of rhetoric, *Dialogues concerning eloquence in general* (1722), François Fenelon indicates that he knows Longinus by way of Boileau and has one of the speakers in the dialogue say that "Longinus does not treat of what is proper to instruct men, but of what is apt to move and seize their passions" (Ch. III, p. 90). (I remind the reader that in Chapter III, I comment several times on the blurring of the boundaries between rhetoric and non-rhetoric in eighteenth-century treatises on oratory and rhetoric.) John Douglas in *Milton vindicated* (1751) states that Longinus "expressly lays down the imitation and emulation of the former great writers and poets as one of the ways that leads to the sublime" (Ch. IV, p. 130). Returning to the work of Upton cited above, I offer the following as an example of rhetoric and the sublime opposed to each other: "I would beg leave to know, what ideas can he be supposed to have of a real sublime in manners and sentiments, who has never gone further for his instruction, than what a puffy rhetorician, who wrote in a barbarous age, can teach?" (p. 135). There is no indication in the context of Upton's passage that his puffy rhetorician is Longinus! Melmoth in his *Letters* writes of Longinus quoting a passage from Homer as an instance of the true sublime, showing that Melmoth does not regard Longinus as a rhetorician unless he holds Homer to be one too (Ch. VIII, p. 167). Bouhours, *The art of criticism* (1705), refers to the fact that Longinus proposes as a model of sublimity a line from Genesis like "that there be light, and there was light", which expresses a magnificent idea with plain words (Ch. XI, p. 203). The import of Bouhour's passage is distinctly not rhetorical.

In connection with the sublime applied to nature before the date of Boileau's translation, it must be admitted that my context does not contain a good example.[1] (This does not mean, as I have said before, that usage of the sublime up to 1674 is rhetorical.) Perhaps the nearest that any passage in the Context comes to filling the bill occurs in Walter Charleton, *Natural History of the Passions* (1674):

> The Reasonable Soul of Man seems to be of a Nature so Divine and Excellent, that it is capable of Understanding all things that are in this life intelligible: but yet so reserved and abstruse withall, that it cannot understand itself; as many most sublime Wits, who had long exercised and perplex'd themselves in enquiries into the hidden and mysterious Essence thereof, have at length ingenuously confess'd. (App. 4, p. 221)

But the success of the passage is only partial; the date is the same as

[1] This is consistent, however, with Frederick Staver, " 'Sublime' as Applied to Nature", *Modern Language Notes*, LXX (Nov. 1955), 484-487, who finds the first example of the word 'sublime' used to express a generalized emotional response to grandeur of visual nature in a letter of Elizabeth Montagu written in 1742.

that of Boileau's translation, and the nature alluded to is nothing else than human nature.

The fifth question I posed near the start of this chapter, Is there a narrowing interpretation of 'hupsous' during the eighteenth century? is best dealt with in general terms. Defining 'hupsous' as 'elevation', it is immediately apparent that, if anything, its interpretation widens during the century, because in addition to the retention of older meanings (see especially the closing pages of Chapters II and III), there is the addition of the psychological school's usage of the word. That is to say that after 1750 can be found references to elevation resulting from causes that range from the sublimities of Homer to the terror of a thunderstorm.

The Context has a number of examples of sublimity residing in the subject matter underlying the production of literature, though fewer than those showing the sublime in the artist and in the literary work proper. If the Context is a worthy gauge, my conclusion here is that, ruling out discussions of the sublime by writers like Burke, the word 'sublime' is not as commonly utilized to treat of the raw material for literature as it is to comment on the writer and his finished product. There is one outstanding instance of the sublime of subject matter in the Context, however. It is in the *Dialogues* of Fenelon where he expresses his desire for a sublime of the familiar, sweet, and simple, where the country laborer is nominated as the subject of a sublime piece. (Ch. III, p. 94).

I close this summary of the conclusions on the sublime suggested by the Context by mentioning three aspects of its usage that are interesting, if less important in the history of the term. There is a considerable amount of criticism in the period that uses the sublime in a satirical fashion. Examples can be found in Chapter III, p. 108 and Chapter VI, p. 156. Satirists' use of the sublime should not, after all, be surprising, since from the beginning of the term's existence critics were wont to warn against the false sublime of bombast, fustian, and indecorum.

A little-regarded aspect of the sublime is that of its usage in the debate between proponents of utility and inutility in art respectively. As in every era, I suspect, the eighteenth century disputed the extent to which literature should serve useful ends. The sublime employed in this connection occurs in Chapter VI, pp. 138-139 and Chapter IX, pp. 172, 186. In three of these four excerpts the sublime apears in the pro-inutility argument. Although the Context's sampling is too small to be positive, I would expect to find this ratio prevail at large.

Lastly, I remind the reader that even in the eighteenth century he can find a kind of thinking that does not seem dated, and even on a subject like the sublime what is more! Chapter II, p. 60 presents a passage on the relativity of men's response to the sublime that does its author credit today.

As a matter of fact, relativity may be the key word in following the long history of the sublime. While Mrs. Langer poses what is probably the central problem for the achievement of the sublime in any age, the artistic unification of form and feeling such as to produce a certain effect, she also allows that this process inevitably results in different forms of the sublime depending on the cultural milieu involved, which fosters its own values and concepts, and symbolizations thereof.

It is hoped that this Context of the word 'sublime' from 1650 to 1760 shows, if nothing else, that the concept formulated by Longinus meant many things to many people in the eighteenth century, but that his idea of the sublime, rightly understood, is not all things to all men.

APPENDIX 1

COLLATION OF FOUR TRANSLATIONS OF *ON THE SUBLIME*

The following passages are collated in the hope of showing the differences among the translators in emphasis on rhetoric. As we might expect, the sections of the treatise on rhetoric proper give the translators less room for individual variation than certain other sections in which rhetoric is not so explicit. It will become apparent that the Smith translation is marked by numerous vocabulary choices closer to the terms of rhetoric and the rules than those of the other three. For identification I use the markings of Roberts only; the equivalent passages can easily be located in their respective texts.

SMITH	ROBERTS	PRICKARD	EINARSON
1.4 For the Sublime not only persuades, but even throws an Audience into Transport. . . . Dexterity of Invention, and good Order and Oeconomy in composition, are not to be discerned from one or two Passages, nor scarcely sometimes from the whole Texture of a Discourse; but the Sublime, when seasonably addressed, with the rapid force of Lightning has borne down all before it, and shewn	The effect of elevated language upon an audience is not persuasion but transport. . . . Similarly, we see skill in invention, and due order and arrangement of matter, emerging as the hard-won result not of one thing or of two, but of the whole texture of the composition, whereas Sublimity flashing forth at the right moment scatters everything before it like a thunderbolt, and at once displays the	For it is not to persuasion but to ecstasy that passages of extraordinary genius carry the hearer . . . Again, skill in invention and power of orderly arrangement are not seen from one passage nor from two, but emerge with effort out of the whole context; Sublimity, we know, brought out at the happy moments, parts all the matter this way and that, and like a lightning	For what is of transcendent genius produces in the hearers not persuasion, but transport . . . And we observe that an author's skill in invention and in the ordering and disposition of his subjects is seen not from a single passage or from two, but scarcely appears even from the whole fabric of his discourse; while sublimity brought forth at the right moment scatters the subjects like a bolt

SMITH	ROBERTS	PRICKARD	EINARSON
at one stroke the compacted Might of Genius.	power of the orator in all its plenitude.	flash, reveals, at a stroke and in its entirety, the power of the orator.	of lightning, and immediately reveals the whole capacity of a speaker at a glance.

Note how the words "not only" in his first sentence render Smith's passage the most rhetorically oriented.

V. All these and such like Indecencies in Composition take their Rise from the same Original; I mean that eager Pursuit of uncommon Turns, which almost infatuates the Writers of the present Age.	All these ugly and parasitical growths arise in literature from a single cause, that pursuit of novelty in the expression of ideas which may be regarded as the fashionable craze of the day.	All these undignified faults spring up in literature from a single cause, the craving for intellectual novelties, on which, above all else, our own generation goes wild.	Yet all such derogations to dignity arise in discourse from a single cause: zeal for novelty in the thoughts, in which above all else our contemporaries run wild.

The above shows even more clearly the progressive de-emphasis of rhetoric in Longinus. Smith's 'uncommon turns' becomes Roberts' 'novelty in the expression of ideas', and ends up in Prickard and Einarson as 'intellectual novelties' and 'thoughts' respectively.

IX. 1 But tho' the first and most important of these Divisions, I mean, Elevation of Thought, be rather a natural than an acquired Qualification . . .	Now the first of the conditions mentioned, namely elevation of mind, holds the foremost rank among them all.	After all, however, the first element, great natural genius, covers far more ground than the others . . .	Yet since the first of our sources, greatness of genius, has a greater portion in sublimity than the rest . . .

And when Smith starts with 'elevation of thought', Roberts makes it 'elevation of mind', and the most recent two translators 'great natural genius' and 'greatness of genius'.

IX.13 The Stile [Homer's] is not so grand and majestic as that of the "Iliad" . . .	He does not in the Odyssey maintain so high a pitch as in those poems of Ilium.	Here [*Odyssey*] the tone of those great lays of Ilium is no longer maintained . . .	For here he no longer preserves a pitch of vigor equal to that of his poem about Troy . . .

Smith is the only translator to use the word 'style'.

SMITH	ROBERTS	PRICKARD	EINARSON
XIII.1 Tho' Plato's Stile particularly excels in Smoothness, and an easy and peaceable Flow of the Words, yet neither does it want an Elevation and Grandeur . . .	Although Plato thus flows on with noiseless stream, he is none the less elevated.	That Plato (to return to him) "flowing in some such noiseless stream", none the less reaches greatness, you will not fail to recognize . . .	That Plato (to return), though he glides onward noiselessly with an expansive current such as we have described, does not for that reason fail to rise to grandeur . . .
XXIX.2 And now, what has been said on this Subject, will I presume, my dear Terentianus, Abundantly shew, of what service Figures may be in producing the Sublime.	But our parenthetical disquisition with regard to the use of figures as bearing upon the sublime has run to sufficient length, dear Terentianus.	Enough however of this disquisition (which came in by way of parenthesis) on the use of figures in producing sublime effects . . .	Let our excursion into ancient literature for the purpose of showing the use of figures for sublimity end here, my dear Terentianus . . .

Interestingly enough Prickard joins Smith in having figures PRODUCE the sublime, while the others translate 'use of figures', which seems less rhetorical in tone. Despite Prickard's reversion in this last passage, however, I feel that the contents of this appendix, taken as a whole, demonstrate the way in which critical interpretation of *On the Sublime* achieves liberal, non-rhetorical possibilities in moving from the early eighteenth century to our own time. I also cite these later translations as support for the thesis of this study that surprisingly liberal interpretations of the sublime can be found in unlikely eighteenth-century sources,[1] and, further, that the work of certain modern interpreters of Longinus that stress his non-rhetorical qualities is worthy of attention.

[1] For the reason that what can occur to the mind of a critic in one age can also occur to the mind of a critic in another.

APPENDIX 2

DICTIONARIES IN WHICH THE WORD 'SUBLIME' DOES NOT APPEAR

The following listing of dictionaries is a comprehensive sampling of those works of this genre among the Folger Library's holdings that do not define the word 'sublime'. I omit certain specialized dictionaries in which the sublime would not be expected to occur.

Henry Cockeram, *The English Dictionary: or, an interpreter of hard English words.* (1655)

Joseph Caryl, *An English-Greek lexicon, containing the Derivations and various Significations of all the Words in the New Testament.* (1661)

Stephen Skinner, *Etymologicon linguae anglicanae.* (1671)

Thomas Wilson, *A complete Christian dictionary: wherein the Significations and several Acceptations of All the Words mentioned in the Holy Scriptures of the Old and New Testament, Are fully Opened, Expressed, Explained ...* (1678)

[Anon.], *Gazophylarium Anglicanum – A new English dictionary* (1691)

The fact that the word 'sublime' is not included in this dictionary is both notable and regrettable because the work is richer etymologically than most of those in Chapter X and this appendix.

Louis Moreri, *The great historical, geographical, and poetical dictionary.* (1694)

N. H., *The Ladies dictionary.* (1694)

Pierre Danet, *A complete dictionary of the Greek and Roman antiquities.* (1700)

[Anon.], *An historical, genealogical and poetical dictionary.* (1703)
This is an example of a type of dictionary, evidently popular in our period, that is not likely to mention the sublime for the reason that most of the word entries are proper names.

[Anon.], *A universal, historical, geographical, chronological, and poetical dictionary.* (1703)
Basically a 'curious miscellany of sacred and prophane history'.

William Willymott, *The peculiar use and signification of certain words in the Latin Tongue.* (1704)

[Anon.], *Thesaurus dramaticus. Containing all the celebrated passages, soliloquies, similies, descriptions, and other poetical beauties in the body of English plays. In two volumes.* (1724)
Not really a dictionary at all, this work is closely enough related in purpose to a lexicon to be listed here. It is organized by categories, none of which treats of the sublime.

Noël Chomel, *Dictionaire oeconomique: or, the family dictionary. Two volumes.* (1725)
Translated from the French, the Dictionaire has a title page which advertises that the dictionary contains, among other things:

All Sorts of Rural Sports and Exercises, conducing to the Benefit and innocent Enjoyments of Life; as also Painting in Miniature, and divers other Arts and Terms of Art explained, for the Entertainment and Amusement of Gentlemen, Ladies, etc.

The Preface to the *Dictionaire* was apparently contributed by one R. Bradley, Professor of Botany in the University of Cambridge. There is a passage in it of interest to us because of the interrelationship of genius, the rules, and the sublime:

If a Man has a bright Genius, he will excell, if he follows his Genius; but where the Genius is either poor or constrain'd, the best Instructions will never bring it to bear good Fruit; one might as well suppose it possible to make a Raphael, a Pope, or a Handel, in Painting, Poetry, and Musick, by Education only. Isocrates, an excellent Greek Writer, gives us a Lesson of the same purport in his Advice to Demonicus, where he says, That Nature is preferable to Law, and a judicious voluntary Choice brings richer Fruit than can be imposed by Necessity.

[Anon.], *A nomenclature English and Italian.* (1726)

Under the category 'of the Liberal arts and Sciences' the words 'rhetoric' and 'eloquence' appear, but not 'sublime'. Nor is it listed in the section devoted to adjectives.

Pierre Bayle, *Dictionaire historique et critique.* (1730)
Bayle's dictionary was available to English readers in English translation, as well as in French.

John Barrow, *Dictionarium polygraphicum: or, the whole body of arts regularly digested. Two volumes.* (1735)
This is primarily a dictionary of the visual arts and crafts.

APPENDIX 3

A SYNOPSIS OF ALFRED ROSENBERG'S DISSERTATION, *LONGINUS IN ENGLAND BIS ZUR ENDE DES 18. JAHRHUNDERTS*

Rosenberg's dissertation is not readily available in the United States to the student of the eighteenth-century sublime. The purpose of this appendix is, therefore, to provide a list of the English writers treated by Rosenberg, along with an indication of how much space he devotes to each. Generally speaking, Rosenberg merely quotes and paraphrases; there is little attempt at interpretation except at the beginning of the three chapters and at the very end, and in these places Rosenberg's summaries necessarily omit frequent or extended discussions of individual writers.

This appendix also presents the citations of nine periodicals in Rosenberg's section "C", "Die Zeit des eigentlichen Einflusses (bis 1800)". These citations supplement the periodicals quoted in Chapter VI, there are no duplications, and three of Rosenberg's appeared later than the terminal limit of my study.

First, the writers:

Addison, 16 pages
Akenside, 2½ pages
Armstrong, 10 lines
Beattie, 1½ pages
Blair, 4½ pages
Blount, 6 lines
Budgell, ½ page
Edmund Burke, 3 pages
Cawthorn, ½ page
Churchill, 9 lines
George Colman, 1 page
Dennis, 2 pages
Dryden, 9½ pages
Fenton, 1 page

Fielding, 4 pages
Gay, 4 lines
Alexander Gerard, 2 pages
Gibbon, 1½ pages
Gildon, ½ page
Goldsmith, 6 pages
Gray, 1 page
James Harris, 2½ pages
Aaron Hill, 7 lines
Henry Home, 4 pages
Richard Hurd, 5 pages
Samuel Johnson, 4 pages
Vicesimus Knox, 6 pages
Robert Lloyd, 1½ pages
Mackenzie, 2 pages
Thomas Parnell, ½ page
Ambrose Philips, ½ page
Christopher Pitt, 7 lines
Pope, 8 pages
Prior, 5 lines
Reynolds, 6 pages
Roscommon, 3 pages
Rowe, 1½ pages
Shaftesbury, 1 page
Sheffield, 1 page
William Smith, 3 pages
Somerville, ½ page
Steele, 2 pages
Sterne, 3 pages
Swift, 2 pages
Sir William Temple, ½ page
Theobald, 1 page
Horace Walpole, 1 page
William Warburton, 3 pages
Joseph Warton, 6½ pages
Gilbert West, ½ page
Robert Wolseley, ½ page
Edward Young, 5 pages

The Periodicals:

Guardian, 121 (July 30, 1713), Longinus on the sublimity of Ajax' silence.

Gentleman's Magazine (August 1735. S. 461), extract from the *Grub-street Journal* of July 31, 1735 on the necessity of the sublime in almost all writings.

Inspector 94 (*Drake*, *Gleaner*, 85–1751),[1] "If Longinus knew anything of the sublime in writing, the scriptures must be full of it, since his whole work, compared with their several parts, seems but a comment on their beauties."

Gray's Inn Journal, 4 (*Gleaner* 92–1752), "enhält eine der in dieser Zeit zahlreichen Parnassvisionen. Shakespeare sitzt dort und 'Longinus admired him to a degree of enthusiasm.'"[2]

Gray's Inn Journal, 51 (*Gleaner* 96–1752), same theme as the preceding: admiration for the great ancient writers, including Longinus.

Gray's Inn Journal, 86 (*Gleaner*, 100–1752), the men are numbered on Parnassus who could represent the republic of letters. Longinus is one of them.

Microcosm 22 (April 9, 1787), "Verfasser George Canning: 'Are we not entertained in the works of Longinus and the Gentleman's Magazine, with delectable dissertations on the weaving of plots and the interweaving of episodes?'"

Microcosm 36 (July 16, 1787), "nennt Longin unter den 'first literary worthies.'"

Observer 134 (Verfasser Richard Cumberland, erste Ausgabe 1785-1790), "bringt eine Besprechung der Werke von Aeschylus: 'As to the tragedy of the seven chiefs against Thebes, it is said to have been the favourite of its author, and we know the testimony of the critic Longinus.'"

[1] In this and the next three citations, Rosenberg does not give the exact date.
[2] In the periodical descriptions, comment not in quotations marks is mine, and quoted in English is taken from the periodical by Rosenberg.

APPENDIX 4

TWO ADDITIONAL ALLUSIONS TO THE SUBLIME

I place the following extracts in an appendix because they do not happen to fit under any of the general headings that comprise Chapters II–XI of the Context.

[Anon.], *Reflections upon reflections.* (1726)

This sixteen-page essay is a rebuttal to another anonymous tract published the same year called *Reflections upon reading the tragedy of Hecuba,* which our author regards as a cheap kind of advertisement for what he says is virtual plagiarism of the Euripides play. While most of *Reflections upon reflections* is a series of quibbles with the earlier work, it does yield the following reference to the sublime.

I have already given you a Proof of that Perfection in Style, in a Scene of Hecuba and Agamemnon; there is another Dialogue of that kind between Polymnestor and Hecuba, at the beginning of the Fifth Act. But what say you now to a touch of sublime Milton – a studied, affected, and unnatural Imitation of his Sublime and Diction.

When the Moon arose,
And shot his cheerless Beams across the Horizon,
Steep we ascend the Summit of yon Rock,
Where the rough Cliff hangs lowring o'er the Main,
And blackens with its Brow the Flood beneath;
As now descending the steep Sharp we travers'd,
The very Spirit and the Shape of Polydor
Appear'd upon the Desart Bourn beneath,
Swift did it glide athwart the Moon-light Gleam,
As Shadows pass across the Glebe in Autumn. –

Note the sharp distinction made by the writer in his prose comment between the sublime on the one hand and diction on the other.

Walter Charleton, *Natural History of the Passions . . . In the Savoy, Printed by T. N. for James Magnes.* (1674)

The source of Charleton's remarks is a combination of his reading in the ancients on the subject of the passions, and his own musings thereon. The treatise is traditional, not reflecting the more advanced thinking of philosophers like Locke and Hobbes.

Now if solid Reasons, Authority Divine, and the judgment of many sublime Wits and profound Philosophers, as well Ancient as Modern, be of any weight to recommend this neither heretical, nor improbable opinion to me; certainly I need not blush to incline thereunto.

(Epistle Prefatory)

The Reasonable Soul of Man seems to be of a Nature so Divine and Excellent, that it is capable of Understanding all things that are in this life intelligible: but yet so reserved and abstruse withall, that it cannot understand itself; as many most sublime Wits, who had long exercised and perplex'd themselves in enquiries into the hidden and mysterious Essence thereof, have at length ingenuously confess'd.

(Section I. Introduction, pp. 2 - 3)

Nor indeed would such a prolix research be consistent with my present design; which principally aim's at a recollection of some notions, that have partly in reading, partly in meditation, occurred to me, concerning the various Passions of the Mind, their Genealogy, their first sources and resorts, their most remarkable Differences, Motions, and Forces, and in fine, by what kind of Connexion and intercourse betwixt two so disparate Natures, the one Incorporal, the other Corporal, it is, that the Rational Soul is respectively coaffected by them. And this with as much brevity, as the amplitude of the Subject can admit; with as much perspicuity, as my weak reason can attain unto, in an argument so sublime and difficult.

(*Ibid.*, pp. 3 - 4)

Bearing in mind that the *Natural History* appeared in the same year as Boileau's translation of Longinus, Charleton's use of the word 'sublime' is remarkable in that it seems more psychologically oriented than the sublime of rhetoric or mere loftiness. However, this is not completely clear in the above passages, and the way they are read determines, most probably, the extent to which my speculation is valid.

BIBLIOGRAPHY

As an aid to the reader the Bibliography is divided into two sections. The first pertains to Chapter I on modern critics and the sublime, and includes all titles, old and new, to be found therein. The second section contains all titles occurring in the Context (Chapters II-XI, and Chapter XII, and the Appendices, provided that they have not been cited in Chapter I.

Section I

Baillie, John, *An Essay on the Sublime* (1747), No. 43, *Augustan Reprints* (Berkeley and Los Angeles, 1953). Introduction by Samuel H. Monk.

Baldwin, Charles S., *Ancient Rhetoric and Poetic* (New York, 1924).

Beers, Cora Lee, *Longinus and the Disintegration of English Neo-Classicism* (Stanford University, 1939).

Bosanquet, Bernhard, *A History of Aesthetic* (London, Sonnenschein, New York, Macmillan, 1910).

Cohen, Ralph, Review article on Walter J. Hipple, Jr.'s *The Beautiful, the Sublime, and the Picturesque, Philological Quarterly*, XXXVII, no. 3, July 1958, 291-4.

Crane, Ronald S., Review article on Samuel H. Monk's *The Sublime, Philological Quarterly*, XV (1936), 165-167.

Donovan, J., "The Festal Origin of Human Speech", *Mind*, XVI (1891), 498-506; XVII (1892), 325-339.

Einarson, B. S., trans., University Classics Edition of *Longinus On the Sublime* and Reynolds' *Discourses* (Chicago, 1945).

Fyfe, W. H., *Longinus on the Sublime* (London, 1927).

Gibbon, Edward, *Journal to January 28th, 1763*, ed. D. M. Low (London, 1929).

Godolphin, F. R. B., "The Basic Critical Doctrine of Longinus 'On the Sublime' ", *Transactions and Proceedings of the American Philological Association*, LXVIII (1937), 172-183.

Hamilton, K. G., *The Two Harmonies: Poetry and Prose in the Seventeenth Century* (Oxford, 1963).

Henn, T. R., *Longinus and English Criticism* (Cambridge, 1934).

Hipple, Walter J., Jr., *The Beautiful, the Sublime, and the Picturesque in Eighteenth-Century British Aesthetic Theory* (Carbondale, 1957).

Hussey, Christopher, *The Picturesque: Studies in a Point of View* (London and New York, 1927).

Langer, Susanne K., *Philosophy in a New Key: A Study in the Symbolism of Reason, Rite, and Art* (Harvard University Press, 1942).

Menuez, Caroline B., "Longinus on the Equivalence of the Arts", *Classical Journal*, XXXVI (1941), 346-353.
Monk, Samuel H., *The Sublime: A Study of Critical Theories in XVIII-Century England* (Modern Language Association, 1935; Ann Arbor, 1960).
Murdoch, Iris, "The Sublime and the Good", *Chicago Review*, XIII, No. iii (1959), 42-55.
Nicolson, Marjorie H., *Mountain Gloom and Mountain Glory* (Ithaca, 1959).
Nitchie, Elizabeth, "Longinus and Later Literary Criticism", *The Classical Weekly*, Vol. 27, No. 16 (1934), 121-126, 129-136.
—, "Longinus and the Theory of Poetic Imitation in 17th and 18th Century England", *Studies in Philology*, XXXII (Oct. 1935), 580-597.
Olson, Elder, "The Argument of Longinus 'On the Sublime' ", *Modern Philology*, XXXIX (1942), 225-258.
—, Introduction to University Classics Edition of *Longinus On the Sublime* and Joshua Reynolds' *Discourses*, One volume (Chicago, 1945).
Prickard, A. O., *Longinus on the Sublime* (Oxford, 1906).
Roberts, W. Rhys, *Longinus on the Sublime. The Greek Text Edited After the Paris MS with Introduction, Translation, Facsimiles and Appendices* (Cambridge, 1899).
Rosenberg, Alfred, *Longinus in England bis zur Ende des 18. Jahrhunderts* (Weimar and Berlin, 1917).
Smith, William, *Dionysius Longinus on the Sublime; translated from the Greek, with notes and observations, and some account of the life, writings, and character of the author* (1743).
Tuveson, Ernest, "Space, Deity, and the 'Natural sublime' ", *Modern Language Quarterly*, XII (1951), 20-38.

Section II

Entries marked with an asterisk are represented here by their short titles only, in order that the Bibliography might be as concise as possible. The location in the Context of their full titles can be determined from the Index by author.

As is the case throughout this study, the name London does not appear when that is the place of publication of seventeenth- and eighteenth-century works.

Anonymous works precede.

The art of speaking in public: or an essay on the action of an orator; as to his pronunciation and gestures. The Second Edition corrected. With an Introduction relating to the famous Mr. Henly's present Oratory. 1727.
An essay on tragedy, with a critical examen of Mahomet and Irene. 1749.
A familiar explanation of the poetical works of Milton. To which is prefixed Mr. Addison's criticism on Paradise Lost. 1762.
Gazophylarium Anglicanum – A New English dictionary (1691).
[A.D.], *Glossographis Anglicana nova: or, a Dictionary, interpreting such Hard Words of whatever Language, as are at present used in the English Tongue, with their Etymologies, Definitions, etc.* (1707).
An historical, genealogical and poetical dictionary (1703).
[N.H.], *The Ladies Dictionary* (1694).

The Many Advantages of a Good Language to any Nation: with an Examination of the present State of our own: As also, An Essay towards correcting some Things that are wrong in it (1724).

Milton's sublimity asserted: in a poem. Occasioned by a late celebrated piece, entituled, Cyder, a Poem; In blank verse, by Philo-Milton (1709).

A nomenclature English and Italian (1726).

An ode on the powers of poetry: To which are prefixed Observations on Taste, and on the present state of poetry and criticism in England (1751).

[T.W.], *The Poet's complaint, a poem* (1682).

Prae-existence. A poem, in imitation of Milton (1714).

Reflections upon reflections (1726).

Rhetoric; or The principles of oratory delineated (1736).

Thesaurus dramaticus. Containing all the celebrated passages, soliloquies, similies, descriptions, and other poetical beauties in the body of English plays. In two volumes (1724).

A universal, historical, geographical, chronological, and poetical dictionary (1703).

A verbal index to Milton's Paradise Lost (1741).

The Adventurer (1752-1754).

Altieri, Ferdinando, *Dizionario italiano ed inglese* (1726).

Armstrong, John, *Taste: an epistle to a young critic* (1753).

*Arnauld, Antoine, *The art of speaking* (1708).

Auerbach, Erich, *Mimesis: The Representation of Reality in Western Literature* (Princeton, 1953).

Bailey, Nathaniel, *An universal etymological English dictionary. Thirteenth edition* (1749).

Baretti, Giuseppi, *A Dictionary of the English and Italian languages, Two Volumes* (1760).

Barnard, Howard C., *The Little Schools of Port-Royal* (Cambridge, 1913).

Barrow, John, *Dictionarium polygraphicum: or, the whole body of arts regularly digested, Two volumes* (1735).

Bayle, Pierre, *Dictionaire historique et critique* (1730).

Benson, William, *Letters concerning poetical translations, and Virgil's and Milton's arts of verse, etc.* (1739).

*Beverley, Thomas, *An exposition of the divinely prophetick song of songs which is Solomons* (1687).

Blackwall, Anthony, *Introduction to the Classic's* (1718).

Blount, Thomas, *Glossographia: or a dictionary* (1681).

Borgerhoff, E.B.O., *The Freedom of French Classicism* (Princeton, 1950).

*Bouhours, Dominique, *The art of criticism* (1705).

Boyer, Abel, *The Royal Dictionary, In Two Parts, First French and English. Secondly, English and French* (1699).

*Boyle, Robert, *Some considerations touching the style of the Holy Scriptures* (1663).

Brightland, John, *A grammar of the English tongue, with the arts of logick, rhetorick, poetry, etc.* (1714).

*Brown, John, *A dissertation on the rise, union, and power, the progression, separations, and corruptions, of poetry and music* (1763).

*Bullokar, John, *An English expositour, or Compleat dictionary* (1671).

Burnet, Gilbert, *Some letters. Containing, an account of what seemed most remarkable in Switzerland, Italy, etc. Rotterdam* (1686).

Cabeen, David C., and Brody, Jules, gen. ed., *A Critical Bibliography of French Literature* (Syracuse University Press, 1961).

Calepini, Ambrosii, *Dictionarium* (Lugduni, 1634).

Caryl, Joseph, *An English-Greek lexicon, containing the Derivations and various Significations of all the Words in the New Testament* (1661).

Charleton, Walter, *Natural History of the Passions ... In the Savoy, Printed by T.N. for James Magnes* (1674).

Chomel, Noël, *Dictionaire oeconomique: or, the family dictionary, Two Volumes* (1725).

Clark, A. F. B., *Boileau and the French Classical Critics in England* (Champion, 1925).

Cocker, Edward, *Cocker's English dictionary* (1704).

Cockeram, Henry, *The English Dictionary: or, an interpreter of hard English words* (1655).

Coles, Elisha, *An English dictionary* (1676).

Cotgrave, John, *Wits interpreter: the English Parnassus. Third Edition* (1671).

Cotgrave, Randle, *A French and English dictionary* (1673).

*Coward, William, *The true test of poetry* (1709).

Crane, R. S., and Kaye, F. B., *A Census of British Newspapers and Periodicals 1620-1800* (Chapel Hill, 1927).

**Critical Club, Letters of* (Edinburgh, 1738).

Crompton, Hugh, *Pierides, or the muses mount* (1658).

*Dalacourt, James, *A prospect of poetry* (Dublin, 1734).

Danet, Pierre, *A complete dictionary of the Greek and Roman antiquities* (1700).

*de Callieres, François, *Characters and criticism upon the ancient and modern orators, poets, painters, musicians, statuaries, & other arts and sciences* (1714).

Defoe, B. N., *A compleat English dictionary* (Westminster, 1735).

Derrick, Samuel, *A poetical dictionary* (1761).

Diderot, Denis, *Encyclopedie* (Paris, 1755).

Douglas, John, *Milton vindicated from the charge of plagiarism, brought against him by Mr. Lauder* (1751).

Edwards, John, *A discourse concerning the authority, stile, and perfection of the books of the old and new testament* (1693).

Edwards, Thomas *The canons of criticism, and glossary, being a supplement to Mr. Warburton's edition of Shakespeare, Fourth edition* (1750).

Edelman, Nathan, ed., Vol. III: *The Seventeenth Century* (of Cabeen and Brody, gen. ed.: *A Critical Bibliography of French Literature*).

*Fenelon, François, *Dialogues concerning eloquence in general* (1722).

Florio, John, *Queen Anna's New World of Words, or Dictionarie of the Italian and English tongues* (1611).

*—, *Vocabolario Italiano & Inglese, A dictionary Italian & English* (1659).

The Free Thinker (1718-1721).

Friedman, Albert B., *The Ballad Revival: Studies in the Influence of Popular on Sophisticated Poetry* (University of Chicago Press, 1961).

Gerbier, Sir Balthazar, *A brief discourse concerning the three chief principles of magnificent building* (1664).

Gouldman, Francis, *A copious dictionary in three parts. Second edition* (Cambridge, 1669).

*Gracian y Morales, Balthasar, *The critick* (1681).

Graham, Walter, *English Literary Periodicals* (New York, 1930).

The Gray's Inn Journal (1752-1754).

The Grub-street Journal (1730-1737).

The Guardian (1713).

Hamm, V. M., Father Dominic Bouhours and Neo-Classical Criticism (*Jesuit Thinkers of the Renaissance; Essays Presented to John F. McCormick, S.J.* [Milwaukee, Marquette University Press, 1939]).

*Harris, John, *Lexicon technicum* (1708).

*Hayward, Thomas, *The British muse* (1738).

*—, *The Quintessence of English poetry* (1740).

Hexham, Henry, *A copious English and Netherduytch dictionarie, composed out of our best English authours* (Rotterdam, 1660).

Hooker, Edward Niles, ed., *The Critical Works of John Dennis* (Baltimore, 1939).

Howell, James, *Lexicon tetraglotton, and English – French – Italian – Spanish dictionary* (1660).

The Inspector (1751).

Jacob, Giles, *The poetical register: or, the lives and characters of the English dramatick poets. With an account of their writings* (1719).

Johnson, Samuel, *A Dictionary of the English Language* (1755).

*Keach, Benjamin, *Troposchematologia* (1682).

Kersey, John, *A new English dictionary* (1702).

Lamy, Bernard, *The art of speaking: written in French by Messieurs du Port Royal: In pursuance of a former Treatise, Intituled, The Art of Thinking* (1676).

Lauder, William, *An essay on Milton's use and imitation of the moderns, in his Paradise Lost* (1750).

Lawson, John, *Lectures concerning oratory. Delivered in Trinity College, Dublin* (Dublin, 1759).

*Le Clerc, Jean, *Parrhasiana: or, thoughts upon several subjects* (1700).

The London Magazine (1733).

Mallet, David, *Of verbal criticism: an epistle to Mr. Pope, Occasioned by Theobald's Shakespear, and Bentley's Milton* (1733).

Marr, George S., *The Periodical Essayists of the Eighteenth Century* (New York, 1924).

Martin, Benjamin, *The General Magazine of Arts and Sciences, Philosophical, Philological, Mathematical, and Mechanical, 6 Vol.* (1755).

Massey, William, *Remarks upon Milton's Paradise Lost* (1761).

Masson, David, *The life of John Milton* (Cambridge, 1859-1894).

Mauger, Claudius, *French and English letters, upon all subjects, mean and sublime . . . Printed by Tho. Royscroft and sold by Samuel Lawndes. Second edition* (1676).

Mears, William, *A catalogue of modern books in divinity, history, law, philosophy, mathematicks, poetry, etc.* (1722).

Melmoth, William, *Letters on several subjects. By the late Sir Thomas Fitzosborne, Bart. Published from the Copies found among his Papers* (1748).

The Microcosm (1787).

Miller, James, *Harlequin-Horace: or, the art of modern poetry* (1731).

Moreri, Louis, *The great historical, geographical, and poetical dictionary* (1694).

The National Journal (1746).

The Observer (1785-1790).

*Oldmixon, John, *The arts of Logick and rhetorick* (1728).

Paterson, James, *A complete commentary with etymological, explanatory, critical and classical notes on Milton's Paradise Lost* (1744).

*Patrick, Simon, *A paraphrase upon the books of Ecclesiastes and the Song of Solomon* (1685).

—, *The Song of Solomon paraphrased. With annotations* (1685).

Peck, Francis, *New memoirs of the life and poetical works of Mr. John Milton* (1740).

Pemberton, Henry, *Observations on poetry, especially the epic: occasioned by the late poem upon Leonides* (1738).

Pennecuik, Alexander, *Streams from Helicon: or poems on various subjects. In three parts. By Alexander Pennecuik Gent. The Second edition* (1720).
Peyre, Henri, *Le Classicisme Français* (New York, 1942).
Phillips, Edward, *The new world of English words: or, A general dictionary* (1658).
Phillips, John, *A reflection on our modern poesy. An essay* (1695).
The Plain Dealer (1730).
Ralph, James, *Sawney. An heroic poem. Occasion'd by the Duncaid. Together with a critique on that poem address'd to Mr. T---d, Mr. M---r, Mr. Eu---n, etc.* (1728).
Richardson, Jonathan, *Explanatory notes and remarks on Milton's Paradise Lost* (1734).
Roberts, John, *An answer to Mr. Pope's preface to Shakespeare. In a letter to a Friend* (1729).
The St. James Journal (1722-1723).
Sewell, William, *A large dictionary, English and Dutch, in two parts (Amsterdam,* 1708).
Sherburn, George, ed., *The Correspondence of Alexander Pope* (Oxford, 1956).
Sheridan, Thomas, *A course of lectures on elocution: together with two dissertations on language; and some other tracts relative to those subjects* (1762).
Skinner, Stephen, *Etymologicon linguae anglicanae* (1671).
Smith, John, *The mysterie of rhetorique unveil'd* (1665).
Spence, Joseph, *An essay on Pope's Odyssey: in which some particular beauties and blemishes of that work are consider'd* (1726).
Staver, Frederick, "'Sublime' as Applied to Nature", *Modern Language Notes*, LXX (Nov. 1955)), 484-487.
Stevens, John, *A new Spanish and English dictionary* (1706).
*Toland, John, *The life of John Milton* (1761).
*Torriano, Gio., *Vocabolario Italiano & Inglese, A Dictionary Italian and English* (1659).
Upton, John, *Critical observations on Shakespeare. By John Upton Prebendary of Rochester* (1746).
*Ward, John, *A system of oratory* (1759).
Webb, Daniel, *Remarks on the beauties of poetry* (1762).
Weed, K., and Bond, R. P., Studies of British Newspapers and Periodicals from their Beginning to 1800: A Bibliography. *Studies in Philology, Extra Series* (Dec. 1946, No. 2, University of North Carolina Press).
Weekes, Nathaniel, *On the abuse of poetry. A satire. Second edition* (1754).
Werenfels, Samuel, *A discourse of logomachys, or controversys about words ... added a dissertation concerning meteors of stile, or false sublimity ... translated into English* (1711).
Willymott, William, *The peculiar use and signification of certain words in the Latin Tongue* (1704).
*Wilson, Thomas, *A complete Christian dictionary* (1678).

INDEX